The Phenomenology of Pain

SERIES IN CONTINENTAL THOUGHT

Editorial Board

Ted Toadvine, Chairman, University of Oregon
Michael Barber, Saint Louis University
Elizabeth A. Behnke, Study Project in Phenomenology of the Body
David Carr, Emory University (Emeritus), The New School
James Dodd, New School University
Lester Embree, Florida Atlantic University†
Sara Heinämaa, University of Jyväskylä, University of Helsinki
José Huertas-Jourda, Wilfrid Laurier University†
Joseph J. Kockelmans, Pennsylvania State University†
William R. McKenna, Miami University
Algis Mickunas, Ohio University
J. N. Mohanty, Temple University
Dermot Moran, University College Dublin
Thomas Nenon, University of Memphis
Rosemary Rizo-Patron de Lerner, Pontificia Universidad Católica del Perú, Lima
Thomas M. Seebohm, Johannes Gutenberg Universität, Mainz†
Gail Soffer, Rome, Italy
Elizabeth Ströker, Universität Köln†
Nicolas de Warren, Penn State University
Richard M. Zaner, Vanderbilt University

International Advisory Board

Suzanne Bachelard, Université de Paris†
Rudolf Boehm, Rijksuniversiteit Gent
Albert Borgmann, University of Montana
Amedeo Giorgi, Saybrook Institute
Richard Grathoff, Universität Bielefeld
Samuel Ijsseling, Husserl-Archief te Leuven†
Alphonso Lingis, Pennsylvania State University
Werner Marx, Albert-Ludwigs Universität, Freiburg†
David Rasmussen, Boston College
John Sallis, Boston College
John Scanlon, Duquesne University
Hugh J. Silverman, State University of New York, Stony Brook†
Carlo Sini, Università di Milano
Jacques Taminiaux, Louvain-la-Neuve†
D. Lawrence Wieder†
Dallas Willard, University of Southern California†

The Phenomenology of Pain

Saulius Geniusas

OHIO UNIVERSITY PRESS   ATHENS

Ohio University Press, Athens, Ohio 45701
ohioswallow.com
© 2020 by Ohio University Press
All rights reserved

To obtain permission to quote, reprint, or otherwise reproduce or distribute
material from Ohio University Press publications, please contact our rights and
permissions department at (740) 593-1154 or (740) 593-4536 (fax).

Printed in the United States of America
Ohio University Press books are printed on acid-free paper ∞ ™

30 29 28 27 26 25 24 23 22 21 20   5 4 3 2 1

Hardcover ISBN: 978-0-8214-2403-2
Electronic ISBN: 978-0-8214-4694-2

LCCN: 2019051766

Library of Congress Cataloging-in-Publication Data available upon request.

For my father,

Algis T. Geniušas

CONTENTS

Acknowledgments ... xi

Introduction ... 1
    Pain as Experience ... 1
    The Phenomenological Approach ... 3
    The Structure of the Following Investigation ... 7

1 Methodological Considerations ... 11
    Fundamental Methodological Commitments:
        Epoché, the Phenomenological Reduction,
        and Eidetic Variation ... 12
    Three Allegations: Psychologism, Introspectionism,
        and Solipsism ... 20
    Revamping Eidetic Variation: From Pure to
        Dialogical Phenomenology ... 25
    The Genetic Method in Phenomenology ... 31

**2 Pain and Intentionality: A Stratified Conception
of Pain Experience** ... 41
    Pain and Intentionality ... 42
    Pain as a Feeling-Sensation ... 44
    Pain as an Intentional Feeling ... 49
    Apprehension–Content of Apprehension ... 52
    Husserl's Analysis of Pain in the *Logical Investigations* ... 54
    Pain as a Stratified Phenomenon ... 59
    Sartre's Phenomenology of Pain in *Being and Nothingness* ... 62

3 The Phenomenology of Pain Dissociation Syndromes ... 68
    Congenital Insensitivity to Pain ... 69
    The Discovery of Pain ... 74
    Lobotomy, Cingulotomy, and Morphine ... 80
    Threat Hypersymbolia ... 83
    Asymbolia for Pain ... 85
    Pain Affect without Pain Sensation ... 93

viii

4 Pain and Temporality — 97

Objective Time and Subjective Temporality — 98

The Different Senses of Presence:
  The Fundamental Levels of Time-Constitution — 100

Implicit and Explicit Presence — 105

The Field of Presence as the Horizon of Pain Experience — 110

Memory and Pain — 112

Anticipation and Pain — 115

5 The Body in Pain: *Leib* and *Körper* — 120

Pain's Indubitability and Bodily Localizability — 121

The Phenomenological Account — 126

The Lived-Body as the Subject of Pain — 127

Pain as *Empfindnis* — 130

Pain's Twofold Localizability — 133

Pain and the Constitution of the Lived-Body — 135

The Structure of Pain Experience — 137

**6 The Phenomenology of Embodied Personhood:
Depersonalization and Repersonalization** — 142

The Phenomenology of Embodied Personhood — 143

Chronic Pain as Depersonalization — 148

Chronic Pain as Repersonalization — 150

Implications for the Phenomenology of Medicine — 154

Pain as an Expressible Phenomenon:
  The Basic Elements of a Phenomenology of Listening — 157

7 Pain and the Life-World: Somatization and Psychologization — 164

Somatization and Psychologization — 166

Somatization, Psychologization, and Their Origins
  in Experience — 168

The Phenomenology of Somatization and Psychologization — 171

The Life-World as the *Wherefrom*, *Wherein*, and
  Whereto of Experience — 172

Between Homeliness and Homelessness:
  Discordance in the Life-World — 175

Masochism and Somatization — 182

CONTENTS ix

Conclusion 188

Notes 195

Bibliography 221

Index 231

ACKNOWLEDGMENTS

Some of the chapters of this book are heavily revised versions of earlier publications. Chapter 2 is a revised version of "Pain and Intentionality" (Geniusas 2017a). Chapter 5 includes material from an earlier study, "The Subject of Pain: Husserl's Discovery of the Lived-Body" (Geniusas 2014b). Chapter 6 is a revised version of "Phenomenology of Chronic Pain: De-Personalization and Re-Personalization" (Geniusas 2017b).

I would like to thank Agustín Serrano de Haro, Gary B. Madison, Simon van Rysewyk, Charles Rodger, and John Quintner, who have read through some chapters of this study. I also owe a word of thanks to Jagna Brudzinska, David Carr, Nicolas de Warren, Dalius Jonkus, Claudio Majolino, Dermot Moran, Luis Niel, Dieter Lohmar, Dmitri Nikulin, Witold Plotka, and Dan Zahavi. Finally, I am grateful to the Research Grants Council of the University Grants Committee in Hong Kong for the General Research Fund grant, which enabled me to devote the time needed to prepare this study for publication.

INTRODUCTION

PAIN AS EXPERIENCE

We can say about pain what Augustine (2006, 242) has said about time: "What is pain? If no one asks me, I know what it is. If I wish to explain it to him who asks, I do not know." Concessions of this kind are common in pain research. For instance, Thomas Lewis begins his *Pain* with the following admission: "I am so far from being able satisfactorily to define pain . . . that the attempt could serve no useful purpose" (1942, v). So also, Johannes J. Degenaar remarks: "I thought I knew what pain was until I was asked to say what the word 'pain' means. Then . . . I realized my ignorance" (1979, 281).

Such statements might take one by surprise, especially in light of the over-abundance of literature on pain that we come across in various sciences. The available literature, however, consists largely of empirical research on various neurological mechanisms as well as other factors that elicit a painful reaction on the part of some organisms. We are flooded with intricate and fascinating details about pain mechanisms, although we know little about the nature of pain experience.

In the phenomenology of medicine, it is common to draw a distinction between *illness* and *disease* and to maintain that while the nature of the disease is determined neurophysiologically, the nature of illness must be fixed phenomenologically (see, for instance, Toombs 1993). We come across no analogous distinction in pain research. Should we take this to mean that the concept of pain is equivocal, that insofar as we think of pain as a biological mechanism, it must be determined neurophysiologically, while insofar as we think of it as experience, it must be determined by some other means? We would avoid much confusion if we conceded that pain as such is *not* neurophysiological in any sense of the term. At its best, pain biology can clarify the neurophysiological causes that give rise to pain as well as provide effective means to minimize pain or even eliminate it. Pain biology, if successful, can shed light on the neurophysiological mechanisms that, presumably, accompany pain experience. However, irrespective of its practical utility, pain biology cannot clarify the nature of pain experience.

Pain biology presupposes that we know *from* experience what pain *as* experience is. Presumably, what we do not know are the causes that trigger it or the influences that shape it. It thus appears that we are in need of knowledge about matters that lie beyond the boundaries of experience. It seems that we are in need of pain biology, not what one might call "pain phenomenology." How legitimate is such a view? To be sure, experience by itself tells us little about the neurological mechanisms that trigger pain experience. For this reason alone, there can be no question about pain phenomenology replacing pain biology. Yet what exactly do we know about pain *as* experience *from* experience? As soon as we try to articulate what is entailed in this implicit understanding, we come to the realization that we are dupes of our own ignorance. What is pain *as* experience? For this, we appear to lack words.[1]

In 1979, with the aim of determining the concept of pain with precision and thereby resolving various ambiguities that have arisen in the science of pain, the International Association for the Study of Pain (IASP) offered the following definition of *pain*, which continues to be the guiding definition to this day: "Pain is an unpleasant sensory and emotional experience associated with actual or potential tissue damage, or described in terms of such damage" (Merskey and Bogduk 1994, 209). Thus, according to the nowadays-dominant definition, pain is an experience.[2] Yet what kind of experience? To qualify it as unpleasant is hardly sufficient to grasp its nature, for, clearly, such a determination is too broad and does not serve to distinguish pain from various forms of psychological suffering. The further stipulation that pain is not just an emotional but also a sensory experience does not resolve the problem, since nausea, vertigo, heartburn, the sensations of excessive heat and cold, of hunger and thirst, even itches and pressure can also be qualified as "unpleasant sensory and emotional experiences." The IASP definition qualifies pain as experience, yet it does not clarify what kind of experience it is. This definition places pain in the genus of sensory and emotional experience, yet it does not provide us with the differentia.[3]

Although it is undeniable that at its core, pain is an experience, our current knowledge of pain is marked by the failure to understand pain as experience. This failure is not accidental. The dominant methodological standpoints in pain research do not provide us with a suitable methodological framework to conceptualize pain *as* experience. Broadly speaking, naturalism and social constructionism constitute the two dominant methodological standpoints in pain research (see Geniusas 2013). While the naturalist focuses on the specific neurological mechanisms that trigger pain experience, the social constructionist traces the social, cultural, and historical influences that shape the experience of pain. In different ways, both the naturalist and the social constructionist conceptualize pain experience as a psychological effect that is activated by different kinds of mechanisms. What both methodological standpoints are interested in is not pain experience as such (they both presuppose that we already know what pain as experience is), but the various neurological mechanisms that trigger it and the particular sociocultural influences that shape it. Yet clearly, if one claims that pain is triggered by these mechanisms and shaped by these influences, then one must have some kind of understanding of what pain as such is. We are thus forced to ask: What can we say about pain *as* experience, considered independently from the mechanisms that trigger it and the influences that shape it? Contemporary pain research does not have the methodological basis to answer this question.

THE PHENOMENOLOGICAL APPROACH

In light of these circumstances, the following study contends that phenomenology is indispensable for pain research. *Neither pain biology nor pain sociology can clarify the nature of pain experience, and, therefore, they must be supplemented with pain phenomenology.* In a general and preliminary way, we can conceive of phenomenology as a method designed to study experience and the different ways in which phenomena manifest themselves in experience. Thus, the often-cited phenomenological refrain, "Zurück zu den Sachen selbst" (Back to the things themselves), must be understood as a solicitation to return to the *field of experience*, conceived of as the fundamental field within which phenomena manifest themselves and their multifaceted meanings originate. According to one of the central phenomenological claims, in the natural course of life, as well as in the sciences, we misconstrue phenomena by transforming them into what they are not, and we do so precisely because we misunderstand how they manifest themselves in experience. Phenomenology's chief ambition is to liberate us from falsifications, which consciousness itself gives rise to in virtue of its absorption in the world of things and its inherent self-forgetfulness, which manifests itself through its tendency to misunderstand itself as a thing among other things. The goal of phenomenology is to liberate consciousness from its self-opacity, to clarify the fundamental structures of experience and recover the lost world of concrete life. Phenomenology proves to be indispensable for pain research because it offers a highly useful methodology to determine the nature of pain experience, irrespective of the specific natural causes that might trigger it and the specific cultural influences that might shape it.[4]

Phenomenology is neither the first nor the only philosophical tradition to be qualified as a philosophy of experience. Various brands of empiricism and pragmatism also merit the same qualification. Are there any reasons to privilege phenomenology over these other philosophical traditions, as far as the philosophy of pain is concerned? Arguably, the reasons are methodological. First and foremost, the phenomenological method is designed to study experience from the first-person point of view. In this regard, it is exceptionally well-suited for pain research, since pain itself is conceivable only as firsthand experience (a pain that is not experienced could be qualified as a painless pain—an expression that is no less self-contradictory than a square triangle). The science of pain is thus in need of phenomenology, for with its help it can inquire into the compatibility in the findings obtained using the first-person and the third-person methodologies (see Price and Aydede 2005). Still, one might object that such a clarification does not fully answer the question, since it leaves the possibility open that introspectionist psychology might fit the bill. In this regard, one should stress that not any description of phenomena from the first-person point of view is to be qualified as phenomenological. There is no phenomenology without the epoché and the phenomenological reduction, conceived of as the two complementary methods designed to provide the researcher with access to experience that is *purified of naturalistic misconceptions*. These sophisticated methods, unique as they are to phenomenology, are designed to suspend the natural way of considering phenomena so as to let them appear without any bias, distortions, or manipulations. As far as pain research is concerned, these methods prove indispensable for any attempt to conceive of pain as *pure* experience, by which we are to understand the experience of pain, considered independently from pain biology and pain sociology.

In light of my foregoing remarks, one cannot help but be surprised by the scarcity of phenomenologically oriented book-length studies of pain. All in all, one can single out just two studies. Christian Grüny's *Zerstörte Erfahrung: Eine Phänomenologie des Schmerzes* was published in 2004. Abraham Olivier's *Being in Pain* appeared in print a few years later, in 2007. Besides Olivier's and Grüny's studies, there are no other book-length investigations that have exclusively focused on the phenomenology of pain.[5] Strangely, a philosophical tradition that prides itself on being attentive to lived-experience, on returning to the things themselves and thereby taking distance from meaningless abstractions that it finds at the heart of many other traditions of thought—this tradition has been remarkably silent as far as the nature of such embodied feelings as pain is concerned. It has certainly contributed less to our understanding of pain than other philosophical traditions, which never claimed that they were striving to offer a reliable account of the nature of experience.

The central ambition of the following study is to break this regrettable silence and to show that phenomenology has an important contribution to make in the framework of pain research in general, and the philosophy of pain in particular. With this in mind, the following investigation will present a philosophical study of pain, which relies upon the phenomenological method. Besides delimiting a phenomenological approach to pain, this study also aims to open a dialogue between the phenomenology of pain and other types of pain research, which we come across in such fields as the analytically oriented philosophy of pain, cognitive science, cultural anthropology, cultural psychopathology, and psychoanalysis. Such a methodological commitment and dialogical orientation carries the demand to situate oneself within the phenomenological tradition, while at the same time being attentive to the developments in other fields of research.

The fundamental goal of this study is thereby delineated: this study aims to demonstrate why phenomenology is indispensable for pain research. Admittedly, there are different kinds of phenomenology, and the complex relation between them continues to raise doubts about the unity and coherence of the phenomenological movement. In the framework of this study, it is not my goal to provide a detailed analysis of the reasons why, despite far-reaching disagreements, the phenomenological tradition as a whole retains its overarching unity.[6] My goal, rather, is to focus on one particular phenomenological tradition, namely, the Husserlian tradition, and to demonstrate why it is of great importance for the philosophy of pain. In such a way, I will aim to complement Olivier's and Grüny's above-mentioned studies, which rely mainly on the resources of Martin Heidegger's and Maurice Merleau-Ponty's phenomenologies. Unless otherwise stated, in this study the concept of phenomenology will be employed as synonymous with Husserlian phenomenology.

Some readers might wonder, Would it not be more appropriate to proceed on a different phenomenological basis and rely on more existentially and less epistemologically oriented phenomenological resources? One of my goals is to show that such stereotypical rejections of Husserlian phenomenology are far from convincing. Appearances to the contrary notwithstanding, Husserlian phenomenology provides a remarkably solid methodological basis for the philosophy of pain. One can single out eight fundamental reasons that make Husserlian phenomenology highly fitting for pain research. Only in Husserlian phenomenology do we encounter the full configuration of these reasons, although, admittedly, some of them can be also found in other philosophical frameworks:

1. Phenomenology is a philosophy of experience, whose fundamental ambition is to clarify phenomena as configurations of meaning that are constituted in experience. As we will see, the methods employed in phenomenology are highly useful to study the nature of pain, conceived not only as a configuration of meaning but also as lived-experience.

2. In contrast to other philosophies of experience, phenomenology provides the methodological basis to study the experience of pain by setting aside naturalistic preconceptions, including all the available theoretical accomplishments, which, for the reasons that will have to be clarified in due course, tacitly reconfigure the nature of experience. Here I am referring to the phenomenological methods of the epoché and the reduction, which enable phenomenology to conceptualize pain in the absence of naturalistic bias and manipulation.

3. Phenomenology primarily relies upon a descriptive method, which is also of great importance for pain research: to this day, the phenomenal nature of pain remains unexplored and it can be surveyed only descriptively.

4. Phenomenological descriptions are not focused on the idiosyncratic characteristics of personal experience. Rather, by virtue of

the method of eidetic variation, phenomenology strives to offer accounts of the *essence* of pain experience. In this regard, too, phenomenology promises to fill a serious gap in pain research.

5. Phenomenology has been celebrated for a long time for overcoming the subject/object dichotomy and for disclosing the centrality of the body in thinking, acting, and feeling. In this regard, too, it proves to be remarkably apt for pain research, since pain in its essence is a bodily phenomenon.

6. Phenomenology provides us with some of the richest—if not *the* richest—analyses of the temporal nature of experience. In this regard, also, it promises to be of great significance for pain research in that it provides the means needed to clarify the temporal structures of pain experience.

7. The groundbreaking distinction in phenomenology between the naturalistic and the personalistic attitudes is of fundamental importance, since pain as experience can be grasped only from the personalistic, and not from a naturalistic, standpoint.

8. Finally, the phenomenological analyses of the life-world are also highly relevant for the philosophy of pain, since these analyses enable us to philosophically conceptualize different ways in which the experience of pain is rooted in cultural worlds.

THE STRUCTURE OF THE FOLLOWING INVESTIGATION

This study will be concerned with three fundamental tasks: it will aim to (1) clarify the fundamental methodological principles that must underlie phenomenologically oriented pain research; (2) develop a new conception of pain on the basis of such methodological principles; and (3) clarify what contribution the phenomenology of pain can make to philosophical anthropology. It is highly important to carry out all these tasks, and for various reasons. As far as the first task is concerned, let us not overlook that in pain research we come across various studies that call themselves phenomenological, even though the exact meaning of this qualification remains unqualified. Various autobiographies, "pain narratives," and empirically oriented studies, as well as introspectionist accounts, are passed off as though they are phenomenological studies of pain. So as to counteract this tendency and the deep confusions it gives rise to, one must stress that phenomenology is first and foremost a method, which means that only insofar as one subscribes to the distinctly phenomenological methodology can one qualify one's study as phenomenological (in the above-mentioned sense).

In chapter 1, my goal will be to lay out those methodological principles that are indispensable for any study that wishes to identify itself as phenomenological in the Husserlian sense of the term. I will contend that the methods of the epoché, the phenomenological reduction, and eidetic variation are the fundamental and indispensable principles of the phenomenological method. Besides clarifying the meaning of these principles, I will further argue that especially in the framework of pain research, these three fundamental methods call for a further twofold supplementation. First, the method of eidetic variation must be supplemented with a method of factual variation, conceived not so much as an independent method, but rather as an important extension of the method of eidetic variation. Second, static methodology in general must be supplemented with what in Husserlian phenomenology is identified as genetic methodology. Taking such a methodological orientation into account, I will maintain that phenomenology is not concerned with the idiosyncratic nature of any particular experience, and in this regard, it should be distinguished from the anthropologically and sociologically oriented pain research that we come across in the literature. In contrast to all empirical research on pain, phenomenology is concerned with essential structures of experience, that is, those structures without which experience as such could not be qualified as painful.[7]

Having clarified the fundamental methodological principles of phenomenological research, we will proceed to the second fundamental task. Our guiding question runs as follows: What is pain, when conceived of as experience and when considered from the phenomenological point of view? Building on the basis of phenomenological descriptions, this manuscript will propose the following answer to this fundamental question: *pain is an aversive bodily feeling with a distinct experiential quality, which can be given only in original firsthand experience, either as a feeling-sensation or as an emotion.*

I should stress that this conception of pain does not rely either on pain biology or on pain sociology. It does not subscribe to the fundamental methodological commitments of either naturalism or social constructionism. All the qualifications entailed in this definition rely upon phenomeno-

PAIN AS EXPERIENCE

logically oriented reflections on pain experience. This conception is meant to articulate the eidetic features of pain experience. I will maintain that the conception of pain proposed here captures the phenomenological essence of pain experience.

To corroborate such a view, the following study will take seven major steps and answer seven central questions. What does it mean to claim (1) that pain is a bodily feeling; (2) that this feeling is aversive; (3) that it has a distinct experiential quality; (4) that it is an original experience; (5) that it can be given only in firsthand experience; (6) that it is originally lived through as a nonintentional feeling-sensation; and, finally (7), that it can also be given as an intentional feeling? Chapters 2–5 of this study deal with these questions explicitly. Chapter 2 conceptualizes pain both as a nonintentional feeling-sensation and as an emotion; it further shows what it means to claim that pain can be given only in firsthand experience. Chapter 3 supplements this conception by showing that pain must be conceived of as a fundamentally aversive feeling that has a unique experiential quality. Chapter 4 supplements the foregoing analysis with an investigation into what it means to qualify the experience of pain as an original experience. Finally, in chapter 5, I will bring this analysis to its end by inquiring into the fundamentally embodied nature of pain experience. By the end of chapter 5, it will have become clear what it means to claim that *pain is an embodied and emotionally stamped bodily feeling, whose fundamentally aversive nature is of a distinct experiential quality.*

Phenomenology's relevance for pain research is not reducible to the conceptual clarification of the nature of pain experience, no matter how important such a task might be. This will bring us to the third fundamental task of this study, which concerns the contribution that the phenomenology of pain could make to philosophical anthropology.[8] *What can the phenomenology of pain contribute to our philosophical understanding of human existence?* This is the central question, to which the final two chapters of this study will aim to offer an answer. Put phenomenologically, what is at stake here are those essential features that make up the core of pain experience, conceived personalistically and not naturalistically. In this regard, it will prove necessary to clarify in detail what it means to claim that the phenomenological category of the person depicts the subject of pain and that the phenomenological concept of the life-world designates the fundamental horizon within which human pain is lived. The last two chapters will address these issues while focusing on chronic pain. Chapter 6 will focus on pain as a depersonalizing and a repersonalizing experience. Chapter 7 will supplement this investigation with a further analysis of the role that somatization and psychologization play in pain experience.

CHAPTER 1

· ·

METHODOLOGICAL CONSIDERATIONS

Let us begin with the analysis of the fundamental methodological principles that must underlie phenomenologically oriented pain research. In the introduction, I have identified this task as one of the three fundamental goals of this study as a whole. Here I want to contend that the methods of the epoché, the phenomenological reduction, and eidetic variation constitute such fundamental methodological principles. These three principles are necessary: only insofar as one subscribes to them does one have the right to identify one's investigation as phenomenological in the Husserlian sense of the term. Nonetheless, these principles are not sufficient; they need to be supplemented with other phenomenological methods. As far as the phenomenology of pain is concerned, these three methodological principles need to be supplemented with two further methodological procedures: what we will here identify as the method of factual variation and the genetic method of intentional implications.[1]

I will take four steps in my analysis. In the first section, I will present the methods of the epoché, the phenomenological reduction, and eidetic variation conceived of as the three principles that make up the methodological core of phenomenologically oriented pain research. In the second section, I will focus on three critiques that have been directed against phenomenology—the contentions that phenomenology is disguised psychologism, camouflaged introspectionism, and veiled solipsism. Responses to these three critiques will solidify the three methodological commitments mentioned above. In the third section, I will argue that the three fundamental phenomenological methods are necessary, yet not sufficient, and that the method of eidetic variation needs to be supplemented with the method of factual variation. We are in need of such a supplementation because in its absence, the method of eidetic variation is all too often understood as an excuse to engage in phenomenological reflections while dismissing (presumably, out of methodological considerations) all other scientific accomplishments that we come across in other fields of research. Phenomenology need not be the victim of its own purity: it must be open to the developments in other sciences—natural, social, and human—as well as to the advances in literature, poetry, cinema, and fine arts. Insofar as phenomenology is cross-disciplinary and cross-cultural, it merits being called *dialogical*. In the fourth section, I will qualify all the methods outlined above as the methodological commitments of static phenomenology, and I will further argue that they need to be supplemented with the methodological principles of genetic phenomenology. In such a way, we will obtain an answer to the first fundamental question of this study, which concerns the identification of the methodological principles of phenomenologically oriented pain research.

Phenomenology has been practiced in a large variety of ways, and, therefore, one cannot exclude the possibility that the phenomenology of pain might rely on some other methodological principles. While admitting such a possibility, I would like to stress two interrelated points. First, phenomenology is a method, and, therefore, anyone who wishes to argue that the static and the genetic methods are expendable must show what other phenomenological methods could replace them. Second, the methods presented here are not only fundamental to phenomenology, but also exceptionally fruitful for pain research, which is in need of a reliable methodology to clarify pain experience independently from pain biology and pain sociology, yet without denigrating it to the empirical level of personal accounts of the idiosyncratic nature of one's own experience.

FUNDAMENTAL METHODOLOGICAL COMMITMENTS: EPOCHÉ, THE PHENOMENOLOGICAL REDUCTION, AND EIDETIC VARIATION

One commonly thinks of phenomenological analyses as reflections on experience, and things given in experience, from the first-person point of view. Such a general qualification all too easily leads to far-reaching ambiguities and confusions. These confusions are especially prevalent in such fields as pain research, where we come across investigations that are labeled as phenomenological simply because they provide a set of reflections on pain experience from the first-person point of view. One is thus left with the impression that any introspective, autobiographical, or even psychologistic set of reflections on pain experience can be characterized as phenomenological. Such a state of affairs has led to a misapprehension of the nature, goals, and function of phenomenology in pain research.

Clearly, not any kind of reflection on experience from the first-person point of view is phenomenological. At least from a Husserlian standpoint, one would say: it is the commitment to specific methodological principles that distinguishes phenomenologically oriented investigations from other studies of lived-experience. Such a standpoint suggests that an investigation can be labeled as phenomenological if, and only if, it subscribes to the fundamental principles of phenomenological methodology. What exactly are those principles?

It is not easy to answer this question. Ever since its emergence, the phenomenological method has been conceptualized in a number of ways, whose compatibility remains a contentious issue. On the one hand, there is the more apparent problem of methodological consistency that runs throughout the phenomenological movement. As Paul Ricoeur (1987, 9) has famously put it, the history of phenomenology is the history of Husserlian heresies. On the other hand, even if one limits oneself to classical phenomenology in general, and Husserlian phenomenology in particular, one nonetheless has to deal with questions concerning the compatibility of different methodological frameworks (say, those of static and genetic phenomenology), as well as of different accounts of the same methodological procedures (say, the account of the reduction as presented in *Ideas I*, *First Philosophy II*, and *The Crisis of European Sciences and Transcendental Phenomenology*). In the present context, it is not my goal to enter into this conflict of interpretations. I believe it is possible to bypass these controversies if one supplements methodological considerations with two qualifications. First, one needs to focus on the identification of the *fundamental* methodological principles, that is, those principles that could be qualified as necessary, although not necessarily sufficient. I will contend that the methods of the epoché, the phenomenological reduction, and eidetic variation are the fundamental principles of Husserlian phenomenology. I do not think that allegiance to these three phenomenological principles is sufficient to clarify what classical phenomenology (to say nothing of the phenomenological tradition as a whole) can contribute to pain research. It is therefore necessary to supplement these three methodological principles with further principles. Second, these three phenomenological principles, while necessary, can be conceptualized in more ways than one. The grandiose task of providing an exhaustive treatment of these principles is unattainable in the framework of a study that focuses on the phenomenology of pain. Here I strive to identify only the essential features of these methodological procedures, while at the same time conceding that they not only can be, but that they also have been, articulated in a number of complementary ways.

A few words on the fundamental goals of Husserlian phenomenology are appropriate here. Husserlian phenomenology is marked by the ambition to be a science of phenomena purified of all unwarranted assumptions, constructions, and interpretation. For this reason, it strives to be a *descriptive* science, which would *present* phenomena the way they appear, without distortions or misrepresentations. It is, however, not enough to describe phenomena in order to grasp them the way they appear, since descriptions all too often succumb to bias and manipulation. Precisely because it strives to describe phenomena *exactly as they appear*, without any contamination, the possibility of phenomenology hinges upon its capacity to design a suitable methodology that would ensure the reliability of phenomenological descriptions. The methods of the epoché, the phenomenological reduction, and eidetic variation are meant to demonstrate the possibility of phenomenology, conceived of as a method for studying pure phenomena in an unbiased way.

The Greek word *epoché* means "suspension, or bracketing." To bracket, or suspend, means to put certain beliefs and commitments out of action and consideration. Husserl uses a number of expressions to characterize the epoché: abstention, dislocation, unplugging, exclusion, withholding, disregarding, abandoning, bracketing, putting out of action, or putting out of play. As all these descriptive approximations suggest, the epoché is a *unique* modification, which should not be confused with either doubt or negation.[2]

First and foremost, the phenomenological epoché is the abstention from all participation in the cognitions of the objective sciences—the putting out of play of any critical position-taking with regard to their truth or falsity. This is of great importance for the phenomenology of pain, since it suggests that phenomenological analysis is possible only if it places in brackets the accomplishments we come across in the science of pain. *Pain phenomenology cannot rely either on pain biology or on pain sociology.* However, such a suspension of scientific validity, radical as it is, does not exhaust the full meaning of the phenomenological epoché. This is because, "in concealment, the world's validities are always founded on other validities, *above* the whole manifold but synthetically unified flow in which the world has and forever attains anew its content of meaning and its ontic validity" (Husserl 1970, 150). We can take this to mean that even if the researcher places all scientific

METHODOLOGICAL CONSIDERATIONS   15

validities in phenomenological brackets, that is, even if he refuses to accept
these validities *as* validities, even under such circumstances, he cannot be assured that his research unfolds in an unbiased way, for even the natural and
seemingly innocent assumption that the phenomena he addresses are *natural*
phenomena (that is, parts of nature) already rests on unclarified presuppositions. This is of great importance for pain research, since it means that a
phenomenologist should not conceive of pain as a natural occurrence, determined by some kind of natural causes, irrespective of whether or not these
causes are known scientifically. Besides requiring that one bracket all scientific knowledge about pain, the method of the epoché also requires that one
put out of action the fundamental presupposition that underlies the science
of pain, namely, the assumption that pain is a natural or, more precisely, a
neurophysiological phenomenon.

Taken by itself, it is unclear where the epoché leaves us. As far as the phenomenology of pain is concerned, it makes clear that a phenomenologist
cannot accept either the scientific results that issue from or the fundamental
assumptions that underlie the science of pain. These are negative determinations. The method of the epoché gains a positive sense when it is coupled
with the phenomenological reduction.[3]

With reference to the phenomenological reduction, Husserl has remarked
that "the understanding of all of phenomenology depends upon the understanding of this method" (1977, 144). This is hardly an overestimation, since
the acquisition of phenomena in the phenomenological sense relies upon the
performance of the phenomenological reduction. In the natural course of life,
I stand on the ground of the world's pregivenness: I accept the world's being as
a matter of course, without inquiring into those acts of consciousness, through
which it obtains its meaning. My interests are exclusively absorbed in the objective world, and not in the flow of experience, through which it obtains the
status of the objective world. We can conceive of the phenomenological reduction as a fundamental change of attitude that enables the phenomenologist to
redirect his interests from objects in the world to his own experience. While
in the natural attitude, I am naively absorbed in the performance of my experience and thus my interests are exclusively absorbed in the objects of my
experience, in the phenomenological attitude, my new interests are redirected
toward those very experiences through which the objects in the world and the
world itself gain their meaning. It thereby becomes understandable why Husserl would contend that "subjectivity, and this universally and exclusively, is my
theme" (1973a, 200). The crude mistake to avoid here is that of conceptualizing

subjectivity as something mysteriously cut off from the world and different types of objectivity. Even though Husserl's phenomenology is often subjected to such a critique, it is hard to come across any analyses of such subjectivity in his writings. Phenomenology is interested in subjectivity's hidden constitutive accomplishments, through which objects in the world, and even the world itself, come to be what they are. The subjectivity thematized in phenomenology should be conceived of as a field of pure experience, or as a field of the world's self-manifestation. By providing access to such a field, the phenomenological reduction opens the way to immanent knowledge.[4]

Besides providing access to the field of immanence, the phenomenological reduction also enables the phenomenologist to keep this field pure of all mundane contaminations. It is crucial to stress that the field of immanence that remains untouched by the epoché is not a region *within* the natural world, but a field of pure experience, within which nature and the world come to self-givenness. One can further qualify this region as *fundamentally unnatural*, comprising not things (natural or cultural), but merely pure phenomena. Phenomenology thematizes the field of pure experience as the region within which things come to their self-manifestation. In this way, phenomenology opens up a new science, "the science of *pure subjectivity*, in which thematic discourse concerns exclusively the lived experiences, the modes of consciousness and what is meant in their objectivity, but exclusively *as* meant" (Husserl 1977, 146).

What is the significance of the phenomenological reduction for such a field of research as the philosophy of pain? *While through the method of the epoché one loses pain as a natural phenomenon, through the method of the phenomenological reduction one regains it as a pure experience.* The fundamental goal of the phenomenology of pain is thereby delineated: its fundamental ambition is to give an account of pain as a pure experience, that is, as an experience purified of all naturalistic apprehensions. The goal is to consistently disconnect all the natural apperceptions, which codetermine our common understanding of pain, conceived of as a natural phenomenon.

Here we stumble across new difficulties. Should one not liken the field of pure experience to a ceaseless Heracleitean flux, to an incomprehensibly streaming life, in which being-thus indefinitely replaces being-so? If pure consciousness indeed is such a stream of experience, then how can one possibly obtain any knowledge of this field? The phenomenologically reduced field of experience appears to be inaccessible to intersubjectively verifiable knowledge. It thereby becomes clear that the possibility of phenomenology is not yet secured by means of the epoché and the reduction. The third methodological procedure, namely, the method of eidetic variation, is designed to provide a solution to this dilemma. Phenomenology does not strive to be a factual science of conscious experiences. Rather, it is meant to be an exploration of the essences of conscious life—a descriptive eidetics of reduced consciousness. Insofar as *phenomenology is an eidetics of experience, the phenomenology of pain must be an eidetics of pain experience*. It does not just strive to give an account of pain, conceived of as pure experience; its fundamental goal is to clarify the essence of such experience.

Still, before turning to eidetic variation, we are in need of a further clarification. Although so far, we have spoken of the reduction in a rather unqualified way, there are good reasons to distinguish between different kinds of reduction, and especially between *phenomenological* and *transcendental* reductions. From the time he discovered the reduction in 1905 until around 1916, Husserl himself did not discriminate between these forms of the reduction. Subsequently, it became clear that insofar as one speaks of the reduction in an unqualified way, it remains an ambiguous concept in that it is associated with two significantly different functions. First, it is associated with the method of bracketing the natural world and of transitioning from a naive naturalistic ontology, which is straightforwardly absorbed in beings, to the analysis of meanings. Second, it is also associated with the further transition from the field of meanings to the ultimate source of all meaning, which Husserl identified with transcendental (inter)subjectivity. From around 1916 onward, Husserl started distinguishing between these two functions of the reduction. The first function was identified as the phenomenological reduction, while the second one was identified as the transcendental reduction. The phenomenological reduction is the method that enables the phenomenologist to transition from the natural world, conceived of as the universe of real things as given in the natural attitude, to the world of pure phenomena. Yet a phenomenologist need not stop with this methodological procedure. One can further supplement the phenomenological reduction with the transcendental reduction by initiating a further transition from the field of phenomena to their ultimate condition, or presupposition, which Husserl associates with transcendental (inter)subjectivity (see Kockelmans 1994, 16–17).

As far as the phenomenology of pain is concerned, it is the phenomenological reduction, and not the transcendental reduction, that is indispensable. The three methods that are here identified as fundamental are those of the epoché, the phenomenological reduction, and eidetic variation. This does not mean that the method of the transcendental reduction is not important in phenomenology; it does mean, however, that one can carry out a phenomenologically oriented study without employing the transcendental reduction. The analysis undertaken in this study will primarily, although not exclusively, rely on the phenomenological reduction.[5]

Let us turn to the third phenomenological method, namely, that of eidetic variation. This method is designed to clarify how one is supposed to move from reflecting on individual instances to grasping essences. According to this method, the kind of example one begins with is irrelevant, just as it is irrelevant if the example derives from actual perception, memory, or phantasy. It is crucial, however, to consider the example as free from all naturalistic explanations: the method of eidetic variation rests on the shoulders of the epoché. Starting with an arbitrary example, one must vary the phenomenon "with a completely free optionalness" (Husserl 1960, 70), while simultaneously retaining the sense of its identity, no matter what kind of phenomenon it might be. This means that one must abstain from the acceptance of the phenomenon's being and change the object into a pure possibility—one possibility among other possibilities. That is, one must vary different aspects of the phenomenon until one reaches the invariant—conceived of as a determination, or a set of determinations, in the absence of which the phenomenon would no longer be the kind of phenomenon it is. Following such a method, one comes to the realization that, for instance, extension is an invariant feature of a material object, or that temporality is an invariant feature of lived-experience. With the discovery of such invariants, the essences of the phenomena come into view.[6]

The method of eidetic variation culminates in the seeing of essences. With the help of this method, phenomenology can become a science of essences. Here we come across the reason why Husserlian phenomenology has often been conceived of as a revival of Platonism. This general characterization, so often employed as a tacit critique of phenomenology, is misleading: in phenomenology, essences are not interpreted in metaphysical terms as *eidai* that belong to an independent realm of true being. They are not paradigmatic things or atoms of true being. By essence, or *eidos*, we are to understand what the phenomenon is in terms of its necessary predicates. Put otherwise, essential predicates refer to those aspects of the phenomenon that belong to it invariantly. It is important not to overlook that Husserl (1983, §74) draws a distinction between *exact essences*, which can be exhaustively defined, and *morphological essences*, whose boundaries are imprecise and which are fundamentally inexact. For Husserl (1983, §§71–75), the kind of exactness possible in mathematics derives from its "ideal concepts" and is unattainable in the descriptive eidetics of the reduced consciousness (see also Bernet, Kern, and Marbach 1993, 86). We can take this to mean that the phenomenology of pain, conceived of as an eidetics of pain experience, need not be conceived of as a discipline that generates exact essences. As we will see, especially when it comes to embodied feelings, the exact lines of demarcation that separate different types of experience from each other are often blurred. As Husserl puts it in *Ideas I*, "An *essence*, and thus a purely apprehensible *eidos*, belongs to the sense of every accidental matter. . . . An individual object is not merely as such an individual, a 'this, here!,' a unique instance. . . . It has its own distinctive character, its stock of essential predicables" (1983, 7). The goal of the phenomenology of pain is to extricate these essential predicables from the concrete flow of experience.

Out of these three methods, the last one is most problematic, and in the history of phenomenology, it has been subjected to diverse criticisms. For instance, consider the phenomenological view that what example one begins with is simply irrelevant. No matter how arbitrary the starting point might be, does the phenomenologist not have to rely on a certain preconceptual understanding of the example's essence? How, otherwise, is the phenomenologist supposed to know what properties of the object can be subjected to imaginative variation? Should the cup of tea on my desk be my starting example, does the method of eidetic variation not rely upon my more basic understanding of the object's perceptual properties and practical functions, thus on my prior capacity to distinguish the cup from the saucer and the teaspoon still before I start varying its different properties, such as its color, shape, texture, size, weight, and so on? Consider also Husserl's own example of the tone used in *Phenomenological Psychology* (1977, 54ff.). Does one not already need to know what a tone is so as to be able to identify it as the starting point of one's analysis as well as to be able to distinguish those properties that belong to it from those that don't? It seems that the method of eidetic variation already presupposes a preconceptual insight into the essence of the phenomenon under scrutiny.

Nonetheless, even if one concedes that the method of eidetic variation presupposes a more original exposure to the essences of phenomena,[7] one nonetheless has to agree that with the help of this method, one obtains a much more solid grasp of the essences in question. Insofar as it results in the insight into what is invariable, the method of eidetic variation solidifies our grasp of essences by transforming our vague and merely preconceptual understanding of phenomena into genuine, reliable, and intersubjectively verifiable knowledge of their essential predicates.

Despite its difficulties, the method of eidetic variation is vital for phenomenology, since in its absence, phenomenology would not be in the position to make any reliable and intersubjectively verifiable claims. What exactly would a phenomenologist be left with if, methodologically, he relied only on the epoché and the phenomenological reduction? Following the methodological guidance of these two methods, one would reach the stream of experience and pure phenomena. Yet what would a phenomenological description of such a stream and such phenomena amount to? One would be left with a pure description of factual experiences and phenomena, yet without any right to claim that the description offered is of any relevance for other experiences or other phenomena. Insofar as one relies upon only the methods of the epoché and the reduction, one can already grasp phenomena in their phenomenological purity, yet one remains restricted to their singularity. Phenomenology is in need of a method that would enable it to transcend what is singular and factual. The method of eidetic variation is designed to take us beyond the Heracleitean flux of experience. The possibility of phenomenology, as a philosophy, rests on the shoulders of insights into essences of phenomena. In phenomenology, the method of eidetic variation is indispensable.

Let us briefly sum up the three methodological procedures that are necessary for phenomenologically oriented research on pain. First, by following the method of the epoché, the phenomenologist puts in brackets all the scientific discoveries about pain and even the fundamental assumption that underlies these discoveries, namely, the assumption that pain is a natural, that is, a neurophysiological phenomenon. Second, with the performance of the phenomenological reduction, the phenomenologist gains access to pain, conceived of as pure experience. Third, the method of eidetic variation enables phenomenology to engender intersubjectively verifiable claims about the essence of pain experience. For our purposes, this brief presentation of the fundamental methodological principles that must underlie the phenomenology of pain will have to suffice.

THREE ALLEGATIONS: PSYCHOLOGISM,
INTROSPECTIONISM, AND SOLIPSISM

The method of eidetic variation has often been subjected to criticism, which left one with the impression that a safer way to proceed is to dispose of this method altogether. I do not see how such a presumably safe route can enable a phenomenologist to beget intersubjectively verifiable claims. With the epoché, the phenomenologist has cut off the possibility of relying on the accomplishments of the objective sciences; with the reduction, he has returned to the stream of pure experiences. Yet what can assure us that this stream is not a Heracleitean flux, into which one cannot set one's foot twice? To make clear the dangers that phenomenology faces when one overlooks the eidetic nature of its claims, let us ask three interrelated questions: (1) When phenomenology is employed in such fields as pain research, does it not degenerate into a form of psychologism? (2) Moreover, can it be anything other than introspectionism? (3) Last but not least, is it not a type of solipsism? Addressing these questions will enable us to bolster the view that the methods of the epoché, the reduction, and eidetic variation are indispensable for phenomenologically oriented pain research.

1. We can answer the first question by opening a brief dialogue between the phenomenology of pain and the phenomenology of illness. In her recent study, Havi Carel bemoans philosophy's indifference to illness. She speaks of the "philosophical tendency to resist thinking about illness" (Carel 2016, 5) and offers an original and highly valuable phenomenological response to this indifference. One should not, however, overlook just how common it is to begin phenomenologically oriented studies of illness with a confession concerning the author's personal experience of pain and/or illness. What exactly is the role of confessions of such nature? To be sure, nobody is a stranger to pain and illness, be it personal or interpersonal. Moreover, any phenomenological account is always grounded in experience. Nonetheless, as far as phenomenologically oriented studies of pain and illness are concerned, one shoots oneself in the foot when one argues, whether openly or discreetly, that only those who suffer from severe forms of illness and/or pain have the right to address these themes philosophically. We face here a crude form of psychologism, conceived of as an illegitimate form of reductionism,[8] which one could describe either as the incapacity to raise one's own personal experience to the eidetic level, or as a matter of diminishing eidetic unities of meaning to the level of psychological experiences. In light of Husserl's sweeping critique of psychologism in the *Prolegomena* to his *Logical Investigations*, anyone in phenomenology who reflects on what such a view implies will be led to discard it.[9]

A phenomenologically oriented study cannot consist of a set of reflections on the idiosyncratic nature of one's own personal experiences, no matter how fortunate or unfortunate they might be. It is not just a question of personal justification that might underlie a phenomenological investigation of such phenomena as pain. What is at stake here is the very nature of an investigation that would make it phenomenological. We face here a deep confusion that continues to haunt phenomenologically oriented pain research. This confusion derives from the misunderstanding of the nature of phenomenologically oriented research. In light of the analysis undertaken in the previous section, we can say that this confusion derives from neglecting the eidetic nature of phenomenological investigations. The stream of pure experiences is not just a Heracleitean flux, which means that the phenomenology of pain is not pain autobiography and it should not be misconceived of as a code word for personal accounts of experience. To be sure, a phenomenologist has a full right to begin the analysis by focusing on first-person experience. Yet only insofar as one's analysis involves some kind of epoché and reduction, and only insofar as it leads to insights into essences, does one have the right to qualify one's account as phenomenological. With this in mind, let us once again stress that a phenomenologically oriented investigation is concerned with the eidetic structures of pain experience.[10]

2. Just as phenomenology is not psychologism, so also it is not introspectionism. This is another implication that follows from the analysis offered in the last section. Here we touch on a confusion that is widespread in the contemporary philosophy of pain, which is marked by a general willingness to enter into dialogue with phenomenology. Such openness to phenomenology relies upon the conjecture that phenomenology can fill a significant void in pain research. One presumes that pain is both physiological and experiential, and on this basis one further claims that the science of pain is in need of both a third-person experimental and a first-person experiential methodology. Within such a framework, one further conceives of phenomenology, along with Eastern meditative practices (see Price and Aydede 2005, 14), as a peculiar type of introspective method.[11] One thus presumes that phenomenology can fulfill an important yet partial task in the science of pain: it can clarify pain's experiential dimensions (what Price and Aydede identify as the horizontal dimension), which then need to be further linked to their neurological underpinnings (what Price and Aydede refer to as the vertical dimension).

While appreciating the general openness toward phenomenology, I would nonetheless claim that we face here a highly misleading appropriation of phenomenology.[12] The confusion in question derives from a misunderstanding of the privilege phenomenology accords to reflection and intuition. One reasons as follows: since phenomenology is a reflective discipline whose fundamental

METHODOLOGICAL CONSIDERATIONS   23

concepts are established intuitively, what else can it be if not introspectionism—a first-person examination of one's conscious thoughts and feelings, which can be given only reflectively and intuitively? But if so, then the devastating critique of introspectionism, and especially in behaviorist psychology, must also apply to phenomenology. This critique has demonstrated that first-person reports appear to rest only on immediate self-givenness, while in truth they entail inferences drawn from overt behavior and from the judgments of others. The recent critiques in the philosophy of mind, which reproach phenomenology for being naively reliant on introspectionist methodology and for failing to find a single universalizable method (see Dennett 1991, 44; Metzinger 2003, 591), thereby become understandable. Supposedly, since phenomenology relies on introspectionist methodology, it inevitably generates inconsistencies, which it has no means to resolve.[13]

We face here widespread confusions. Francisco J. Varela (1996, 334) is fully justified when he maintains that one mixes up apples and oranges when one puts phenomenology and introspectionism into the same bag. Even though it privileges reflection and intuition, phenomenology is not introspectionism. While introspection is focused on individual instances of subjective experience, phenomenology is concerned with experiential essences, that is, with invariants. As Shaun Gallagher has it, "Phenomenology is not simply about subjective experience understood as an internal felt sensation or phenomenal consciousness" (2012, 58). Or as Dan Zahavi maintains, "All the major figures in the phenomenological tradition have openly and unequivocally denied that they are engaged in some kind of introspective psychology and that the method they employ is a method of introspection" (2013, 25–26).[14]

This should not be taken to mean that introspectionism and phenomenology do not have anything in common. Both introspectionism and phenomenology could be qualified as methods designed to examine one's thoughts and feelings as they are given through the first-person perspective. So also, both could be qualified as analyses of essentially nonextensive phenomena, which can be given only reflectively and intuitively. Yet these significant affinities should not overshadow fundamental differences between them, which are both methodological and thematic. Put in the language common in the philosophy of mind, one could say that both introspectionism and phenomenology obey the *mentality condition*: both are concerned with generating knowledge about conscious experience, and not about physical events that lie presumably outside one's conscious experience. Yet phenomenology does not obey two other important conditions that introspectionism obeys, namely, the *first-person condition* and the *temporal proximity condition*. First, we need to draw a clear distinction between what in phenomenology is called the first-person perspective and what in the philosophy of mind is called the first-person condition. Introspection meets the first-person condition in that it is a process that is aimed at generating knowledge or beliefs about *one's own mind only*, not anyone else's. By contrast, phenomenology is not concerned with the idiosyncratic nature of anyone's experience, be it my own or anyone else's; it is not meant to offer a description of anyone's mind in particular, but is exclusively focused on generating knowledge about the eidetic structures that must underlie any experience whatsoever. Second, introspectionism obeys the *temporal proximity condition* insofar as it is *a process* of learning about one's own *currently ongoing, or very recently past*, mental states or processes. By contrast, phenomenology is not concerned with a particular group of temporal experiences, but with the temporality of experience as such.

To this twofold distinction between phenomenology and introspectionism, one can add a third point of divergence. It concerns the breadth of introspective and phenomenological research. Introspectionism has been employed to study only relatively simple phenomena (for instance, the responses of different subjects under the same and/or different conditions to the same stimulus), while much more complex phenomena (for instance, those that concern mental disorders and personality) could not be addressed introspectively. By contrast, the phenomenological method is meant to enable the researcher to address the essences of any experience, irrespective of how simple or complex it might be.

3. What does it mean to assert that phenomenology, claims to the contrary notwithstanding, cannot escape the charge of solipsism? To clarify the meaning of this accusation, let us open a brief dialogue between the phenomenology of pain and the phenomenology of medicine by turning to Tania Gergel's recent critique of the phenomenological method. With reference to the phenomenology of illness, Gergel contends that one of its fundamental goals is "to give an account and help us understand illness as it is experienced by the ill individuals themselves" (2012, 1104). However, as Gergel sees it, phenomenological sensitivity to the experiential dimensions of illness does not facilitate, but rather impedes the capacity to understand and relate to ill individuals. "Far from enabling empathy and understanding, if the true conception of illness resides in the ill individual's personal experience of the phenomena, we might well ask how it can ever be truly communicated and

understood by another" (Gergel 2012, 1104). As Gergel sees it, this is not only a methodological difficulty that afflicts phenomenological studies of illness, but a problem that also impedes phenomenology's ambition to facilitate a dialogue between patients and health-care practitioners. If illness is confined within the boundaries of experience, then we inevitably come to confront *the challenge of solipsism*: the experience of illness seems to be inaccessible to anyone except the individual subject of that experience.

Let us extend this critique from the phenomenology of illness to the phenomenology of pain and let us ask: Does phenomenology truly maintain that the concepts of illness and pain *reside* in the ill individual's personal experience in a way that those concepts would elude interpersonal understanding? In light of the foregoing account of the phenomenological method, we can see that we face here a misleading characterization of the phenomenological standpoint. The suggestion that the concepts in question *reside* in the experience of the patient is a clear instance of psychologism. Phenomenology aims to *ground* the concepts of illness and pain *in experience*, yet not to bound them within personal experience. Illness and pain are not confined within, but rooted in, experience.

Gergel's characterization of the phenomenology of illness represents the widespread tendency in the philosophy of illness to misidentify phenomenological analyses as types of empirical description of factual experiences pain patients live through. We need to reassert the fundamental methodological commitments that underlie phenomenologically oriented studies. In light of these commitments, the task of the phenomenology of pain is to provide insight into what is essential about pain experience. A study can be qualified as phenomenological, in the Husserlian sense of the term, insofar as it subscribes to the methods of the epoché, the reduction, and eidetic variation. Much confusion would be avoided if not only the critics of phenomenology, but also those who take themselves to be practicing phenomenology, recognized the indispensable role that these methods must play in phenomenologically oriented research.

REVAMPING EIDETIC VARIATION: FROM PURE TO DIALOGICAL PHENOMENOLOGY

My defense of the method of eidetic variation does not entail that I take this method to be free of difficulties. So far I have left the most severe limitation out of consideration. All too often, this method is understood as an excuse to practice phenomenology in isolation from other intellectual debates and controversies. One thinks that this method proscribes the possibility of any kind of dialogue between phenomenology and other sciences, be they human, social, or natural. Presumably, insofar as these sciences do not rely on the methods of the epoché and the reduction, phenomenologists do not have the right to accept their results in their own research. It appears that phenomenologists are destined to carry out their research not only in methodological loneliness, but also in thematic seclusion. Needless to say, all of this carries regrettable consequences for phenomenological research. When viewed from the perspective of other sciences, phenomenological findings all too often appear extraneous and dispensable. We thus need to ask: Does the phenomenological method place a requirement on the phenomenologists to practice phenomenology in such an insular way?

If it is indeed true that the method of eidetic variation places such a requirement on the part of the researcher, then I would contend that this method cannot achieve its fundamental objective, namely, it cannot generate insights into the essences of the phenomena. When interpreted in the above-mentioned way, this method becomes entirely dependent upon the phenomenologist's *factual* cognitive abilities, which limit the range of possible variation. Even worse: when interpreted in such an insular way, the method of eidetic variation places the investigator back in the arms of psychologism. These remarks call for some further elucidation.

Husserl claims that at a certain point in the process of eidetic variation, the researcher comes to see the essence of the phenomenon, and, when this happens, no further variation is needed. Yet how can one ever be assured that the process of imaginative variation is no longer necessary and that one has, presumably, attained insight into the essence of the phenomenon? In this regard, the distinction Husserl draws between open and motivated possibility is highly helpful.[15] No matter how carefully one might follow the eidetic method, there always seems to be an open possibility that one might be misidentifying the presumably essential characteristics of the phenomenon. It seems that the method of eidetic variation, especially when practiced in the insular way as described above, is just not capable of closing off such an open possibility and thereby reassuring us that we are avoiding possible pitfalls. What is more, when this method is practiced in private seclusion, the general insights attained come into conflict with the results achieved in scientific research. With regard to Husserl's (1977, 75) eidetic claim that colors and sounds cannot change into each other, Shaun Gallagher writes:

> Simply because he cannot *imagine* this possibility, however, doesn't mean that it is *actually* impossible. Here we can see the importance of intersubjective verification, since in fact, one can find people who experience synaesthesia, and for whom colors and sounds do change into each other. Empirical research on synesthesia [*sic*] can also indicate the range of possibilities and can demonstrate that the regional (ontological) boundary between colors and sounds can be more malleable than might be ordinarily expected. (2012, 51)

Do conflicts of this kind between phenomenological claims and the results of empirical research compel us to abandon eidetic variation as an unreliable method that cannot secure the reliability of its own pronouncements? Such a conclusion would be detrimental for phenomenology, for, as I have argued earlier, if phenomenology relies only on the methods of the epoché and the reduction, then it is not in the position to make any reliable claims that could obtain intersubjective verification. Yet such a conclusion would be both hasty and illegitimate. Conflicts that emerge between phenomenologically oriented claims and the results achieved in other sciences compel us to abandon *a certain interpretation* of eidetic variation, namely, the interpretation that presumes this method places a demand on the researcher to engage in phenomenological reflections while taking safe distance from all other intellectual discussions. The recognition that the method of eidetic variation does not warrant the reliability of phenomenological insights into the essence of the phenomena requires that we find a way to open a dialogue between phenomenology and other sciences. Methodologically, we can achieve this goal by showing that there is a fully legitimate way in which imaginative variations could be supplemented with factual variations, namely, those variations that draw on the accomplishments in other fields of research. Such factual variations can derive from highly diverse sources, such as the natural, social, and human sciences, literature and poetry, fine arts and cinema, or even (auto) biographies. Insofar as phenomenology is open to such supplementation, one has all the reasons needed to call it *dialogical phenomenology*.

We are in need of such a phenomenological approach that would stay faithful to the fundamental methodological principles (the epoché, the reduction, and eidetic variation) while at the same time being open to the developments in other fields. What I identify here as dialogical phenomenology is a philosophical approach that meets both conditions. Yet how feasible is such an approach? How can phenomenology accept the results from other disciplines? Would this not require one to give up one's commitment to the methods of the epoché and the reduction? It might seem that dialogical phenomenology is a *contradictio in adjecto*. It appears to compromise phenomenology's purity, since it forces one to accept the results from other fields that were obtained on the grounds of the natural attitude. Since the phenomenological method requires one to put in brackets the natural attitude, including the presuppositions that underlie and the results that follow from the natural, social, and human sciences, either one can strictly adhere to the fundamental phenomenological principles, or one can build on the basis of the results obtained in the sciences of the natural attitude. It seems that these are the two approaches between which one must choose.

Admittedly, phenomenology cannot, and should not, accept the insights derived from these highly diverse sources as straightforward validities. However, one has a full right to incorporate these insights into the phenomenological field *by transforming them into possibilities*, which in their own turn would enable the researcher to expand the horizons of eidetic variation. Insofar as one accepts the results from diverse sciences *as possibilities*, one does not treat them as matters of fact or as reliable conclusions that follow from sound arguments. If accepted as mere possibilities, scientific discoveries can enlarge the horizon of those imaginative possibilities, which the phenomenologist must take into account while employing the method of eidetic variation. In this sense, and in this sense alone, dialogical phenomenology's openness to the results that stem from other fields of research does not compromise its methodological orientation.

The fact that scientific findings can be accepted in phenomenology only *as possibilities* means that factual variations should not be conceived of as an independent method alongside the method of eidetic variation. Rather, the coupling of these procedures enables one to give up a certain conception of the method of eidetic variation as illegitimate; it enables one to reject the view that eidetic variation closes off all possibilities of opening a dialogue between phenomenology and other sciences and that therefore, presumably, a phenomenologist must be an intellectual hermit, whose research must unfold in methodological and thematic solitude. By supplementing imaginative variations with factual variations, one liberates phenomenology from its insularity and opens the way to pursue a dialogue between phenomenology and other sciences.[16]

The coupling of imaginative variations with factual variations is especially needed when one turns to such complex phenomena as pain. Especially then the need arises for dialogical phenomenology, which would be open to descriptions and analyses we come across in other fields of research. Consider in this regard Dan Zahavi's following observation about thought experiments:

> It might, occasionally, be better to abandon fiction altogether and instead pay more attention to the startling facts found in the actual world. . . . If we are looking for phenomena that can shake our ingrained assumptions and force us to refine, revise, or even abandon our habitual way of thinking, all we have to do is to turn to psychopathology, along with neurology, developmental psychology, and ethnology; all of these disciplines present us with rich sources of challenging material. (2005, 141–42)

Many other disciplines besides the ones mentioned here can also oblige us to revise our cognitive habits. To repeat, revisions of this kind can also be triggered by the resources provided in fine arts, literature, poetry, cinema, or any kind of (auto)biographies. In principle, any instituted framework can provide the resources to supplement imaginative variations with factual variations and thereby enable us to obtain more reliable access to the essence of the phenomenon. In general, the more complex the phenomenon, the less reliable the merely personal imaginative variation and the greater the need to enrich it with factual variations. To follow up on Zahavi's analysis, "If we wish to test our assumptions about the unity of mind, the privacy of mental states, the nature of agency, or the role of emotions, far more may be learned from a close examination of pathological phenomena such as depersonalization, thought insertion, multiple personality disorder, cases of apraxia, or states of anhedonia than from thought experiments involving swapped brains or teletransporters" (2005, 142). As we will see in chapter 3, a lot is to be learned about the essence of pain from pain dissociation syndromes, such as congenital insensitivity to pain, threat hypersymbolia, or asymbolia for pain. By incorporating such themes into phenomenologically oriented pain research, we can supplement the analysis built on personally motivated imaginative variations with phenomenological reflections that rely on factual variations.

To repeat, we should not think of factual variation as a separate method that is set alongside the method of eidetic variation. Rather, it is an addendum, or qualification, that enables one to liberate oneself from a certain—to my mind, illegitimate—conception of eidetic variation. By supplementing imaginative variation with factual variation, we are in a good position to respond to the hermeneutical critique, which suggests that phenomenology does not sufficiently acknowledge its own embeddedness in the structures of particular languages. This critique runs along the following lines: the phenomenologist who employs the method of eidetic variation cannot help but do so while using a particular language. Yet languages have their own particular grammatical and syntactical structures, which tacitly determine the style and limits of phenomenological descriptions. Such being the case, just as eidetic intuition can never be pure, so also, phenomenological descriptions can never be pure descriptions.

To appreciate the significance of this critique, we could think here of the notorious critiques of Descartes that highlight the philologically questionable employment of the concept of the ego in Descartes's account of the "ego cogito." We could also think of Nietzsche's contention that the philosophical distinction between substance and attribute is not as innocent as it might seem. Presumably, this distinction is of philological origins: it derives from the distinction between the subject and the predicate that is characteristic of Indo-Germanic languages, although this distinction is missing in many other languages that belong to other language groups. Philological critiques of such kind bring into question the possibility of pure descriptions. They suggest that all intuitions and experiences are always already shot through with structures that derive from particular languages. We are thereby invited to concede that the seeing of essences, which is meant to result from eidetic variation, is also predetermined by these structures. Presumably, we can never reach the assurance that these structures do not disfigure the phenomenological descriptions of the alleged essences of the phenomena.

Dialogical phenomenology, which is willing to supplement imaginative variations with factual variations, is in a good position to answer this critique. A concrete phenomenological analysis that is built upon the methods of the epoché, the reduction, and eidetic variation (conceived only in terms of one's own imaginative variation) might indeed fail to provide us with reliable insights into the essence of the phenomena, and the reasons for this failure might concern the grammatical and syntactical structures of language. Precisely, therefore, dialogical phenomenology must be open not only to research undertaken in other disciplines, but also to research undertaken in other cultural settings and in other languages. Besides being cross-disciplinary, dialogical phenomenology also needs to be cross-cultural—open to the possibility that descriptions of the phenomenon undertaken in other cultural settings and other languages might provide the incentive to refine and revise the results obtained in one's own eidetic analysis.

We can say about eidetic variation what Merleau-Ponty (1962, xiv) famously said about the reduction: the greatest lesson of the eidetic variation is the impossibility of a complete eidetic variation. Insofar as dialogical phenomenology is open to descriptions offered in other disciplines and other languages, it is never in the position to foreclose its own analysis of the phenomenon. As a phenomenologist, one must risk making eidetic claims, yet one cannot foreclose the possibility that these claims will have to be refined and revised. A phenomenologist is a perpetual beginner.

THE GENETIC METHOD IN PHENOMENOLOGY

Although indispensable for phenomenologically oriented pain research, the methods outlined above do not exhaust the methodological resources of the phenomenological standpoint. We could qualify these methods as the fundamental methodological principles of static phenomenology, and to this we could add that they need to be supplemented with the fundamental methodological principles of genetic phenomenology.[17] It is, however, extremely difficult to qualify the fundamental methodological orientation that makes up the core of genetically oriented analyses.[18] We can avoid serious confusion if we recognize that genetic phenomenology is meant not to replace, but to supplement, the static method. More precisely, the genetic method is meant to clarify some of the fundamental presuppositions that underlie static methodology. In this section, I will take a detour to the fundamental methodological principles of genetic phenomenology, and only at its very end will I return to the question that is of central importance for our purposes, namely, the question concerning the significance of the genetic method for phenomenologically oriented pain research.

In his early writings, Husserl did not consider genetic investigations appropriate to phenomenology. He thought genetic investigations were of an empirical nature, that they had to rely on empirical methods, and that their significance was also only empirical. Such was the view Husserl held in the

Logical Investigations (2000; first published in 1900–1901), where phenomenology, conceived of as descriptive psychology, was methodologically compelled to exclude all genetic considerations.[19] In the first volume of the *Ideas* (1983; first published in 1913), Husserl also defended such a perspective.[20] According to Husserl of *Ideas I*, questions about essences are fundamentally different from questions about facts.

The recognition that genetic considerations need to be incorporated into phenomenology was triggered by the realization that static phenomenology relies upon presuppositions that call for genetic clarifications. Phenomenology is a study of consciousness, yet consciousness is not just a field of experience, but also a *stream* of experiences, and insofar as it is a stream, it must be studied not only in terms of its essential structures, but also in terms of its development. The synchronic study of consciousness that we come across in static phenomenology needs to be supplemented with a diachronic investigation.

Recall my earlier observation about eidetic variation. As an investigator, I must already have a vague grasp of the phenomenon before I subject it to the method of eidetic variation. Yet, precisely because this vague understanding is inexplicit, that is, precisely because I do not know what is entailed in my largely preconceptual understanding of the phenomenon, I am in need of eidetic variation—a method that would enable me to purify the phenomenon's essence from various confusions and misapprehensions. This means that the method of eidetic variation hangs on the shoulders of the investigator's mundane grasp of phenomena: it is a method for testing, revising, and refining the already pregiven understanding of the phenomena.

What does phenomenology have to say about this preconceptual understanding? As far as the method of eidetic variation is concerned, phenomenology merely relies on its availability, without inquiring into its possibility. Precisely, therefore, we are in need of genetic considerations. Such a supplementation is necessary, since in its absence we would have to conclude that phenomenology itself rests on presuppositions that can be handled only by means of other kinds of investigations. That is, we would have to concede that the phenomenological analysis of essences is possible if, and only if, one already has a largely preconceptual grasp of phenomena that can be clarified only nonphenomenologically. Such a state of affairs would compromise phenomenology's aspiration to be a fundamental science of pure experience, which neither rests on naturalistic preconceptions nor limits itself to filling in the gaps left open in other fields of research, but which clarifies the

METHODOLOGICAL CONSIDERATIONS

fundamental concepts and fundamental presuppositions that are at work in other investigations. We thus need to ask: *How does preconceptual understanding originate, and how does it develop?* Genetic phenomenology is meant to answer these two questions.

Genetic considerations arise from the need to supplement the analyses of being with reflections on becoming.[21] Questions about the genesis of the preconceptual understanding of phenomena can be appropriated in phenomenology if, and only if, one demonstrates that the sphere of becoming can itself be studied, not at the factual, but at the eidetic level.[22] To demonstrate that the sphere of becoming is a legitimate phenomenological theme, one must show that the genesis of the preconceptual understanding of phenomena is itself ruled by certain *principles*, which can be clarified phenomenologically.

Husserl (2001, 629) identifies genetic phenomenology as *explanatory*, as opposed to static phenomenology, which he qualifies as *descriptive*. These qualifications suggest that insofar as one follows the principles of static phenomenology, one must zero in on the intuitively given phenomenon, and, following the method of eidetic variation, one must describe its essential characteristics. By contrast, the genetic method requires that one trespass the boundaries of pure description. As seen from the genetic standpoint, it does not suffice to describe; rather, one must explain. Insofar as genetic explanation is a matter of interpretation, one could characterize genetic phenomenology as genetically oriented hermeneutics of subjective life and the life-world (see Luft 2004, 226). Yet, obviously, not any kind of explanation or interpretation is phenomenological in the genetic sense of the term. Here we turn to the crucial question: *What, then, are the fundamental principles that make up the methodological core of genetic phenomenology?* Despite the basic nature of this question, it is extremely difficult to answer.[23]

The fundamental *methodological* difference between static and genetic phenomenology can be clarified by focusing on the different paths to the phenomenological reduction.[24] While static phenomenology relies upon the so-called Cartesian path, genetic phenomenology offers two alternative paths, which Husserl identifies as the path through psychology and the path through the life-world.[25] A detailed account of these two paths is not possible in the present context. Fortunately, it is also not necessary. My task here is to portray these two genetic paths in broad strokes and to highlight their common methodological features. It is these common features, I will suggest, that make up the methodological basis of genetic phenomenology.

Both genetic paths to the reduction are alternatives to the Cartesian path, which is dominant in static phenomenology. The Cartesian path is motivated by the recognition of the irrevocable contingency that characterizes the general thesis of the natural standpoint. This thesis runs as follows: "the" world as actuality is always already there (see Husserl 1983, §30; and Husserl 1959, §33). The recognition that this thesis is irretrievably contingent calls for a radical alteration of the natural thesis, which Husserl conceptualizes under the heading of the phenomenological epoché. In its own turn, the epoché provides us with the possibility to turn our attention to the field of pure experience, conceived of as the phenomenological residuum. The phenomenological reduction is nothing other than this "universal overthrow" (Husserl 1959, 68) of the natural attitude, which one could also characterize as the radical deliverance of attention from its worldly absorption and its redirection to the newly discovered field of transcendental experience.

As seen from the genetic standpoint, the Cartesian path to the reduction suffers from two chief limitations. First, it gives the false impression that the transcendental field of experience is empty of content (or at least any content that would clearly correspond to the content of mundane experience). It thus seems that phenomenology is reinvigorated Platonism, which liberates us from the shadows in the cave and directs us away from the field of everyday experience to another world of ideas and essences. Second, the conception of the reduction that prevails in static phenomenology, and especially when coupled with the method of eidetic variation, gives the misleading impression that phenomenology can conceptualize the field of pure experience only synchronically (that is, in terms of eidetic structures, which characterize all possible experience) and not diachronically. It thus seems that such an approach to the reduction overlooks the full-fledged significance of the temporal nature of the experiential field, conceiving of it only as a pure form, and not *as a field of genesis*.

The path to the reduction through psychology is marked by the refusal to suspend the thesis of the natural attitude in one go. This path prefigures transcendental phenomenology. It invites the investigator to focus on specific acts phenomenologically, even before one performs the universal epoché and the universal reduction.[26] To follow this path is to engage in *mundane phenomenology*, which still hasn't brought into question the belief in the world (see Held 2003, 28–29). We can thereby see how the genetic approach overcomes the first limitation of the static approach I have identified above. Anything and everything we come across in the natural attitude can be reabsorbed within the field of transcendental experience and thereby transformed into a phenomenological theme.[27] Following the psychological path, one demonstrates that the field of experience is not empty of content: there is absolutely nothing in the field of mundane experience that cannot be redeemed phenomenologically. Moreover, following the genetic path also enables one to overcome the second limitation, which concerns the prospects of a diachronic analysis of the field of experience. If it is indeed true that all acts of mundane experience can be "translated" into transcendental acts, then we can say the following: "Just as I in the natural attitude, as I-this-person, retrospectively and prospectively know about my past and future life, so also, as I practice the transcendental reduction, I know about my transcendental being or life in the *past* and the *future*; and I know this from my transcendental experience" (Husserl 1959, 84; my translation—SG). The goal of the psychological path to the reduction is to unveil the full content of universal transcendental experience: to deliver the transcendental present, past, and future and thereby provide the resources needed to further conceptualize the field of experience *as a field of genesis*.

The ontological path to the reduction is also marked by the refusal to suspend the general thesis of the natural attitude at the outset. While the path through psychology directs the phenomenologist's attention to the psychological acts of mundane consciousness, the ontological path leads to the general correlate of all mundane acts, namely, it leads to the life-world. The life-world is to be understood as the world that the natural attitude has as its correlate. It is the subjective-relative world, conceived of as being at once the ground and the horizon of all human action, both natural and scientific. The ontological path to the reduction leads us to the life-world, conceived of as the forgotten ground of scientific accomplishments, and further thematizes the life-world as the constitutive accomplishment of transcendental subjectivity. In this regard, one may rightly claim that the ontological path faces a twofold task. Its first central task is to purify such a world of all idealistic and naturalistic misconceptions, to recover its original meaning prior to that meaning having been covered up by the "veil of ideas" that experience itself has imposed on the world. Put paradoxically, the first task is to offer *a science of the prescientific world*, which would provide us with the understanding of its most essential structures. Yet this first task must be coupled with the second one, namely, to demonstrate that such a prescientific world is itself a hidden accomplishment of transcendental (inter)subjectivity. As seen from the perspective of genetic phenomenology, our understanding of the life-world remains limited for as long as we do not recognize that the life-world is an intentional correlate of transcendental (inter)subjectivity.

In light of the above, one can say that the second and the third ways to the reduction are complementary in three ways: they both begin at the level of mundane experience, they are both regressive, and they both culminate at the level of transcendental (inter)subjectivity.[28] What makes such a methodological orientation genetic is its regressive nature, and so as to understand it more precisely, we need to supplement the foregoing analysis with reflections on the method of *intentional implications*.[29] At first glance, this method might appear inconsequential. To follow up on Husserl's own examples, within the field of reduced experience, my act of recollection intentionally implies my foregoing act of perception; so also, my act of anticipation intentionally implies my future perception (although, admittedly, with a different kind of evidence). Thus, "I recall having a conversation with you in the hallway" intentionally implies "I had such a conversation with you in the hallway." Claims of this nature border on being trivial. Nonetheless, the method of intentional implications proves to be remarkably resourceful, and it would be hardly an overstatement to qualify it as the engine of genetic methodology in general. What is ultimately at stake in this method is not just the recognition of the double-sided complexity inscribed in the reproductive acts of recollection, phantasy, and anticipation.[30] Of much greater methodological significance is the realization that the method of intentional implications enables us to conceive of present experiences as configurations of sense that rely upon more basic experiences. Conceived of from a genetic point of view, each and every intentional experience always intends more in the object than is given in pure intuition, and this surplus of meaning points to the intentional accomplishments of foregoing experiences. The method of intentional implications is designed to demonstrate that my whole past is intentionally implicated in each and every one of my present intentional experiences. In the final analysis, the method of intentional implications provides the methodological basis upon which to thematize the realm of pure experiences as a developmental field of apperceptive accomplishments.

We thereby obtain the methodological basis for studying the formation of preconceptual understanding in terms of "lawful regularities that regulate the formation of apperceptions" (Husserl 2001, 624). Apperceptions are intentional lived-experiences that prescribe to the given phenomenon dimensions of sense that exceed their intuitive justification. The phenomenological concept of apperception is meant to capture the excess of meaning that

METHODOLOGICAL CONSIDERATIONS

trespasses the boundaries of the phenomenon's intuitive self-givenness.[31] As seen from the standpoint of genetic phenomenology, each and every consciousness is apperceptive: "We cannot even conceive of a consciousness that would not go beyond the strict present in its essential flux from presence to new presences" (Husserl 2001, 626). It is, however, not enough to characterize apperceptive consciousness as a consciousness of the surplus of meaning that exceeds the bounds of intuition and that accompanies each and every experience. Apperceptive consciousness is focused on what is given intuitively and it finds within the intuitively given a *motivation* for a consciousness of something that exceeds the boundaries of intuition. That is, apperceptive consciousness is not just conscious of something intuitively given and in addition still conscious of dimensions of sense that exceed the boundaries of intuition; rather, it is a consciousness that intentionally points toward the nonintuitive as that which is motivated intuitively (see Husserl 2001, 627). To a large degree, the goal of genetic phenomenology is to discover the fundamental principles in accordance with which apperceptions are formed and in accordance with which ever-new apperceptions necessarily arise from other apperceptions.[32] They can be formed at different levels of experience, which Husserl (2001, 631) identifies as the level of pure activity, the intermediary level between passivity and activity, and the level of pure passivity.

At this point we can come back to the twofold question raised at the beginning of this section: *How does preconceptual understanding originate, and how does it develop?* Having addressed the fundamental methodological principles that underlie genetic phenomenology, we are in the position to appreciate the remarkably rich answer genetic phenomenology offers to this question. This answer is fundamentally twofold. On the one hand, by focusing on the hidden accomplishments of transcendental subjectivity, genetic phenomenology demonstrates that preconceptual understanding originates and develops within the framework of subjective experience. Genetic phenomenology focuses on the field of transcendental experience from a diachronic standpoint and inquires into the fundamental laws and principles in accordance with which transcendental experience develops. On the other hand, genetic phenomenology also strives to show that preconceptual understanding originates and develops in the life-world. In this regard, the questions that prove central to phenomenology concern the life-world's fundamental structures, the way in which objects in the life-world obtain their meaning, and the way in which our basic rootedness in the life-world prefigures our theoretical activities.

We are finally in the position to ask: Of what significance is the genetic method for phenomenologically oriented analyses of pain? What we just said about preconceptual understanding in general, we can also say about such bodily experiences as pain. We can ask: How does the experience of pain originate and how does it develop? The second and third paths to the reduction, coupled with the method of intentional implications, provide us with the methodological basis for addressing these questions phenomenologically. Following the guidelines of genetic methodology, we can investigate how the experience of pain originates both in the field of experience in general and in the life-world. In this regard, in what follows it will be important to show that pain originates as a rupture in the field of experience that unsettles one's otherwise natural absorption in the world of things. In the natural course of life, we are, for the most part, delivered from internal life. Everything for us is outside, in the world, on the road, in the town, in the midst of the crowd (see Sartre 1970, 5). The emergence of pain puts a stop to our natural excentricity: the door through which we used to naturally fly out into the world is now, as it were, blocked with a mirror, in which we see reflected the incapacity of the inborn movement to get off the ground. Pain belongs to a group of feelings that compel us to discover our own immanence. Yet pain does not only occur, it also lingers, which means that one cannot grasp its nature without understanding its temporality. Following the genetic method, we can investigate the temporal nature of pain experience not only in terms of its formal structures, but also in light of its development, paying close attention to the significance of retention and protention, as well as memory and anticipation. Moreover, following the genetic method, we can also investigate how the experience of pain is incorporated into various apperceptions—both conceptual and affective—and how these apperceptions codetermine the nature of pain experience. The analysis of these themes will require that we understand pain not only as a depersonalizing, but also as a repersonalizing experience: not only as an experience that robs us of our selfhood, but also as an experience that invites us to reconstitute ourselves anew. Last but not least, the genetic method also invites us to examine the significance of the person's immersion in the life-world. In this regard, a genetically oriented phenomenology of pain can demonstrate to what extent the processes of somatization and psychologization codetermine the nature of pain experience.

As my references to such processes as depersonalization and repersonalization, as well as somatization and psychologization, suggest, genetically oriented phenomenology of pain must be pursued in dialogue with other disciplines—such as cultural anthropology, cultural psychopathology, and psychoanalysis—which study the same processes on the basis of other methodological principles. In this regard, genetic phenomenology, much like the method of factual variation, liberates phenomenology from insularity by opening exchanges with other fields of research.

~

Let us sum up these methodological considerations. I presented the methods of the epoché, the phenomenological reduction, and eidetic variation as the three fundamental methodological principles that make up the basic core of phenomenologically oriented investigations. I further argued that these three principles are necessary, although not sufficient. In virtue of inherent limitations, they need to be supplemented with further methodological considerations. As we saw, even though the method of eidetic variation is meant to provide the researcher with access to the essence of the phenomenon, it cannot guarantee that the investigator will not confuse this essence with a generalized factual description. Such being the case, the method of eidetic variation needs to be supplemented with the possibilities opened up by factual variation. Such a supplementation significantly enriches the phenomenological field of analysis, even though, admittedly, it does not close off the open possibility that the phenomenological insights might still fail to reach the essence of the phenomenon. Such a methodological supplementation, which reconceptualizes factual variation as a necessary ingredient of eidetic variation, imparts upon phenomenology a much-needed dialogical orientation. Phenomenology need not be disadvantaged by its own purity. Insofar as it is willing to supplement imaginative variations with factual variations, it can build on the basis of accomplishments derived from other sciences by transforming these accomplishments into pure possibilities. Insofar as phenomenology is willing to take on such a methodological orientation, it loses its insularity and becomes dialogical.

Such a dialogical approach is especially called for in pain research. As Gallagher has it, "Phenomena that pertain to biological and specifically human behavior and experience are so complex, that we cannot always grasp the imaginative possibilities in a unified intentional act" (2012, 55). Pain is such a phenomenon. Thus, even though I will begin my analysis in chapter 2 by building phenomenological descriptions in line with the first three fundamental phenomenological methods, it will soon become apparent that a dialogue between phenomenology and a number of other disciplines—such as cognitive science, cultural anthropology, and psychoanalysis—is of great importance for phenomenologically oriented pain research. In addition to supplementing eidetic descriptions with resources obtained from other disciplines, it will also prove necessary to supplement static analyses with genetic investigations. In phenomenology, it does not suffice to clarify the nature of pain experience in terms of its fundamental structures. This is a great task in itself, and it can be achieved by following the methodological guidelines of static phenomenology. Nonetheless, the phenomenological determination of the nature of pain experience remains formal in the absence of genetic investigations, and it therefore needs to be supplemented with an inquiry into the origins and development of pain experience. Such a genetic inquiry supplements the static account by demonstrating the astonishing degree to which pain experience is nested in apperceptions and rooted in the life-world. Genetic phenomenology provides us with the methods needed to study these apperceptions in terms of the fundamental laws that guide their development.

In the introduction, I suggested that the science of pain is in need of phenomenology for two central and interrelated reasons: first, it does not have a reliable method to study the nature of pain experience; and second, it is not in the position to inquire into the compatibility of the findings obtained by means of the first-person and third-person methodologies. The methodological considerations offered in this chapter provide the science of pain with the methodological foundation that it can rely upon as it strives to accomplish both tasks.

CHAPTER 2

PAIN AND INTENTIONALITY

A Stratified Conception of Pain Experience

Having clarified the fundamental methodological commitments that must underlie phenomenologically oriented pain research, we are now ready to turn to our second task. We are ready to raise the fundamental question: *What is pain?* According to the definition proposed by the International Association for the Study of Pain (IASP), "Pain is an unpleasant sensory and emotional experience associated with actual or potential tissue damage, or described in terms of such damage" (Merskey and Bogduk 1994, 209). This established definition, however, cannot be accepted at face value in phenomenology. We know one reason for this from the introduction. Although this definition admits that pain is an experience, it does not clarify the nature of pain *as* experience. It is not enough to qualify pain experience as sensory, emotional, and unpleasant since many other experiences, such as nausea, bodily exhaustion, various kinds of bodily illness, and psychological suffering could also be qualified the same way. The IASP definition does not give us an account of the *explanandum*, which could then be provided with further *explanans*.

One can single out additional reasons why this definition cannot be relied upon in phenomenology. With the performance of the phenomenological epoché, one can no longer clarify the nature of pain experience on the basis of associations with actual or potential tissue damage. The claim that pain experience is associated with actual or potential tissue damage relies on the assumption that the body that experiences pain is composed of tissues—body cells that are organized in accordance with a specific structure and function—and that the experience of pain either is, or derives from, damage that affects these tissues. Such a conception of pain is grounded in pain biology. Yet, as we know from the methodological investigations offered in chapter 1, pain phenomenology cannot rely on pain biology. There are, thus, not only thematic but also methodological reasons why the IASP definition of pain cannot be relied upon in phenomenological research.

What, then, is pain, when conceived in accordance with the fundamental phenomenological principles? The answer that I wish to offer runs as follows: *pain is an aversive bodily feeling with a distinct experiential quality, which can be given only in original firsthand experience, either as a nonintentional feeling-sensation or as an intentional feeling.* The legitimacy of such an answer must be established on the basis of phenomenological descriptions, which would rely on the methodological principles outlined in chapter 1. To offer such descriptions and thereby justify the phenomenological legitimacy of the proposed conception of pain, one must proceed by asking seven questions, which I will list here in the order in which I will pursue them in this study. What does it mean to claim (1) that pain is a nonintentional feeling-sensation; (2) that it is an intentional feeling; (3) that it can be given only in firsthand experience; (4) that this feeling is fundamentally aversive; (5) that it has a unique experiential quality; (6) that it is an original experience; and (7) that it is localized in the body? This chapter will be concerned with the first three questions. Chapter 3 will turn to the fourth and fifth questions, and chapter 4 will offer an analysis of the sixth one, while in chapter 5 we will complete the analysis by turning to the seventh question. At the end of chapter 5, we will have justified the phenomenological conception of pain proposed here.

PAIN AND INTENTIONALITY

Few other questions are as germane to the phenomenology of pain as the question concerning the intentional structure of pain experience. Should pain be qualified as an intentional feeling, namely, as a "consciousness of something," or should it be characterized as a nonintentional feeling-sensation, a mere "experiential content," or a pure "affective state," which does not intend anything? This is the oldest question in the phenomenology of pain. We come across this question in a controversy between two of Edmund Husserl's teachers: Franz Brentano and Carl Stumpf.[1] While Brentano was committed to the view that pain is an intentional feeling, Stumpf argued that pain is a nonintentional sensation, which he called a "feeling-sensation" (*Gefühlsempfindung*). As Stumpf (1924) was subsequently to observe, although in virtually all other regards he considered himself Brentano's follower, the question concerning the intentional status of such feelings as pain marked an uncompromising disagreement between him and Brentano.

This unresolved controversy had far-reaching repercussions for the subsequent development of the phenomenological analyses of pain. Three sets of illustrations should suffice as a clear confirmation that the oldest question in the phenomenology of pain never reached a clear resolution. First, consider Max Scheler's reflections on pain. In his *Formalism in Ethics and Non-Formal Ethics of Values*, Scheler (1973, esp. 328–44) sides with Stumpf when he argues that pain is a nonintentional feeling state. However, in his later works, most notably in "The Meaning of Suffering," Scheler (1992) conceptualizes pain as a particular form of suffering, conceived of as an intentional experience. In "The Meaning of Suffering," Scheler takes over the Brentanian point of view and interprets pain through the prism of intentionality. Second, consider Frederik J. J. Buytendijk's (1962) and Michel Henry's (1973) reflections on pain. Much like the later Scheler, Buytendijk also follows Brentano when he argues that pain cannot be conceived of as a nonintentional feeling-sensation, which, allegedly, affects only the body-self. According to Buytendijk, to clarify pain's personal significance, one must address the meaning that pain has for the sufferer. To do so, one must address pain in various intentional frameworks that bind the sufferer to his or her body, to others, and to the sociocultural world at large. By contrast, Michel Henry radicalizes Stumpf's position and argues that pain is the paradigm of worldless self-affection, conceived of as a purely immanent feeling that living beings have of the concrete modes of their lives. No other experience exemplifies auto-affection as purely as the experience of pain.[2] Third, consider Elaine Scarry's (1985) and Abraham Olivier's (2007) studies of pain. On the one hand, Scarry provides one of the strongest defenses of Stumpf's view. As she puts it in her classical study, *The Body in Pain*, "Desire is desire of x, fear is fear of y, hunger is hunger for z; but pain is not 'of' or 'for' anything—it is itself alone" (Scarry 1985, 161–62). On the other hand, in direct contrast to Scarry, Olivier presents us with a concept of pain as a "disturbed bodily perception bound to hurt, affliction or agony" (2007, 198). Conceiving of pain as a form of perception, Olivier defends the Brentanian line and argues that pain is an intentional experience.

Thus, in the phenomenological literature on pain, the question concerning the intentional status of pain experience remains to this day unresolved. One might be tempted to interpret this seemingly endless controversy as a failure on the part of phenomenology to determine one of the central issues that lie at the heart of the phenomenologically informed pain research. Yet one can also interpret it as a clue that the question concerning the intentional status of pain simply cannot be answered unequivocally.

Such, indeed, is the view that I wish to present in this chapter: there are good reasons why the question concerning the intentional status of pain could not reach a clear resolution. I will defend two interrelated claims. First, pain is a *sensory feeling*. The qualification of pain as sensory relies upon Stumpf's determination of pain as a feeling-sensation. Yet pain is also a feeling, which means that pain also entails emotive dimensions. In this regard, the qualification of pain as a feeling already relies on Brentano's claim that pain is an intentional emotion. However, the conception of pain as a sensory feeling only sharpens the question: How can pain be both a nonintentional feeling-sensation (*Gefühlsempfindung*) and an intentional feeling? To resolve this apparent contradiction, it will be necessary to supplement the first claim with a second one, which will suggest that pain is a stratified experience. This claim means that the experience of pain is composed of two fundamental strata: while its founding stratum is nonintentional, the founded stratum is marked by intentionality. I will maintain that such a stratified conception of pain provides the necessary basis to reconcile Stumpf's and Brentano's standpoints.

PAIN AS A FEELING-SENSATION

What phenomenological evidence underlies the claim that pain is a nonintentional feeling-sensation? I do not raise this question as a preamble to an exegetical study. Rather than limiting myself to Stumpf's analysis, I will strive to present the view that pain is a nonintentional experience as a live option. Arguably, there are at least seven reasons to interpret this position as a living possibility.

First, as the proponents of the Stumpfian standpoint have always maintained, just try to offer a phenomenological description of pain experience, and you will see that pain has no referential content. Elaine Scarry formulates this point especially forcefully. She does not doubt that most of our feelings are intentional. Thus, "love is love of x, fear is fear of y, ambivalence is ambivalence about z" (Scarry 1985, 5). Yet, according to Scarry, no matter how extensive the list of intentional feelings might be, physical pain interrupts it. While intentional feelings are feelings *for* somebody or something, physical pain is "not *of* or *for* anything" (1985, 5). Physical pain takes no referential content; rather, it "resists objectification in language" (1985, 5).

Is it true that physical pain is not "*for* or *about* anything"? Brentano and his followers disagree with this characterization and argue that the standpoint of Stumpf's followers is built upon a fabricated phenomenological description. They argue that pain is an intentional feeling, whose correlate is one's physical body. Thus, if I have abdominal pain, the intentional correlate of my feeling-intention is an area in my stomach; if I have a migraine, the intentional correlate of my pain is an area in my head. Pain has the structure of perceptual consciousness: just as seeing is seeing of x, and hearing is hearing of y, so having pain is related to z. One could say that the intentional correlates of physical pain are surface or nonsurface bodily areas (see Janzen 2013, 864).

However, according to Stumpf's followers, the structure of pain experience is by no means identical with the structure of perceptual consciousness. Here we come across the second reason that supports their position. In the case of perception, consciousness is first and foremost absorbed in the intentional object and only secondarily conscious of its own experiential contents. In the case of pain, the situation is reversed: one is first and foremost absorbed in one's experience and only secondarily conscious of one's body, conceived of as the object of pain experience. This absorption in experience itself, rather than in the objects of experience, intimates that in the case of pain, we are faced not with intentional consciousness, but with a feeling-sensation.

Stumpf's followers do not deny that pain can be interpreted as a way of being aware of an object, namely, of one's own body. However, they assert that this interpretation is an accomplishment of reflective consciousness. They claim that prior to reflection, pain is experienced neither as an intentional feeling nor as an object of this feeling, but as a nonintentional experiential content. At this basic experiential level, pains do not appear, they are just lived through.

Third, one could point out that there is an essential structural difference between intentional consciousness and pain experience. Intentional consciousness is marked by the distinction between the intentional act and the object of this act. In the case of pain experience, one cannot draw an analogous distinction. While we distinguish between the seeing and the seen, the judging and the judged, the loving and the loved, we do not distinguish between the "paining" and the "pained." Being a feeling-sensation, pain does not lend itself to the same kind of structural analysis as do intentional experiences.

Fourth, to provide this view with further support, one could point to the disruptive effects of intense pain experience. As Scarry (1985) puts it, pain obliterates all intentional contents of consciousness, leaving one with a nonintentional experience. Indeed, the more intense one's pain, the more it forces one to withdraw from any intentional object one might have been contemplating. Admittedly, only in exceptional cases do such annihilating powers of pain bring about a complete obliteration of consciousness. Yet as Agustín Serrano de Haro insightfully points out, "In regard to the whole field of consciousness, a pain experience either takes full possession of the conscious foreground, or it strives to actually do so" (2011, 390). Put otherwise, any experience of pain, no matter how weak or intense it might be, manifests a *tendency* to obliterate and take possession of consciousness, and this tendency can manifest itself in a more or less pure form. Insofar as one resists this tendency and retains the capacity to contemplate the intentional object one was contemplating, one transforms pain into what it is not, namely, into a mere uneasiness or discomfort. Insofar as this tendency wins over one's resistance and one succumbs to pain, one experiences a growing distance from all intentional objects, which leaves one with affective sensations as the sole experiential content. In the extreme case, pain is all there is.

Pain would not be pain if it did not unsettle other feelings, perceptions, thoughts, or activities. Moreover, pain disrupts not only wakeful consciousness, but also consciousness that is asleep. When pain intrudes, it forces consciousness to withdraw from any intentional content it had been contemplating, no matter if this content was perceived, contemplated, imagined, or just dreamed. This obtrusive nature of intense pain casts another shadow of doubt over the view that pain is a nonintentional feeling-sensation. Stumpf and his followers claim that pain is a sensation. Yet sensations do not enter the field of consciousness as objects in the foreground. They do not appear, but are lived through; they are not perceived, but experienced. However, while one can objectify one's sensed contents only through reflective acts, pain emerges in the thematic field of consciousness as though in a flash and forces one to immediately objectify it. Indeed, pain intrudes the field of experience very much like other events in our surroundings, such as sudden noises that interrupt calmness, or unexpected movements that disrupt stillness. Does this fact not compel one to admit that pain is not a feeling-sensation, but an object of intentional consciousness? Using Husserl's terminology from *Ideas I*, one can ask: Should one not abandon the view that pain is a *hyle* and replace

PAIN AND INTENTIONALITY 47

it with the realization that it is a *noema*, conceived of as the objective correlate of an intentional act?[3]

Stumpf's followers have the resources needed to answer this objection. We say that the pain in the abdomen is dreadful, or that the headache is unbearable. The language we employ suggests that pain is an intentional object. Yet one should not be misled by the grammatical structure of such descriptions. As Stumpf observed (1907, 9), everybody knows that the sentence "Sugar is sweet," means that sugar *tastes* sweet, and when it comes to pain, the situation is no different. Whatever else pain might be, it is first and foremost a feeling, and therefore, to clarify what pain is, one must clarify not the nature of an object, but the nature of a feeling. Admittedly, such a response leaves it undecided whether the feeling in question should be determined as an intentional act or as a nonintentional feeling-sensation. Yet, as the foregoing analysis has shown, the structure of pain is essentially different from the structure of intentional acts. If this is accepted, one has to admit that pain is a nonintentional feeling-sensation.

Arguably, one of the reasons why Stumpf qualifies pain as a unique kind of sensation, namely, as a feeling-sensation, is so as not to lose sight of the obtrusive nature of pain experience. Other sensory contents do not impose themselves upon us by stealing our attention. So as to distinguish between the obtrusive and the nonobtrusive sensations, Stumpf identifies the former as feeling-sensations. One can thus respond to Brentano and his followers by pointing out that the obtrusive nature of pain does not contradict the fact that it is a sensation. Appearances to the contrary notwithstanding, there are obtrusive sensations; they are called feeling-sensations.

Let us turn to the fifth reason that supports the view of Stumpf's followers. Those who suffer from pain live through their pains *indubitably*. As Scarry puts it, "For the person in pain, so incontestably and unnegotiably present is it that 'having pain' may come to be thought of as the most vibrant example of what it is to 'have certainty'" (1985, 4). To be in pain means, among other things, to have no doubt that one is in pain. Yet indubitability is a mark of inner rather than outer perception. This means that such an intentional object as one's own body cannot be given indubitably. Moreover, this also means that insofar as pain is marked by indubitability, it cannot be qualified as an object of experience but must be either an intentional act, which intends an object, or a nonintentional content of experience. Yet, as we already know, pain cannot be an intentional act. If so, one has to conclude that pain is a nonintentional feeling-sensation.

One might object that Stumpf's followers build their case by paying attention only to the most gruesome forms of intense pain, which obliterate all other forms of consciousness. Would one not be led to different conclusions if one focused on milder and much more common forms of pain? With this question, we are led to the sixth reason that underlies the standpoint of Stumpf's followers. No matter how mild or intense pain might be, it is experienced not as an object but, to use Hermann Schmitz's (2009, 23–27) fitting expression, as an *atmosphere* that colors intentional objects. Consider, for instance, how, after a sleepless night, one experiences a migraine while nonetheless being forced to engage in regular activities. Under such circumstances, one does not relate to the pain in one's head as an intentional object of one's consciousness. Rather, pain creates a particular atmosphere, which "is without place, yet nonetheless spatial,"[4] and thus embraces and affects any object one might perceive or be contemplating. Consider the pain in one's eyes, of which Jean-Paul Sartre (1956, 309) speaks in *Being and Nothingness*. If I experience this kind of pain while reading a book, then the object of my consciousness is the book, while pain is neither to the right nor to the left of it, nor is it one of the truths enclosed in it. Rather, pain manifests itself as the quivering of the letters on the page or as the difficulty in understanding their meaning. Thus, as Sartre explicitly puts it, "Pain is totally void of intentionality" (1956, 308), by which we are to understand that pain is not an intentional object among others. Nonetheless, I experience it as a "contingent attachment to the world" (Sartre 1956, 309), or, to return to Schmitz, as an *atmosphere* that covers my act of reading. One thus lives one's pain as a pure affective state, which refuses to be characterized as intentional.

To what has been mentioned above, let us add a seventh and last reason that supports the standpoint of Stumpf's followers. This reason concerns what Scarry (1985, 15) has called the "as if" structure of the existing vocabulary for pain. We qualify our pains temporally as quivering, pulsing, throbbing, or beating; we qualify them spatially as jumping or shooting; with an eye on their pressure, we speak of them as cramping, cutting, drilling, gnawing, pinching, pressing, pricking, pulling, or stabbing. Yet the primary meanings of these and many other terms, which are employed in the McGill Pain Questionnaire with the aim of identifying the sensory, affective, and cognitive contents of pain experience, are related to objects and not to any kind of experience, including pain experience. These terms can be meaningfully employed in characterizing pain only because of the metaphorical transference of sense, that is, only because of the "as if" structure of the vocabulary for pain. But why does this transference provide us with the only available vocabulary for pain? Arguably, here we are in need of metaphors precisely because language is designed to name what is referential. As Scarry puts it, "Physical pain is not identical with (and often exists without) either agency or damage, but these things are referential; consequently, we often call on them to convey the experience of the pain itself" (1985, 15).[5] In short, to speak of pain, one must objectify pain with the help of those terms that do not apply to it, which, by implication, means that to speak of pain, one must objectify what is not an object at all. We cannot help but find the means to speak about pain. Yet, as soon as we give it a name, we falsify and misrepresent a nonintentional experience as an intentional object. We must keep our guard up so as not to become "victims to the seduction of language" (Husserl 1970, 362).

Such, then, are the central reasons that underlie the view that pain is a nonintentional feeling-sensation. Pain has no referential content; it does not share the same structure with other kinds of intentional consciousness; its disruptive effects are such that in the extreme case, pain empties consciousness of any intentional content; the indubitable evidence characteristic of its givenness is essentially different from the evidence that applies to the givenness of intentional contents; it covers all intentional relations as a nonintentional atmosphere; last but not least, the language we employ to characterize our pains is yet a further testament to the nonintentional nature of pain experience. These reasons make it understandable why the perspective that was first introduced by Stumpf retains its credibility to this day. Nonetheless, this fact need not be conceived of as an invitation to abandon the Brentanian position. In the following section, we will consider the reasons that underlie Brentano's standpoint.

PAIN AS AN INTENTIONAL FEELING

There are three fundamental ways in which one can understand pain as an intentional experience. First, one could argue that pain is neither a nonintentional feeling-sensation, nor an object of feelings, but a particular way one is conscious of one particular object, namely, of one's own body. After all, one never experiences pain in midair: one cannot simply "be in pain." One can feel pain only in one's head, neck, abdomen, and so on. We can feel pain only *in* our bodies, conceived of as intentional correlates of our feelings. The experience of pain thereby proves to be an instance of our acquaintance with intentionally constituted reality.

As we saw in the previous section, Stumpf's followers reject this line of reasoning by pointing out that pain experience does not share the same structure with perceptual consciousness. While seeing is always seeing of something, and hearing is always hearing something, feeling pain is not a matter of intending something through pain experience, but a matter of living through a particular feeling. Even more: the very way we live through intense pain tends to block our access to any intentional object we might have been contemplating. Small wonder, then, that Stumpf and his followers consider pain to be a nonintentional experience. Yet Brentano's followers consider such a response an instance of a misplaced criticism. One does not need to think that the structure of pain experience is analogous with that of perception in order to recognize pain as an intentional experience. It is much more significant to highlight the fact that the structure of pain experience is analogous with that of other intentional emotions. Consider such emotions as pride and shame, attraction and disgust, or joy and sorrow. In the case of each, the subject of experience is absorbed more in one's own feelings than in their intentional correlates. Nonetheless, this structural difference between emotions and perceptions does not imply that emotions are bereft of intentionality. Clearly, we are proud or ashamed *over something*, attracted or disgusted *by something*, overjoyed or sorrowed *by something*. So also, just because those who suffer from pain are first and foremost absorbed in their experience, and only secondarily conscious of their bodies, does not imply that the experience of pain is nonintentional. Quite on the contrary, just like the above-mentioned emotions, the experience of pain is intentional through and through. For this very reason, Brentano and his followers invite us to concede that pain is an intentional emotion.

Second, besides identifying pain as an intentional feeling, one can also thematize it as an intentional correlate of feelings. That is, besides thematizing pain noetically, one can also address it noematically. Serrano de Haro has referred to such a conception of pain as the "pure intentional model" and qualified it as the view that conceives of pain as a "disturbing event that one notices in some part of one's body and which monopolizes one's attention" (2011, 392). One could single out two central reasons to support such a view. First, without recognizing pain as a *noema*, one could not make sense of pain's obtrusive characteristics. Only what appears can obtrude consciousness and

PAIN AND INTENTIONALITY

obliterate all of its other contents. Yet, by definition, whatever appears is the correlate of one's intentional experiences.[6] Second, without recognizing pain as a *noema*, one can only partly make sense of the bodily nature of pain. If it is indeed true that pain has bodily localizability, then it must be given in our bodies, conceived of as intentional correlates of experience.[7]

Third, one can also conceive of pain as a feeling, through which one intentionally relates not only to one's body, but to all possible experiential objects. While this view is especially strongly defended by Merleau-Ponty and his followers, the phenomenological origins of this conception can be found in Husserl's reflections on sensings (*Empfindnisse*) that we come across in *Ideas II*.[8] As far as the philosophy of pain is concerned, Abraham Olivier's (2007) *Being in Pain* provides the most elaborate analysis of such a conception of pain experience. Building his case against both the materialists and the dualists, who either directly (materialists) or indirectly (dualists) privilege the physiological conceptions of pain (see Olivier 2007, 2–6), Olivier thematizes pain as a "disturbed bodily perception bound to hurt, affliction or agony" (2007, 6). Relying on Merleau-Ponty's phenomenology of perception, Olivier (2007, 27) understands perception in a remarkably broad way, which covers all intentional acts, and identifies the subject of experience as a perceiving body. Within such a conceptual framework, to argue that pain is a disturbed perception is to suggest that pain disturbs how the subject of experience senses, feels, and thinks. Thus, pain affects not only the sufferer's body; it also disturbs anything that emerges in the field of sensations, perceptions, or thoughts.

Such a conceptual framework invites us to reinterpret Sartre's and Schmitz's contributions to the phenomenology of pain as clarifications of the intentional nature of pain experience. Although Sartre explicitly qualifies the most basic experience of pain as nonintentional, one can conceive of the pain-in-the-eyes of which he speaks as an illustration of the intentional structure of pain experience. Pain covers each and every object one might be sensing, perceiving, or contemplating. So also, with regard to Schmitz, one can conceive of the atmosphere of pain as a horizon that covers all of pain's intentional effects. Itself being without place, pain covers everything that emerges in perceptual, imaginary, or conceptual spaces. In this sense also, pain proves to be irreducibly intentional.

Thus, even though there are good reasons to hold on to the standpoint of Stumpf's followers, there are also strong reasons that support the Brentanian view. It is not enough to state that pain can be conceived of as an intentional experience. One must stress that it can be so conceived of in no fewer than three ways: either as an intentional feeling, or as an intentional object, or, finally, as an intentional atmosphere that covers all intentional feelings and intentional objects. Since both the Stumpfian and the Brentanian positions are grounded in phenomenological descriptions, it is hardly surprising that the question concerning the intentional structure of pain experience remains to this day without a definite resolution.

APPREHENSION—CONTENT OF APPREHENSION

We seem to be faced with two incompatible standpoints. If the position of Stumpf's followers is correct, then it seems that the standpoint of Brentano's followers must be mistaken, and vice versa. Nonetheless, there is a way to resolve the obvious divergences between the Brentanian and the Stumpfian positions and, as I have already argued elsewhere, such a way is not unprecedented. Section 15 of Husserl's Fifth Logical Investigation, which offers the first explicitly phenomenological analysis of pain (Brentano's and Stumpf's accounts being protophenomenological), is nothing other than an attempt to reconcile Stumpf's and Brentano's positions (see Geniusas 2014a). However, since in the *Logical Investigations* Husserl is only marginally interested in clarifying the intentional structure of feelings and emotions, the resolution he offers is nothing more than a blueprint. My goal here is to develop this blueprint further by building on the basis of Husserl's schema "apprehension–content of apprehension" (*Auffassung/ Auffassungsinhalt*).

Husserl introduced this schema in the *Logical Investigations* with the aim of clarifying the structure of intentionality. In this schema, the content refers to sensible materials, which Husserl defines as *real* (*reel*) experiential contents. Here the term "real" (*reel*) stands for what is immanently given in consciousness (color-data, tone-data, touch-data, or algedonic-data, to use Husserl's own illustrations). By contrast, intentional contents are identified as "irreal": they are not the contents consciousness lives through, but phenomena consciousness intends. Otherwise put, they are not given in consciousness, but appear to consciousness.

According to Husserl of the *Logical Investigations*, experience obtains intentional character by means of "apprehension," "interpretation," or "animation" (these are all English renditions of the German "*Auffassung*"), which bestows sense upon the real (*reel*) contents of consciousness. This does not mean that apprehension objectifies real contents of consciousness. For Husserl, apprehension does not transform either sensations or acts of apprehension into objects of consciousness. Rather, through apprehension, consciousness reinterprets its own sensations as particular acts that are intentionally directed at their intentional correlates. Thus, according to the view Husserl endorses in the *Logical Investigations*, what appears to consciousness as an object is based upon the prereflective application of the apprehension–content of apprehension schema. The function of this schema is to enable consciousness to grasp the meaning of the intended object (see Gallagher 1998, 45).

Husserl's followers, as well as Husserl himself, have repeatedly questioned the validity of this conceptual model. Aron Gurwitsch (1964, 265–73) famously maintained that Husserl's doctrine of the contents of consciousness is equivalent to the Constancy Hypothesis, which the Gestalt psychologists had already shown to be false. Presumably, by this Gurwitsch meant that Husserl had no right to maintain, as he did, that the same nonintentional contents can lend themselves to different kinds of apprehension, since nonintentional data display no structure at all and thus cannot be said to remain constant in the stream of experience. So also, Sartre maintained that "in giving to the *hyle* both the characteristics of a thing and the characteristics of consciousness, Husserl believed that he facilitated the passage from one to the other, but he succeeded only in creating a hybrid being which consciousness rejects and which cannot be a part of the world" (1956, lix). Quentin Smith provided yet another influential critique of this schema when he argued that no consciousness could ever access its own nonintentional contents. In order to thematize them, one would need to separate them from intentional apprehensions while simultaneously subjecting them to such apprehensions (see Smith 1977, 356–67). Besides these three established critiques, it is also worth pointing out that Husserl himself questioned the schema's legitimacy. Nonetheless, despite this seemingly radical critique, the question concerning its legitimacy remains to this day an unsettled issue.[9]

Even though Husserl subsequently questioned the legitimacy of this schema, and especially in the frameworks of his phenomenological analyses of phantasy and time-consciousness, in other frameworks of analysis he continues to endorse its legitimacy (see Lohmar and Brudzi ska 2011, 119). For our purposes, it is important to see that this schema provides much-needed resources to reconcile the controversy over the intentional structure of pain experience. How does the apprehension–content of apprehension schema help us understand pain experience? I would like to flesh out an answer to this question by first turning back to §15 of Husserl's *Logical Investigations*. If only because this section provides us with the first explicitly phenomenological analysis of pain in phenomenological literature in general, it deserves our careful attention.

HUSSERL'S ANALYSIS OF PAIN IN THE *LOGICAL INVESTIGATIONS*

In §15 of the Fifth Investigation we come across Husserl's first explicit analysis of pain. In this analysis, Husserl does not strive to articulate an unprecedented philosophical approach to pain but to resolve the controversy between Stumpf and Brentano. It is this controversy, taken along with Husserl's attempt to resolve it, that constitutes the origins of the phenomenology of pain.

The position Husserl ends up endorsing comes close to the one that Stumpf defended in his analysis of feeling-sensations. Stumpf aimed to situate his position between two extremes—the Jamesian view, which reduces *all* emotions to sensations (see James 1980, 442–86), and the Brentanian view, which suggests that *all* feelings, including pleasure and pain, are not sensations, but emotions. In contrast to both James and Brentano, Stumpf draws a distinction between intentional emotions and nonintentional feeling-sensations. In this regard, Husserl follows Stumpf. On the one hand, he suggests that there is a group of essentially intentional feelings. Taking over Brentano's terminology, Husserl calls such feelings *feeling-acts*. For instance, "Pleasure without anything pleasant is unthinkable"; "*The specific essence of pleasure demands a relation to something pleasing*" (Husserl 2000, 571). On the other hand, Husserl also maintains that there are nonintentional feelings. Taking over both Stumpf's distinction and terminology, Husserl labels such feelings *feeling-sensations*. Just as for Stumpf, so also for Husserl, pain constitutes the chief example of such feelings: "[The] sensible pain of a burn can certainly not be classed beside a conviction, a surmise, a volition etc., but beside sensory contents like rough or smooth, red or blue etc." (Husserl 2000, 572). Thus, Husserl's central thesis in §15 of the Fifth Logical Investigation echoes Stumpf's position: *the notion of feelings is equivocal*. Some feelings are intrinsically intentional, while other feelings lack this property. This fundamental distinction lends itself to a two-fold clarification.

First, one could distinguish between intentional and nonintentional feelings on the basis of *ascription*. When we describe the landscape as beautiful, or the weather as gloomy, we ascribe feeling-qualities to the *objects of experience*. By contrast, in the case of such feeling-sensations as pain, we ascribe feelings not to objects, but to the *subject of experience*. In the first case, we are dealing with intentional feelings, and in the second case, with nonintentional feelings.

Second, the distinction in question is also *structural*. Intentional feelings are logically and epistemologically *founded* experiences. When a politician is delighted about the election results, his joy, which is itself an intentional experience, is founded upon a more basic intentional presentation—the hearing of the news that he has won the election. By contrast, although nonintentional feelings might be founded "ontologically" upon more basic intentional presentations, they are not founded upon them logically or epistemologically.[10] This means that feelings such as pain are to be conceived of as the immediate givenness of sensory content in the absence of more basic sensory acts.

Thus, in the debate between Stumpf and Brentano, Husserl *seems* to take Stumpf's side. Such is the view defended by both Denis Fisette (see especially Fisette 2010) and Agustín Serrano de Haro (2011) in their notable contributions.[11] Here I would like to develop an alternative interpretation, which would demonstrate that Husserl's goal in the *Logical Investigations* is not to reiterate Stumpf's standpoint, but to resolve the conflict between his most important teachers. Husserl does not resolve this conflict by contending that pain is nothing more than a feeling-sensation, as Stumpf had put it, and as many others were later to repeat. Rather, Husserl maintains that not only the notion of feelings, but *the notion of pain is equivocal* as well: it can be conceived both as a feeling-sensation and as an intentional experience.

An analogy drawn between pain and tactile sensations can help explain how pain can be conceived of as both a nonintentional feeling-sensation and an intentional experience. When I wake up in the middle of the night in a pitch-dark hotel room and when my hand searches for the light switch, I grasp a number of unfamiliar objects. Insofar as I refrain from asking what objects my hand has just touched, I experience purely tactile sensations. However, I can also interpret these tactile sensations as properties of particular objects. I can recognize the object my hand has just touched as a glass of water that I left on the bedside table before falling asleep. In this manner, the tactile sensations function as presentative contents of particular acts of consciousness. Due to such acts of "taking up," I transform pure sensations into intentional experiences. Just as tactile sensations, so pain sensations, too, can be transformed into intentional objects of experience. Insofar as I do not objectify my pains, I experience them as pure sensations. Yet, according to Husserl of the *Logical Investigations*, pains can be also apperceived, or taken up, within an intentional interpretation.[12]

One could object that this analogy between pain and other tactile sensations conceals an important difference. I can experience tactile sensations just at their sensory level, or, alternatively, I can apperceive them as presenting tactually intended objects, such as the bedside table or the glass of water on it. Yet, clearly, pain does not present any object the way these other tactual sensations do: it does not make any sense to suggest that through my pain, I intend the bedside table, or the book lying on it. Nonetheless, how exactly should we understand the difference in question? Is it the case that while tactual sensations are objectifying, pain sensations are not? Or, alternatively, is it the case that both tactual sensations and pain sensations can be objectifying, although in significantly different senses of the term? I consider the first alternative unacceptable. If pain sensations were not objectifying in any sense of the term, we would not be in the position to point at the pain in our bodies, nor could we say that we are suffering, say, from a toothache or from the pain in the abdomen. Of course, to this one could still object that pain's bodily localizability need not be conceived perceptually: we can simply *feel* our pain's bodily location (we will still return to this issue in chapter 5). Yet, clearly, besides being felt, pain's bodily location can also be *indicated* (when I find myself in the dentist's office, I can point at the tooth that hurts). This basic capacity to indicate our pains and speak about them expresses in the most direct way our capacity to apprehend our pains intentionally. We can objectify our pains, although in a fundamentally different sense than we objectify other tactual sensations. Most of the pains that we suffer from are precisely such objectified pains—the kinds of pain that bother us, that limit our capacities, that enslave us. These are the kinds of pain that we have already transformed into intentional objects while at the same time we continue to feel them sensuously.

The notion of pain turns out to be equivocal. Building on the basis of Husserl's analysis, one could clarify this ambiguity as follows: while pain conceived of as a feeling-sensation is a *simple* experience, pain taken up in an objectifying interpretation is a *complex* experience. Moreover, when pain is conceived of as a complex phenomenon, it turns out to be a *stratified phenomenon* that entails both sensory and intentional components. When it comes to such experiences as pain, while the sensory stratum is the founding one, the intentional stratum is founded upon the sensory one.

The interpretation I propose here suggests that, in contrast to Stumpf, for whom pain's sensuousness signals its *nonintentional* essence, for Husserl, pain's sensuousness forms pain's *pre-intentional* character. To qualify pain as pre-intentional is to suggest that it *can* undergo an objective interpretation (although, admittedly, it need not—we can *feel* our pains without apprehending them), due to which we can localize a particular pain in our bodies, conceived of as intentional objects of experience. The intentionality of pain is founded upon pain's pre-intentional givenness.[13]

How, then, does Husserl resolve the controversy between Stumpf and Brentano? He does this on the basis of the realization that the intentionality of feelings can be understood in two different ways. Besides being founded on presentations, it can also be founded on feeling-sensations. Arguably, both Brentano and Stumpf overlooked the second possibility, and precisely because they both overlooked it, they found themselves in a seemingly irresolvable controversy. Husserl's proposed solution derives from the realization that pain sensations can function as presentative contents that can give rise to pain as an intentional object of experience.

The proposed conception of pain as a stratified phenomenon relies upon *two distinctions*. On the one hand, there is the *distinction between intentional and nonintentional feelings*, which Husserl defends in the Fifth Logical Investigation. On the other hand, there is the not so visible *distinction between simple and complex experiences*. Pain is not an intentional experience, insofar as intentionality is conceived in line with the Brentanian model, which suggests that all intentional feelings are founded on presentations. In this regard, Husserl's opposition to Brentano cannot raise any doubt.[14] This does not mean, however, that pain should be characterized as an essentially nonintentional experience. To be sure, insofar as pain is conceived of as a simple experience, it is a pure feeling-sensation. Nonetheless, pain can also be conceived of as a complex experience—an intentional object, founded upon pain sensations.

According to the view I defend here, we should not interpret the central distinction between intentional and nonintentional feelings in §15 of the Fifth Logical Investigation as a suggestion that alongside essentially intentional feelings, there is a group of essentially nonintentional feelings. Rather, these nonintentional feelings, understood as feeling-sensations, can be taken up in an objectifying interpretation and transformed into components of intentional consciousness. There are two essentially different types of feelings: essentially intentional feelings, which are founded upon presentations; as well as nonintentional feelings, which are not founded on other presentations, yet which can found complex feeling-presentations. Husserl's conception of pain as primarily a feeling-sensation, which can also become a complex intentional feeling, is to be understood as a critique, which is simultaneously directed at Brentano's and Stumpf's views, a critique that provides a viable resolution to a seemingly irresolvable dispute.

Consider Husserl's observation in one of the appendixes that accompany his *Logical Investigations*: "The perceived object is not the pain as experienced, but the pain in a transcendent reference as connected with the tooth" (2000, 866). The distinction Husserl draws here between pain-as-experienced and pain-as-an-object-of-experience is a clear indication that pain can be conceived not only as a sensed content but also as an intentional object. Husserl introduces this distinction with the aim of qualifying the type of evidence that accompanies one's pain experience. Husserl's goal here is to replace Brentano's distinction between internal and external perception with the distinction between adequate and inadequate evidence. While for Brentano, only acts of consciousness can be given through internal perception (and thus, given indubitably), for Husserl, not only conscious acts, but also nonintentional contents of experience can be said to be given adequately. According to Husserl, insofar as pain is conceived of as a lived-experience, it is given adequately (that is, given indubitably). By contrast, insofar as pain is conceived of as an object of experience, its evidence is inadequate (one can therefore easily mistake the tooth that hurts for the one that does not hurt).[15]

In contrast to Stumpf and his followers, Husserl refuses to characterize the experience of pain as an *essentially* nonintentional experience. In contrast to Brentano and his followers, Husserl rejects the view that pain is an *essentially* intentional experience. The apprehension–content of apprehension schema underlies his view that feelings such as pain can be experienced both nonintentionally and intentionally. Moreover, according to Husserl, intentional feelings can be founded not only upon presentations

PAIN AND INTENTIONALITY

but also upon feeling-sensations. Yet, clearly, only if feelings are stratified phenomena can they be conceived both as sensations and as intentional objects.

This detour to Husserl's analysis of pain in the *Logical Investigations* provides us with the resources needed to fix the third characteristic of the phenomenological conception of pain proposed in the introduction. To the qualifications that (1) pain is a pre-intentional sensation and (2) an intentional feeling, we can further add that (3) pain *can be given only in firsthand experience*. This means that one can experience pain only as *one's own*: pain, as such, is fundamentally *unshareable*. To be sure, if I see you writhe in pain, I can suffer for you; if I hear you squeal, I can even bring about pain in my own body. Nonetheless, just as my suffering is not your pain, so the pain I feel is not the same as yours. We have already come across the fundamental phenomenological reason that underlies these undeniable facts of experience. As we saw, before it is anything else, pain is a feeling-sensation. It is, however, undeniable that I can experience only *my own* sensations. If, by impossibility, I were to experience anyone else's bodily sensations, I would thereby reabsorb the other's body within my own. Insofar as pain is a feeling-sensation, it can be lived only in firsthand experience.

PAIN AS A STRATIFIED PHENOMENON

Let us return to the earlier question: What exactly does it mean to conceive of pain as an irreducibly ambiguous phenomenon? The phenomenological investigation we have undertaken invites us to maintain that pain can be conceived *both* as a non- or a pre-intentional sensation and as an intentional feeling. With an eye on my foregoing analysis, one could provide the pre-intentional experience of pain with five fundamental determinations:

1. At the most basic level of experience, pain is lived as a mere sensation: pain is not what appears to consciousness, but only what consciousness lives through.
2. Insofar as it is lived as a feeling-sensation, it is not *of* or *for* anything; it "does not take on any object" and "resists objectification in language."
3. Insofar as pain is a sensation, its structure is fundamentally different from the structure of perceptual consciousness: at this level of experience, pain does not take on noetic/noematic structures.

4. At the pre-intentional level of experience, pain can be given as obtrusive, yet pain's obtrusiveness is fundamentally different from the obtrusiveness of appearances. While unexpected sounds or sudden movements obtrude us from without, pain disturbs us from within.[16]

5. Insofar as it obtrudes us from within, pain is experienced indubitably, which in its own turn means that to be in pain is to have no doubts that one is in pain.

Insofar as pain is lived as a nonobtrusive sensation, it remains either largely unnoticed or largely nonthematic. In the first case, we might be dealing with an experience consisting of unnoticed bodily affects. Thus, one's sleeping body can manifest all the signs of pain, even though the subject of experience might not be explicitly conscious of pain. When it is lived as an unnoticed sensation, pain escapes the grasp of consciousness, although it does not escape the grasp of bodily awareness. In the second case, we are faced with pains, which one lives through only in the background of experience. Thus, a soldier may disregard his pain during combat, just as an athlete may neglect his pain during the competition. Both are aware of their pains, yet only through bodily awareness, that is, only nonthematically or implicitly.

The more obtrusive the pain, the more it has the tendency to change its character and transform itself into an intentional experience.[17] The apprehension–content of apprehension schema enables one to account for this metamorphosis. Once the experience of pain becomes the content of apprehension, it can no longer be identified as a non- or a pre-intentional content of experience. It now obtains noetic and noematic characteristics. At the founded level of experience, the structure of pain turns out to be not that different from the structure of perceptual consciousness. With an eye on the foregoing analysis, one can say that at this level of experience, pain can be given in three fundamentally different ways: (1) either as an intentional feeling; or (2) as one's body-object, conceived of as an object of one's feelings; or (3) as the atmosphere that embraces any intentional object that consciousness-in-pain might be sensing, perceiving, or contemplating.

Such an intentional model might strike one as counterintuitive. The model seems to suggest that pain experience largely relies upon active and spontaneous configurations of pregiven materials. Does this mean that we activate our pains through conscious decisions and interpretive activities? Such

PAIN AND INTENTIONALITY

a view would plainly contradict the evidence of experience, which suggests that we live our pains passively and receptively. Yet such an objection is an instance of misplaced criticism. One needs to stress that the apprehension of the contents of experience is not carried out at the level of willful spontaneity. It takes place "behind one's back," at the level of passive experience, which precedes one's cognitive interpretations or willful decisions. As seen from the perspective of mundane reflection, one lives one's pains passively and receptively. Yet, as far as phenomenological clarification of this experience is concerned, this passivity and receptivity are shown to entail levels of basic spontaneous activity.

According to the view I am presenting here, the question concerning the intentional nature of pain experience failed to reach a satisfactory resolution due to the absence of a clear recognition of the stratified nature of pain experience. The question concerning the intentional structure of pain should be answered differently depending on whether one addresses pain as the unapprehended content of experience, or as an intentional feeling, or as an object of intentional feelings, or, finally, as an atmosphere that colors all possible objects of one's feelings. The question concerning the intentional structure of pain, just as the question concerning the intentional nature of experience in general, does not lend itself to a univocal determination.

In his noteworthy study "Is Pain an Intentional Experience?," Serrano de Haro (2011) was led to similar conclusions. He argued that the three main categories of Husserlian analysis of intentionality in *Ideas I*—*hyle*, *noesis*, and *noema*—are needed for the basic phenomenological description of pain experience. However, according to Serrano de Haro, these categories are required "without internal division—and this is the very core of the problem" (2011, 387). The problem pertains to the fact that (1) insofar as pain is determined hyletically, it cannot be conceived of either noetically or noematically; (2) insofar as it is determined noetically, it cannot be conceived of either hyletically or noematically; and (3) insofar as it is determined noematically, it cannot be conceived of either hyletically or noetically. According to Serrano de Haro, pain simultaneously *should be* and *cannot be* determined in the three above-mentioned ways.

The recognition of the stratified nature of pain experience resolves this dilemma. I am in full agreement with Serrano de Haro when he claims that from a phenomenological point of view, "pain experience cannot be adequately described either as pure sensation or as an intentional act or as a peculiar intentional object" (2011, 387). However, as I have argued above, the hyletic, noetic, and noematic descriptions of pain address one and the same phenomenon, yet at different levels of its manifestation. According to the perspective I am here developing, pain *must* be and *can* be determined in the three above-mentioned ways.

The concrete analyses that we come across in classical phenomenological texts lend the reading I am here proposing further support. A look at Jean-Paul Sartre's phenomenological analysis of pain will enrich our understanding of pain, conceived of as a stratified phenomenon.[18]

SARTRE'S PHENOMENOLOGY OF PAIN
IN *BEING AND NOTHINGNESS*

We come across Sartre's analysis of pain in the framework of his account of the body in *Being and Nothingness* (1956). Sartre argues that our philosophical understanding of the body remains distorted for as long as we do not address the differences between (1) how I relate to my own body; (2) how I relate to the body of the Other; and (3) how I internalize the Other's perspective in my understanding of my own body. Similarly, when it comes to the phenomenon of pain, Sartre distinguishes between (1) how pain is experienced prereflectively; (2) how it is thematized as an object of personal and affective reflection; and (3) how it is experienced once I internalize the Other's perspective on my own body. Let us look at this threefold phenomenality of pain in more detail.

Slightly modifying Sartre's own guiding example, let us consider the following scenario: You are suffering from insomnia, and after a long and sleepless night, you need to begin the day by delivering an important lecture. You can hardly keep your eyes open and the pain in your head makes it difficult to gather a single thought. What can be said about pain experience under such circumstances? Building on the basis of Sartre's analysis, let us draw a distinction between four closely related features:

    1. The original manifestation of pain is *prereflective*. Pain does not arise the moment you turn to it and reflect on it. Rather, by the time you reflect on it, you recognize pain as an *ongoing* experience. This means that turning-toward-pain is already motivated by pain experience, which allows us to say that reflection-on-pain arises as a modification of a more original prereflective experience.

2. Insofar as pain is prereflective, it is also *preobjective*. To return to the above-mentioned scenario, when you find yourself in the lecture hall, the pains you live through do not appear in the right or the left corner of the room or among the claims you are trying to articulate. The original experience of pain lacks intentionality, and thus, pain is neither a real nor an ideal object. Far from constituting an object of experience, at the prereflective level pain is lived as a characteristic that marks the subject's embodied relation to the world. Thus, as you struggle to deliver the lecture, the fatigue-in-your-eyes that accompanies your migraine manifests itself as the quivering of the figures in front of you, as the frustration that accompanies your failure to articulate the ideas as clearly as you usually do, and as the irritation that follows the puzzled looks and questions of the audience.

3. Although pain is not experienced as an object of experience, *it marks, or colors, each and every object of experience*. Just as the body-in-pain is spread across all things in the world, yet at the same time condensed in one point, so pain is also everywhere in the world—in every object that the pain-in-the-eyes is directed to, in every thought that the body-in-pain is contemplating.

4. Just as the body, as it manifests itself prereflectively, is *lived rather than known*, so pain as well, in its original manifestation, is also lived and not known. On the one hand, at the prereflective level of experience, pain cannot be known because pain does not belong to the category of what is definable or even describable. On the other hand, even though it escapes thematic consciousness, pain nonetheless affects each and every object of consciousness. As it qualifies the relation to any object in the world, pain is lived as *a mark of facticity*—as a mark of the contingent way in which you relate to objects around you.[19]

For the most part, only moderate and short-lived pain unfolds exclusively on the prereflective level of experience. Pain stands out from other experiences in that it motivates the subject to transform his or her own body into an object of experience.[20] The more intense the experience of pain, the more likely is the subject to transform it into an object of reflection.

Arguably, it is the *abnormality* of pain that motivates consciousness to transform consciousness-in-pain into pain-as-object-of-experience. Insofar as your body functions normally, you do not apprehend it as an object. Without being conscious of it as a worldly object, you remain related *through* it to worldly objects. Yet an intense pain breaks apart the *normal* flow of experience and thereby motivates consciousness to transform the body-in-pain into an object of reflection. This means that insofar as your body is what it *normally* is, it is not an object of reflection; insofar as it is an object of reflection, it has already become something *other* than what it normally is. Let us take a closer look at the transformations that reflection brings forth.

It is important to distinguish between different types of reflection. First, we need to distinguish between what one could call *primordial* and *intersubjective* reflection. On the one hand, you can abstract from how you are given to Others and limit your reflection to how you are given to yourself. On the other hand, you can reflect on yourself by appropriating the perspective of the Other. In the first case, you face *primordial* reflection; in the second case, your reflection is *intersubjective*. Second, we also need to distinguish between *affective* and *cognitive* reflection. On the one hand, you can turn to pain and try to endure it, or you can hate it, or you can apprehend it as unbearable. On the other hand, you can also turn to pain with the aim of discovering the causes that have given rise to it. In the first case, your reflection is *affective*; in the second case, it is *cognitive*. Let us begin with the *primordial* reflection and afterward turn to *intersubjective* reflection.

At this level of reflective experience, pain is not yet given as a physiological phenomenon. Rather, at this level, you reflect on pain as a mere experience— as a *psychic* phenomenon. Once you do this, you apprehend concrete pain as a manifestation of *suffering*.[21] So as to grasp what pain as suffering means more precisely, let us attend to one of Sartre's (1956, 303) striking metaphors: *Suffering is like a melody, while each and every concrete pain is a note in the melody.*

This metaphor suggests two things: First, as soon as we reflect on pain, we do not grasp each and every concrete pain as a distinct object of experience. Rather, we conceive of diverse sensations as *expressive* of one and the same experience. Second, even when it comes to the concrete experience of pain, its intensity varies, sometimes reaching almost unbearable levels, sometimes diminishing to states of painlessness. In this regard, the experience of pain is also much like a melody: reflective consciousness does not interpret these painless states as the terminations of suffering; rather, just as silence constitutes a part of a melody, so the brief moments of relief are part of suffering.

One can distinguish five closely interrelated aspects of such a reflective givenness of pain, conceived of as suffering:

1. The pain you suffer is given as something *transcendent*—as an irresistible force that overpowers your own body.

2. Actual suffering is given as something *passive*. It is not an active force that absorbs you, but a passivity that follows the inability to resist the force of pain.

3. Borrowing Sartre's metaphors, we can further qualify suffering as "magical." On the one hand, if you no longer see a particular object in front of you, it is because you have turned away from it. On the other hand, if for an extended period of time you no longer experience any pain, it is because *suffering itself has left*. Thus, the person suffering from pain can proclaim: "*It* is gone; I am free from *it*."

4. Still with reference to Sartre's vocabulary, we can further describe suffering as "animistic." By this we are to understand that even when the pain we suffer magically withdraws from the field of experience, it *can* return and be recognized as the same pain. Thus, the suffering person can exclaim: "I know what it is, and I can't believe it's coming back."

5. Besides being *transcendent, passive, magical*, and *animistic*, suffering is also given *without distance*. Thus, even though you reflectively identify suffering as something other than your own body, suffering nonetheless absorbs and penetrates your own consciousness and your own body. Suffering derives from the *abnormality* of pain; yet what you experience is *your own abnormality*, that is, *your own otherness*. As Sartre ever so elegantly puts it, suffering "fastens on to consciousness with all its teeth, penetrates consciousness with all its notes; *and these teeth, these notes are my consciousness*" (1956, 442).

Let us turn to how pain is given to *intersubjective* reflection. At this level, pain is no longer interpreted as merely lived-pain or as an affective object. Rather, one's experience of pain is transformed into a manifestation of a *disease*. It becomes such a manifestation when you take on the perspective of the Other, when you view your own body from the third-person point of view and see a particular pain as a sign expressing a malfunction in the body. At this level, the pain in your eyes is no longer experienced either as the blurring of the figures in front of you or as an expression of ongoing suffering; now pain becomes a manifestation of, say, blepharitis or a corneal ulcer. Far from being just lived, or just given as an affective object, at this point *pain is known*, and so as to express this knowledge, you employ instrumental concepts that neither are nor could be derived from the manner in which your body is lived by you.[22]

Once pain is interpreted as a sign that expresses a malfunction in the body, pain can be *localized*. Yet the *physiological* localization is possible only once you take on the perspective of the Other.[23] Thus, you might *know* that your pain lies in the open sore on the cornea, yet this is something that, strictly speaking, you cannot experience. On the one hand, insofar as pain is an experience, it tells me nothing about the physiological structure of my body; on the other hand, insofar as pain is a disease, it tells me nothing about how pain is experienced.

We can thus say that the differences between Husserl's and Sartre's philosophical projects notwithstanding, both conceive of pain affectively and cognitively, both as a pre-intentional experience as well as an intentional object. Just as for Husserl, so also for Sartre, the experience of pain is irreducibly ambiguous. It is the stratified nature of pain that renders this irreducible ambiguity intelligible.

~

The account of pain presented in this chapter was largely built on classical phenomenological reflections that we come across in Brentano, Stumpf, Husserl, and Sartre. This account relies upon three central insights: (1) pain is a stratified phenomenon; (2) while at the founding level, pain is lived through as a nonintentional *hyle*, at the founded level, it is marked by intentionality; and (3) the schema "apprehension–content of apprehension" explains the relation between these experiential strata. At the beginning of this chapter, I argued that such an approach enables one to resolve the controversy over the intentional status of pain experience; toward the end, I maintained that the proposed resolution leads to the realization that pain is an irreducible stratified phenomenon. The historically oriented excursus that has been undertaken here provides us with a clarification of the first two determinations of the phenomenological conception of pain that I outlined in the introduction to this chapter: pain is both a nonintentional feeling-sensation and an intentional feeling. The stratified conception of pain that relies upon the Husserlian model of apprehension–content of apprehension allows us to understand the phenomenological legitimacy of both the Stumpfian and the Brentanian conceptions. Moreover, this analysis also provides the means needed to clarify the third determination of the phenomenological conception of pain: pain can be lived only as *firsthand experience*.

Following Sartre, one has good reasons to argue that *pain is a stratified experience that affects the embodied subject and that unfolds on three different levels of experience*: (1) originally, pain is merely lived prereflectively and preobjectively; (2) once transformed into an affective object, it becomes a form of suffering; and (3) finally, once transformed into a cognitive object, it is conceived of as disease. In chapter 3, we will see how such a stratified conception of pain enables us to clarify the experiential structure of various pain syndromes, such as threat hypersymbolia, pain asymbolia, and congenital analgesia. Opening a dialogue between phenomenology and cognitive science on such a basis will also enable us to address two further qualifications that belong to the proposed phenomenological conception of pain: besides being fundamentally *aversive*, pain must also be further determined as *a feeling with a distinct experiential quality*.

CHAPTER 3

· ·

THE PHENOMENOLOGY OF PAIN
DISSOCIATION SYNDROMES

By offering an investigation that was concernced at the same time with the intentional nature of pain experience and with the historical origins of the phenomenology of pain, the last chapter demonstrated that pain (1) can be given only in firsthand experience; (2) either as a nonintentional feeling-sensation; or (3) as an intentional feeling. In this chapter, I wish to supplement such a conception of pain with two further qualifications: pain is (4) an aversive feeling; and (5) it has a distinct experiential quality. The fourth qualification appears self-evident. How could anyone argue against it? Precisely because of the apparent self-evidence of the claim, it proves highly promising to follow the guidelines of what I have identified in chapter 1 as dialogical phenomenology and open a conversation between phenomenology and cognitive science. Within such a framework, we can focus on pain dissociation syndromes, which bring into question the validity of this seemingly self-evident claim. I do not want to rule out the possibility of alternative philosophical explanations. My goal is more modest: I wish to show only that the conception of pain proposed here enables us to make good sense of these syndromes.

For the most part, pain is lived as a complex experience, composed of sensory, emotive, and cognitive dimensions (see Grahek 2007; Hardcastle 1999; Trigg 1970). Nonetheless, as we know from chapter 2, pain can also be experienced as a mere feeling-sensation, devoid of emotive and cognitive components.[1] One therefore has no right to qualify pain at the eidetic level as a stratified phenomenon. This realization invites us to ask: What are the conditions that need to be met for a pain sensation to be lived as a "whole pain experience" (see Trigg 1970), that is, a complex experience that comprises sensory, emotive, and cognitive dimensions? For this to happen, pain sensations must be apprehended emotively and cognitively. Yet is such a clarification sufficient? *Must consciousness always apprehend its pain sensations the same way, which would transform these sensations into a "whole pain experience"?* By opening a dialogue between phenomenology and cognitive science, we will come to realize how complicated the relation between pain sensations and their apprehension can be. In its own turn, this realization will bring into question the seemingly self-evident view that pain cannot help but be an aversive feeling, with a distinct experiential quality.

We will focus on five pain association syndromes. We will begin with the analysis of *congenital insensitivity to pain* (CIP), and we will see that patients who suffer from this pain syndrome are neither capable of apprehending nor living through their sensations as painful. Second, we will turn to lobotomized, cingulotomized, and morphinized patients, and we will see that even though they can experience their sensations as painful, they cannot apprehend these sensations as painful. Third, we will address the condition known as *threat hypersymbolia*, and we will see that in some cases, one can live through pain sensations and apprehend them as painful even though no harm is inflicted on the body. Fourth, we will turn to *asymbolia for pain* (AP) and see that in some cases, patients can recognize that harm is inflicted on their bodies, even though this recognition is not accompanied with pain experience at either the sensory, the emotive, or the cognitive level. Finally, we will also consider the legitimacy of the syndrome known as "pain affect without pain sensation." Is it possible to live through the emotion of pain in the absence of pain sensation? I will contend that there is no phenomenological evidence to corroborate such a view.

On the basis of such a dialogical approach, we will be able to address the question concerning the aversive nature of pain experience: *Why does pain hurt, and should it?* The common answer runs as follows: pain must hurt if it is to perform a biologically useful function, so much so that in its absence, an organism could not survive. Since phenomenology cannot rely on biology, it must provide an alternative answer to this question.

CONGENITAL INSENSITIVITY TO PAIN

At first glance it might seem that the pain syndrome George Dearborn discovered in 1932 and termed "congenital pure analgesia" provides incontestable evidence against the fourth qualification of pain defended in this study, which suggests that by its very nature pain is an aversive feeling. Those who suffer from congenital insensitivity to pain (CIP) feel no unpleasant sensations, in any sense imaginable, when they bite deep into the tongue while chewing food, when they kneel on hot radiators, when their bodies are subjected to strong electric shock, or when they walk on legs with cracked bones until they break completely (see Melzack and Wall 2008, 3–7). Those who suffer from this condition are not numb: they can distinguish between hot and cold sensations, and they know when they are subjected to a pinprick. However, patients with CIP experience these and other sensations without any dislike or distress. Patients born with this condition chew off their tongues, the inside of their cheeks, or their hands, yet events of this kind are not accompanied with any aversive feelings. McMurray provides us with the best-documented case of CIP, which concerns Miss C.—a twenty-two-year-old Canadian student at McGill University:

> The tip of the tongue was deformed from severe biting, which occurred during childhood. The hands, legs and feet showed multiple scars, which had been produced by cuts, bites and scratches, many of which were unnoticed. After a day on the beach she had to inspect her feet carefully for cuts. . . . At no point had she ever reported any form of ache or pain, such as headache, earache, toothache, stomach ache or menstrual pain. . . . Frostbites in winter were frequent. Burns from hot objects and from overlong exposure to the sun had also been numerous. (1950, 654)

This condition is so rare that, according to an article published in the *Independent* in May 2015, only about twenty cases have been reported in scientific literature. However, there are other conditions that are similar in nature. Episodic analgesia is much more common. It occurs when one is injured yet does not undergo any aversive feelings until minutes or hours afterward. Moreover, "such conditions as leprosy, diabetes, alcoholism, multiple sclerosis, nerve disorders and spinal cord injury can also bring about the strangely hazardous state of insensitivity to pain" (Brand and Yancey 1997, 5–6). Here is how Paul Brand describes his encounter with a leprosy patient in India, who was working as a young weaver:

> "May I see your hand," I yelled to the weaver. He released the pedals and set down the shuttle. . . . He held out a deformed, twisted hand with shortened fingers. The index finger had lost maybe a third of an inch in length and as I looked closer I saw a naked bone

> protruding from a nasty, septic wound. This boy was working with a finger cut to the bone! "How did you cut yourself?" I asked. He gave a nonchalant reply: "Oh, it's nothing. I had a pimple on my finger, and earlier it bled a little. I guess it's opened up again." (Brand and Yancey 1997, 89)

It is crucial to stress that CIP and similar conditions mentioned above do not provide us with any evidence against the view that averseness constitutes an essential characteristic of pain experience. It is a matter of dangerous equivocation to suggest that CIP patients manifest the most thorough indifference to pain. Such a qualification attributes to these patients what they lack, for as both Trigg and Grahek rightly observe, one must feel pain if one is to be indifferent to it. CIP does not provide us with an instance of indifference to pain, but rather, with a case of *indifference to pain-inducing stimuli*. As McMurray argued still in 1950, sensitivity to pain must meet three criteria: (1) a verbal report to painful experience; (2) overt behavioral reactions (such as wincing, withdrawal, or restlessness); and (3) physiological responses, as seen in the blood pressure, heart rate, and respiratory changes (1950, 652–53). CIP patients do not manifest sensitivity to pain in any of these three senses.

Patients suffering from CIP do not live through pain sensations: when they are subjected to pain-inducing stimuli, their bodies manifest no changes in blood pressure, heart rate, or respiration (see Melzack and Wall 2008, 4). Precisely because they do not live through pain sensations, they cannot intend their own pains as objects of cognitive or emotive intentionality. In contrast to pain asymbolics, to whom we will soon turn, CIP patients cannot laugh at their pain (strictly speaking, there is nothing to laugh at); in contrast to masochists, they cannot love their pain (there is nothing to love); and in contrast to typical pain patients, they can neither hate nor suffer from their pain (there is nothing to hate or suffer from). Their attitude is marked by a thorough insensitivity to pain. If there is anything that these patients hate, it is their incapacity to live through pain, which Steven Pete, one of the patients suffering from this condition, describes as "the agony of feeling no pain" (2012).

Here is one typical report of this condition: "The patient said that six days previously he had inadvertently held his left hand in a gas flame, while heating glue, but when he saw this, he felt no discomfort, and was aware only of a tingling sensation in the fingers" (Jewsbury 1951, 339). Here is another, no less typical account, this time about a patient who agreed to participate in physiological experiments:

> At no time during any of the experiments using noxious stimuli did the subject report a sensation or feeling, which could be interpreted as a report of pain. Ache, unpleasantness, unbearableness, or pain itself was never described. Consistent with this was the complete absence of any observable sign of painful experience. (McMurray 1950, 660)

The patients suffering from this condition might not identify any sensation as unpleasant, yet they nonetheless distinguish between "good days" and "bad days," qualifying their bad days as a nuisance and, in this sense, unpleasant. As Steven Pete remarks, "It feels like a compression, a throbbing compressed feeling in my joints. On a bad day it makes me very cranky when I have that feeling all day, because it's just a nuisance. It limits your mobility and your joint isn't able to move as much as it should" (2012).

We should consider it a genuine scientific breakthrough that in 2015 pain scientists discovered the genetic causes that trigger this condition (see Chen et al. 2015). Pain scientists identified the PRDM[11] gene as the pain-sensing gene and further traced specific mutations in this gene, which are involved in activating genetic switches. This research led to the conclusion that CIP is passed on genetically and that the parents of the patients suffering from this condition are the unaffected carriers of the defective gene. The mutation of this gene results in all the pain sensors of the body being turned off from birth. While many other genes might also play a role, the PRDM1[2] gene plays a key role in modifying the chromatin protein, which becomes attached to the DNA of the chromosomes. The chromatin protein acts as a control switch that activates or deactivates other genes on the chromosome.

A scientific investigation of the state of painlessness proved to carry far-reaching therapeutic significance. Recent research conducted on mice demonstrated that genetically modified mice, who could not feel any pain, had an increase in the expression of genes for opioid peptides, known as the body's natural painkillers. A drug called naloxone was administered to the mice, which blocked their opioid receptors, thereby also stalling the body's natural painkiller. As a result, the sensation of pain was again triggered in the genetically modified mice. Admittedly, what works for rodents does not always work for humans. However, the researchers also administered the very same drug to a thirty-nine-year-old CIP patient. After receiving the same treatment, she felt pain for the first time in her life (see Minett et al. 2015). The scientific discovery of the causes that trigger CIP is of great importance for medical research, and not only because it gives hope of a cure to those who suffer from the agony of *not* feeling pain. If pain science can identify the mechanisms that underlie pain sensations, then, potentially, besides enabling patients to feel pain that is necessary for their survival, it can also control and reduce unnecessary pain.

Although a phenomenological analysis of this curious condition does not carry therapeutic implications (at least as far as biomedical modes of treatment are concerned), it can nonetheless shed some light on the structures of pain experience. The apprehension–content of apprehension schema suggests that for pain to be lived as a "whole pain experience," the sensations of pain must undergo a specific kind of cognitive and emotive apprehension. With this in mind one can identify two basic phenomenological reasons why the patients suffering from CIP are incapable of living through a "whole pain experience." First, they are incapable of living through pain sensations; and second, since they do not have pain sensations, the content is missing that they could apprehend in any way, appropriate or inappropriate. Therefore, these patients can neither laugh at their pains, nor love their pains, nor, finally, hate them.

Put in terms of the Brentano-Stumpf debate, the patients suffering from CIP feel no pain, conceived either as a feeling-sensation or as an emotion. These patients cannot know what pain experience is because they are incapable of living through pain sensations. We can take this to mean that the "whole pain experience" is not just a multidimensional but rather a stratified phenomenon, which comprises not just multiple, but rather founding and founded strata of experience. A phenomenological analysis of CIP suggests that the sensory dimension is *fundamental* to pain experience: it forms the experiential basis that underlies the emotive and cognitive strata. Thus, while one can live through pain sensations without intending pain as an emotive or cognitive object of experience, one cannot intend one's pain emotively or cognitively if one does not have pain sensations. The sensory dimension is the experiential bedrock of pain experience in general.

Does this realization not enable us to answer the question concerning the painfulness of pain? *Does pain have to hurt? If so, why? And if not, why not?* As mentioned above, the common answer points to pain biology. One claims that the ability to sense pain as an aversive sensation is fundamental to our self-preservation: if pain did not hurt, we would not survive. However, since it cannot rely on pain biology, pain phenomenology cannot accept this common answer, which we come across already in Aristotle. The phenomenological analysis of CIP offered here provides us with another possibility: the realization that the "whole pain experience" is not just a multidimensional but a stratified phenomenon suggests that *there must be something about pain sensations themselves that motivates consciousness to apperceive them as painful*. Precisely, therefore, CIP does not provide any counterevidence against the claim that pain is an aversive feeling. A CIP patient undergoes no unpleasant sensations precisely because she is incapable of living through pain sensations, and being incapable of sensing pain, this patient is also incapable of having a "whole pain experience." To follow up on this clue, let us consider one of the most curious case histories in the literature on pain dissociation syndromes. It concerns a CIP patient, who, after suffering many years from the agony of painlessness, came to the unfortunately false conclusion that she was in the process of being liberated from her affliction and had learned how to sense pain.

THE DISCOVERY OF PAIN

This curious case was documented by Gordon A. McMurray in 1950. The young woman suffering from CIP "expressed the belief that, to a large extent, her sensitivity to painful stimuli was increasing" (1950, 654). What was her belief based on? Apparently, it "was largely due to the greater success she had had in later years in avoiding serious tissue damage. Later evidence made it appear much more likely that this was due to more adult behavior patterns, and to learning to use other cues as a warning of potentially damaging stimuli" (McMurray 1950, 654). Her belief that she had learned how to sense pain was based on three fundamental factors: (1) on the observation of the behavior of others in pain; (2) on the imitation of this behavior; and (3) on the realization that this imitation leads to avoiding serious tissue damage. The patient would withdraw her hand from a flame rather than leaving it there to be burned; she would no longer stick objects into her nostrils. Yet for what reason? The reason, apparently, had to do with the realization that these actions would result in injury, rather than pain. As Trigg put it while commenting on this case, the patient "would realize that she was behaving in a similar way to other people in such situations, and because she had been taught that their behavior meant that they were feeling pain, she could easily conclude that she too was feeling pain. She would be making an inference from her behavior" (1970, 170).

This, indeed, is the crucial point: the very fact that the patient was *inferring* that she was in pain provided sufficient proof that she was *not* in pain. Norman Malcolm insightfully remarks,

> If the man gives an answer (e.g., "I knew it must be pain because of the way I jumped") then he proves by that very fact that he has not mastered the correct use of the words "I feel pain. . . ." In telling us how he did it he will convict himself of a misuse. Therefore the question "How did he recognize his sensation?" requests the impossible. (1958, 977)

We do not live through pain sensations as conclusions to arguments; rather, we live through them either as pure feeling-sensations, or as stratified experiences that comprise sensory, emotive, and cognitive components. We do not require any external evidence to verify the fact that we feel pain when we actually feel it. The principle "Esse est percipi" fully applies to pain. The problem with the CIP patient is that her belief that she was in pain was not grounded in the feeling of pain. The gap that separated her belief and her experience was sufficient proof that she was not in pain.

Nonetheless, the patient under consideration was quite likely feeling *something*, and this something in question—be it a feeling of pressure, or a feeling of warmth—was what she identified as a feeling of pain. But if so, then the belief that one is feeling pain can be mistaken not only because it is conceived of as an inference, but also because it might be grounded in a *false feeling*— a feeling that the patient misidentifies as pain. A person suffering from CIP might learn from others that pain is a disagreeable and unpleasant sensation. Yet recall Steven Pete's account, quoted above, of his good days and bad days as well as his description of a throbbing, compressed feeling in his joints. Presumably, this feeling of compression is experienced as a disagreeable and unpleasant sensation by even those who suffer from CIP. A person suffering from this condition could certainly conclude that this unpleasant sensation is exactly what others identify as pain. We are faced with an even more curious scenario: here is a person who feels no pain, yet is convinced that she is in pain, and her conviction is grounded in immediate experience. On what basis are we to distinguish between appropriate and inappropriate convictions that one is in pain?

This scenario invites us to rethink some established commitments in the literature on pain. One can put the question as follows: Does the claim "I have pain" have the same meaning as the claim "I am convinced that I have pain"? Is one right to identify the claim "I am convinced that I have pain" as incorrigible? *Is it possible to be convinced that one is in pain and nonetheless be wrong?*

In her classical study *The Body in Pain*, Elaine Scarry famously maintained that "to have pain is to have certainty; to hear about pain is to have doubt" (1985, 13). Can we modify the first claim and say: "If one is certain that one is in pain, then one is in pain"? The person under consideration is certain that she is in pain, although all the evidence points to the contrary. Consider also Norman Malcolm's observation:

> A man cannot be in *error* as to whether he is in pain; he cannot say, "My leg hurts," by mistake, any more than he can groan by mistake. It is senseless to suppose that he has wrongly identified a tickle as pain. . . . True, he may be undecided as to whether it is best described as an "ache" or a "pain" . . . , but his very indecision *shows* us what his sensation is, i.e. something between an ache and a pain. (1958, 542ff.)

Yet insofar as one can misidentify pain as any other highly disagreeable and deeply unpleasant feeling, one can certainly be in error as to whether one is in pain, and one can certainly "groan by mistake," if by this one means groaning from a painless although deeply unpleasant, horrendous, and intolerable feeling, while at the same time thinking that one is groaning from pain. We are thereby led to the realization that the conviction that one is in pain is not incorrigible. First, the proposition, "I am in pain," is neither clear nor distinct. One might utter it and be convinced of its truth, despite the absence of feelings to support it: it might refer to one's behavior, which in its own turn would copy the behavior of others, who are, presumably, in pain. Second, this proposition does not become incorrigible when one adds to it a conviction that it is grounded in actual pain experience.[2] One might misidentify the concept of pain and employ it to characterize any kind of unpleasant feeling. We thus need to ask: On what basis is one to distinguish between appropriate and inappropriate convictions that one is in pain?

Phenomenology provides helpful resources to resolve this impasse. It invites us to admit that the experience of pain has a peculiar experiential *quality*, and it is this quality that distinguishes pain from other disagreeable and unpleasant sensations.[3] The sensation of pain *feels* differently than an itch, just as it feels differently from how tingling, pricking, or numbing sensations feel. The differences in question cannot be accounted for in terms of intensity; rather, we face here different sensations, with different qualities. Pain is not *any* kind of a disagreeable and unpleasant sensation, and thus we need to supplement what I have identified above as the fourth qualification of pain with the fifth qualification: (5) Pain is a disagreeable and unpleasant sensation with a specific experiential quality. Pain sensations have a unique quality, and it is precisely the capacity to recognize this quality that distinguishes an appropriate and inappropriate contention that one is in pain.

Admittedly, in some cases, as in those described in the above-quoted passage from Malcolm, one might not know whether one is living through pain or a different kind of an unpleasant sensation. Yet one should not misinterpret uncertainty of this kind as proof of inability to distinguish between different kinds of unpleasant sensations on the basis of their quality. Rather, the uncertainty in question points to the largely porous borderlines that distinguish different kinds of unpleasant sensations from one another, and thus, in light of the colorfulness of the life of sensations, we often do not know in which category the sensation under consideration should be placed. This does not mean, however, as Bruce Aune (1965) in a Kantian fashion contends, that there is nothing we could possibly say about pain sensations as such.[4] If this were true, we would not have the experiential basis to draw distinctions between different types of sensations. Yet distinctions of this nature are neither conceptual nor linguistic. Rather, the categorization of sensations—that is, the distinctions we have drawn between them—largely rests on the qualities of sensations themselves.

Mutatis mutandis, one could say about pain what John Locke says about solidity: "If anyone ask me what this solidity is I send him to his sense to inform him; let him put a flit or a football between his hands and then endeavor to join them, and he will know" (2005, 95). I do not want to suggest that pain is a primary quality in Locke's sense, namely, that the experience of pain quality corresponds to pain quality as such, whatever that might be. In contrast to Locke's primary qualities, pain *is* an experience *tout court*, and for this very reason, to find out what it is, we must consult experience.

Admittedly, the task of articulating the quality of pain in detail confronts severe difficulties, and the reason for this concerns the nature of language. We simply do not have at our disposal an appropriate language for pain sensations or, more generally, for sensations as such. As it becomes especially clear once we turn our attention to the McGill Pain Questionnaire, most of the terms we employ to characterize our pain sensations are first and foremost meant to describe objects of experience, rather than the peculiar quality of bodily feelings. This is something we have already touched upon in chapter 2. Temporally, we describe pains as quivering, pulsing, throbbing, beating, or pounding; spatially, we describe them as jumping, flashing, or shooting; in terms of their pressure, we characterize them as drilling or stabbing, sharp or cutting, pinching or pressing; so also, we describe our pains as dull, sore, heavy, or splitting; as tiring, sickening, or exhausting; as terrifying, cruel, and excruciating, et cetera. Even a cursory look at this list of terms, which is not meant to be exhaustive, makes clear that the language we use to characterize our pains is an object-related language, which only figuratively can be said to characterize the quality of pain experience. Yet no matter how conceptually unrefined our understanding of the quality of pain might be, and no matter how daunting the task of conceptually fixing the quality of pain might be, it is nonetheless crucial to admit that pain sensations share a unique quality, for it is precisely this quality that enables us to differentiate pain from what is sometimes called "mental" suffering as well as from other related, yet different types of "physical" sensations. In the absence of a specific quality, we could no longer consider CIP in any way unusual, and the curious case history of the young woman who learned how to experience pain would be characteristic of everybody's experience. We would all "feel" pain without actually feeling it, and even excessive dozes of naloxone could not improve our lot.

The different types of pain of which we have just spoken might very well make one wonder: Do the differences in question not provide sufficient proof that there is no unique quality of pain? Such, indeed, is the view defended by the functionalists, such as Paul and Patricia Churchland (1981); Norton Nelkin (1986, 1994); and Michael Tye (2005), all of whom in different ways argue against what I have identified as the fifth qualification of pain experience (see Grahek 2007, 96–98). According to their view, pain does not have a unique quality; presumably, our qualification of pains as dull and sharp, or jumping and flashing, or quivering and heavy, provides sufficient proof that it must be something else besides the quality of pain that unifies this group of sensations. According to the functionalist account, the unity in question is ensured by a similar stimulus-response pattern of our behavior, which has joined qualitatively distinct types of experiences, which were all given one and the same name: "pain." Yet, as Grahek insightfully observes, the differences we draw between

THE PHENOMENOLOGY OF PAIN DISSOCIATION SYNDROMES 79

drilling and stabbing, sharp and cutting, pinching and pressing, and all other types of pain are meaningful only insofar as they are assumed to be "qualitative differences *within* the modality of pain, designating different kinds of pain within the same genus" (2007, 98). We face here "experiential *determinates* of the experiential *determinable* modality of pain" (Grahek 2007, 106). Sharp and dull pains, just as stinging and burning pains, certainly differ from each other qualitatively; nonetheless, there must be something in common between them, and this something in question must be the quality of pain itself, for otherwise one would simply feel the sensations of sharpness and dullness, of stinging and burning, without feeling them as painful. We face here *intramodal differences within the modality of pain.*

At this point we are in the position to return to our principal question: Why does pain hurt? It hurts not only, and not primarily, because of biological reasons, which relate to self-preservation. Another reason that underlies its inherently abhorrent nature concerns the quality of pain sensations themselves. Here I fully concur with Grahek's view, which suggests that pain quality is "the triggering point which sets the machinery to 'go,' and it sets apart the machinery that wears its sign from those that are similar to it, but do not carry its signature" (2007, 95). Pain, conceived of as a whole experience, rests on the shoulders of pain sensations, which themselves have disagreeable and unpleasant characteristics.[5] Pain's refusal to cease and its intensification constitute the two chief and complementary ways in which a mere pain sensation transforms itself into a "whole pain experience." We face here a transformation from disagreeableness to distress, from unpleasantness to torment and agony. This transformation provides us with a phenomenological clarification of the difference between a mere pain sensation and a "whole pain experience."

Still in 1939, a famous French surgeon, René Leriche, argued that the biological explanation of the painfulness of pain is so severely constrained that it must be rejected. As he put it,

> Physicians too readily claim that *pain is a reaction of defense, a fortunate warning, which puts us on our guard against the risks of disease.* . . . Reaction of defense? Against whom? Against what? Against the cancer which not infrequently gives little trouble until quite late? Against heart afflictions, which always develop quietly? . . . One must reject, then, this false conception of beneficent pain. (quoted in Melzack and Wall 2008)

Since a large variety of pains do not serve any biological function, one cannot make sense of the painfulness of pain on the basis of pain biology. Nonetheless, even when confronted with biologically incomprehensible forms of pain, we can make sense of the painfulness of pain phenomenologically. It is the apprehension of pain contents as painful that transforms pain sensations into the "whole pain experience." Since the contents apprehended are themselves inherently unpleasant and disagreeable, the more intense our pain sensations, the stronger the motivation to apprehend them as agonizing, distressing, and tormenting experiences. Our pains are inherently painful, just as our orgasms are inherently pleasant. The link that binds pains to their biological function is just as contingent as the link that binds orgasms to the reproductive function. While in some cases the link that binds these feeling-sensations to their biological function is incontestable, in other cases it is just as incontestably absent.

LOBOTOMY, CINGULOTOMY, AND MORPHINE

The smooth and typical movement of experience from what Grahek calls *feeling pain* to *being in pain*—from the having of painful sensed-contents to a painful apprehension of these contents—can be interrupted. Lobotomized, cingulotomized, and morphinized patients provide us with good examples of how such a typical transition in apprehension can be suspended in midair. The curious thing about these patients is that although they are capable of painful experiences, their painful experiences do not trouble them. As Kurt Baier puts it, "In cases of prefrontal lobotomy, patients claim that they have the same feelings as before, but they no longer mind" (1962, 7). Or as David Armstrong has it, "There are situations where people report that they have pains but they say that the pain is not giving them any sort of concerns" (2002, 101). In a strange way, although they experience their sensations as pains, they do not find their pains bothersome. Put in the language of the Brentano-Stumpf debate, these patients live their pains as feeling-sensations, but not as emotions. Thus, if we ask again if pain is necessarily aversive, lobotomized, cingulotomized, and morphinized patients provide us with further evidence that pain does not have to be painful, disturbing, or troublesome. Paradoxically, we face here a case of painless pains. And thus it seems the fourth qualification does not hold.

Given that the patients under consideration do not intend their pains as painful, do we have any evidence to claim that they nonetheless experience

THE PHENOMENOLOGY OF PAIN DISSOCIATION SYNDROMES

painful sensations? Can we claim that the sensations they live through are indeed unpleasant and disagreeable? If patients' reports are to be trusted, then we have to answer these questions affirmatively. Consider in this regard the following: when Paul Brand asked one lobotomized patient about her pain, "she smiled sweetly and chuckled to herself. 'In fact, it's still agonizing. But I don't mind'" (Brand and Yancey 1997, 210). By identifying her pain as *agonizing*, the patient leaves us in no doubt about the unpleasant and disagreeable nature of her experience. This point is further confirmed by Walter Freeman and James W. Watts in their observation that "after prefrontal lobotomy, these patients can apparently feel pain just as acutely, but they are no longer afraid of pain, nor concerned over the possible consequences. . . . The emotional component is attenuated and the fear of pain is no longer disabling" (1950, 360). Consider also Hardy, Wolff, and Goodell's telling report. Basing their study on thirty-eight lobotomies performed in a New York hospital, they observed that "of these, 17 admitted experiencing pain only when asked; four had no pain at all" (1952, 310). As they further remark, "Some patients, although ostensibly tranquil before being asked about their pain, overreacted with a show of grimacing and fears when their attention was focused upon it by a direct question concerning its quality and its intensity" (1952, 316). We come across a similar report in Theodore Barber's (1959) study, which suggests that insofar as lobotomized patients are not asked about their pain, they seem to be free from it; however, as soon as asked about it, they often start showing discomfort.[6]

Cingulotomized patients manifest a similar indifference toward their pain. Much like the lobotomized patients, they report that even though they sense pain, their pain is neither distressing nor bothersome. In this regard, morphinized patients are no different.

How is one to make sense of the curious fact that here we face patients who simultaneously appear to feel and not to feel pain? The "apprehension–content of apprehension" schema provides the resources needed to clarify the possibility of such pain syndromes phenomenologically. With this schema in the back of one's mind, one can claim that the patients in question continue to live through pain, insofar as pain is an experiential content, yet they fail to constitute pain as an intentional object of experience. It is the discrepancy between what the patients live through at the pre-intentional and intentional levels of experience that provides the basis for a phenomenological clarification. Lobotomy, cingulotomy, and morphine block the otherwise natural transition from one level of pain experience to the other. The fact that, as the above-mentioned anecdotes suggest, many patients suffering from this condition become conscious of their pain only when asked about it provides further reason to support the proposed interpretation. After all, we can become thematically conscious of the sensed contents only through reflection, and this is exactly why many patients become intentionally conscious of their pains only when asked (that is, only when *forced to reflect*). Otherwise, these patients manifest an almost complete indifference either to the past or to the future; as Hardy, Wolff, and Goodell put it, these patients manifest a remarkable capacity to "forget" about their experiences (1952, 317). This confinement to one temporal modality and the almost complete lack of concern for what lies outside the immediate present is therapeutically effective, although, clearly, besides liberating the patient from painfulness, it also transforms the patient's personality. It thus seems that lobotomized, cingulotomized, and morphinized patients are capable of constituting their pains as intentional objects *only through reflection*. They lack the straightforward capacity to intend their own pains as objects of emotive and cognitive intentionality.[7]

I do not want to suggest that the patients under consideration are not capable of apprehending their pain sensations. Rather, their apprehension of the painful content is pathological in that once they transform their pains into intentional objects, these objects turn out to be free of all painfulness.[8] As Grahek has it, "The sensation of pain remains, but the dread, anxiety, or fear that formerly accompanied pain has disappeared" (2007, 133). Or as Freeman and Watts have it, "The pain was still present, but it was a sensation rather than a threat" (1950, 134). For this very reason, the patients under consideration simultaneously feel pain and don't feel pain; therefore, they maintain that they feel pain, yet it does not bother them. They feel pain, insofar as pain is conceived of as a nonintentional content of experience; yet they feel no pain, insofar as pain is conceived of as an object of experience. For better or worse, these patients are incapable of carrying their painful experiences from the pre-intentional to the intentional level.[9] And thus, their testimony to the contrary notwithstanding, lobotomized, cingulotomized, and morphinized patients do not provide counterevidence to the fourth essential qualification of pain experience, which suggests that in its very essence, pain is an aversive experience.

THREAT HYPERSYMBOLIA

I borrow the concept of threat hypersymbolia from Grahek (2007), who attributes its discovery to Tjaard U. Hoogenraad. In a study conducted in 1994, Hoogenraad, L. M. Ramos, and J. van Gijn addressed the case of a patient who had suffered from infarction and who would nonetheless experience burning pain in the numb side of the body, yet only on those rare occasions when he would see the doctor's hand approach his numb arm. We face here an instance of pain being stripped of its biological function, although, in contrast to CIP, not because of pain's absence, but on the contrary, because of its hyperpresence. Threat hypersymbolia illustrates how pain can become an inadequate and hyperprotective response. Patients suffering from this syndrome experience excruciating pains in the numb parts of their bodies when they visually identify a threatening object approaching their bodies.

Threat hypersymbolia does not provide any counterevidence to the fourth qualification of pain experience. On the contrary, to claim that patients suffering from this condition feel excruciating pain is to contend that the experience they undergo is fundamentally aversive. Still, we need to address this pain dissociation syndrome in the present context because it brings into question another claim defended in this study, namely, the claim concerning the stratified nature of pain experience. Does pain hypersymbolia not illustrate that pain can be experienced intentionally, and *only* intentionally—as an object of cognitive and emotive intentionality—in complete absence of a sensory component? We are in need of some further clarification.

A forty-six-year-old construction engineer had moved his head with a jerk so as to avoid a falling beam in the construction site. This commonplace experience was followed by a persistent headache, and three days later the patient's hand had become clumsy. While taking a bath a few days after the incident, he could no longer identify the left hand as his own. While lying in bed he was once again taken aback by the misapprehension of his hand as being that of a stranger. He soon lost all sensations in his arm. Yet the consequences of this seemingly trivial accident were even stranger than that:

> He had no feeling in the arm and could not use it, but when he saw the arm being approached by someone it would suddenly move sideways as if it had been stung; simultaneously, he experienced a burning pain. The involuntary withdrawal movements of his left

84 THE PHENOMENOLOGY OF PAIN

> arm were so embarrassing that he tied it to his belt. (Hoogenraad, Ramos, and Van Gijn 1994, 851)

This is not just a case that illustrates the general role that *anticipation* plays in pain experience. As we know, it sometimes suffices to hear the dentist's drill and to see it approach us to experience pain. In such circumstances the dentist, faking surprise, might proclaim that she hasn't even touched us. Yet she cannot fool us so easily: we know, just as she does, that it's just a question of time until the drill hits the tooth. Yet pain hypersymbolia is not just a matter of visual stimuli inducing actual feelings of pain. The patient finds the situation deeply embarrassing because his body reacts contrary to how he wants it to react. Moreover, his body appears to identify each approaching object as a threat-inducing stimulus. As Grahek points out, we face here "a case in which the human pain protective system has gone irreparably awry, causing permanent misery to the unfortunate sufferer" (2007, 23).

Are we then to conclude that while lobotomized, cingulotomized, and morphinized patients live their pains pre-intentionally, and only pre-intentionally, threat hypersymbolia patients relate to their pains intentionally, and only intentionally? Such a view seems to be supported by the fact that in the case of pain hypersymbolia, pain is evoked exclusively by visual stimuli. Thus, the feeling of pain withdraws as soon as the patient closes his eyes; yet as soon as he opens them and identifies the visual object approaching his arm, the burning pain reappears. If this means that in this case pain is experienced in the absence of pain sensations, then threat hypersymbolia provides a strong counterargument to my contention in chapter 2 that pain is a stratified phenomenon. If it is indeed true that when it comes to the "whole pain experience," the sensory dimension is foundational, then it should not be possible to experience pain without pain sensations. If pain is indeed a stratified phenomenon as described above, then threat hypersymbolia seems to be impossible, and vice versa. Or put in Grahek's terms, if pain is indeed a stratified phenomenon, then (this goes against one of Grahek's central claims) it should not be possible to be in pain while feeling no pain.[10]

Arguably, we find ourselves at an impasse because of an ambiguity that lies at the heart of the concept of sensations. In a set of lectures delivered in 1908, Edward Titchener maintained that psychology and psychophysics employ the notion of sensation in two fundamentally different ways. While in psychology, sensations refer to the most basic psychological data of experience, in psychophysics, sensations are conceived of as physical phenomena,

THE PHENOMENOLOGY OF PAIN DISSOCIATION SYNDROMES 85

or, more precisely, as the physical correlates of psychological data. According to Titchener, "The failure to distinguish between psychophysics and psychology proper has led to much confused argument" (1973, 8). This very ambiguity between different concepts of sensation is exactly what has led us to the current impasse. For let us ask, in which sense are we to understand the assertion that those who suffer from threat hypersymbolia feel no painful sensations? Insofar as pain-inducing *stimuli* are missing, these patients do not live through any painful sensations in the psychophysical sense. However, if it makes any sense to claim that these patients experience pain, they must live through painful sensations in the psychological sense, for otherwise we would simply lack any reasons to claim that it is precisely pain, and not, say, anguish, despair, or any other kind of emotion that these patients live through. To return to Hoogenraad, Ramos, and Van Gijn's patient, only if he feels a painful sensation in the psychological sense *in the left side of his body* can his body manifest clear signs of pain. Moreover, the very fact that the patient finds his bodily reaction embarrassing provides further proof that this patient experiences pain sensations in spite of the efforts to escape them. Phenomenological reflections on pain hypersymbolia provide further proof that in the absence of pain sensations, pain as such is inconceivable. Threat hypersymbolia provides incontestable evidence that even in the absence of pain-inducing stimuli, one can nonetheless live through pain sensations in the psychological sense, and for this very reason, one can apprehend these sensations as excruciatingly painful.[11]

ASYMBOLIA FOR PAIN

Paul Schilder and Erwin Stengel were the first to describe this pain syndrome:

> In 1927, we observed a patient with sensory aphasia who would have hurt herself severely if left alone. She pushed everything that came into her hand against her eyes, heedless of the pain she thus inflicted on herself. When we studied this patient more carefully, we found that she did not react to pain or only in an incomplete and local way. (1931, 598)

At first glance it might seem that we face here another case of CIP, yet a closer look reveals a striking difference. In contrast to CIP patients, Schilder and

Stengel's patient recognized pain, even though she lacked appropriate motor and emotional responses to pain. The patient felt pain, even though it appeared not to bother her. This seemingly impossible unity of the presence of pain, accompanied with emotional indifference, differentiates asymbolia for pain (AP) from other syndromes. As Robert Hemphill and Erwin Stengel put it, AP consists "in the lack of adequate reactions to painful stimuli which are obviously perceived correctly by the patient as pain" (1940, 257). Or as Jack Rubins and Emanuel Friedman have it, AP is a condition that "denotes the inability to recognize the unpleasant or disagreeable component of a painful or threatening stimulus, with the result that little or no defense reaction is produced, although the noxious stimulus itself is perceived" (1948, 554). We need to ask again: Must the experience of pain be aversive? Does AP not provide us with an example of how pain can be experienced without any negativity?

A person suffering from AP can hold a lit match until her fingers would almost burn without dropping it, yet would not mind the sensation of pain that an experience such as this one would normally provoke. So also, when pricked in the palm of her hand, the patient would smile joyfully, then start laughing, and while reaching the hand out to the investigator in full complacency, she would proclaim, "Oh, pain, that hurts" (see Schilder and Stengel 1928, 147). Special pain-producing tests, such as the intravenous injection of histamine or the artificially produced muscle ischemia, would seemingly incite the sensation of pain in AP patients, yet would nonetheless fail to spur an adequate emotional and behavioral reaction. Those diagnosed with AP commonly claim during the examination that the pinprick does not hurt even after prolonged application. As in one case examined by Rubins and Friedman, the patient can say "Ouch" and grimace when severely pricked to the point of drawing blood; nonetheless, she would never withdraw her limbs or turn her head away (1948, 561). It is especially perplexing that the patients with AP often respond to the pains inflicted by the examiners with laughter. All the mentioned characteristics of AP seem to suggest that the patients diagnosed with this condition sense pain, yet do not react to the pain sensation appropriately. It seems that AP is a behavioral pathology that affects not the patient's pain sensation, but pain behavior as well as cognitive and emotional reactions to pain.

While CIP is (as the term suggests) an instance of insensitivity to pain, AP is an instance of indifference to pain. This means that while the CIP patients do not sense any pain, the AP patients sense pain, yet are indifferent to what they sense. The indifference admits of degrees: it can take the form of complete indifference, or it can manifest itself as partial indifference, coupled with verbal exclamations (such as "Ouch," or "That hurts all right") and some partial movements of escape. As, for instance, the study by Berthier, Starkstein, and Leiguarda revealed, "After prolonged deep painful stimuli, 2 patients showed a local and incomplete withdrawal response of the leg, while 3 patients showed only an incomplete unilateral defense reaction. One patient not only failed to show a withdrawal response but also exhibited a reaction of 'approach' to the painful stimuli" (1988, 43).

Can we consider AP to be an instance of *apraxia*, understood as the loss of ability to carry out learned purposeful bodily movements? Rubins and Friedman (1948) have considered this possibility and were drawn to a negative conclusion. When it comes to apraxia, only the motor movements are of importance, and the considerations of the nature of sensations are nonessential. By contrast, when it comes to AP, the sensation of pain appears to be just as important as the motor reaction. As Rubins and Friedman further observe, "Pain sensation as evaluated by our routine criteria—namely, ability to distinguish between sharp and dull on application of a pointed object or to perceive sharpness with the same intensity—was normal" (1948, 566).

Thus, AP appears to be an instance of a pain sensation lived in the absence of emotional and behavioral responses. In Grahek's (2007) words, it appears to represent in the purest form how one can feel pain while at the same time being not in pain. But if so, then AP brings into question the fourth qualification of pain experience introduced in this chapter—the thesis concerning the inherently unpleasant nature of pain sensations. The very fact that patients suffering from AP can be indifferent to their pains and even laugh at their pains seems to provide sufficient phenomenological evidence against this thesis.

In the recent philosophy of pain, one can single out two competing interpretations of this syndrome. The first interpretation was put forth by Grahek (2007), while the second one has been recently defended by Colin Klein (2015a, 2015b). Grahek's treatment of AP relies upon his commitment to the idea that pain is a complex experience that comprises sensory-discriminative, emotional-cognitive, and behavioral components. While in the normal pain experience these components are tied to each other, in some pathological cases they can also exist independently from one another. Pain dissociation syndromes arise when the sensory part dissociates from the emotional and the behavioral parts. This means that, according to Grahek, there are in principle two, and only two, different types of pain dissociation syndromes: (1) pain without painfulness; and (2) painfulness without pain. In the first case, one feels pain while one is not in pain; in the second case, one is in pain while nonetheless not feeling any pain. According to Grahek (2007), AP provides us with the only pure example of pain without painfulness, that is, of feeling pain while not being in pain.

Grahek's basic commitment to the idea that pain is a complex experience corresponds to the phenomenological thesis presented in this study: pain is a multidimensional phenomenon. However, Grahek's interpretation of AP as an instance of pain without painfulness constitutes a serious challenge to the phenomenological claim that the painfulness of pain is rooted in the quality of pain sensations. If it is indeed true that AP is an instance of pain without painfulness, then we are to conclude that pain sensations as such are bereft of any painfulness, that they are free of disagreeable and unpleasant characteristics. As Grahek elegantly puts it, "The pure juice or essence of pain experience thus extracted has turned out to be a blunt, fleshless, inert sensation pointing to nothing beyond itself, leaving no traces in the memory and powerless to move the body and mind in any way" (2007, 76). This is a highly counterintuitive realization, since if one were asked, What exactly is this "pure juice of pain"?, one would be led to respond: It is nothing painful! In fact, those who experience it in its purity often cannot help themselves and laugh at it.

While Grahek's (2007) interpretation of AP is rooted in his commitment to the idea that pain is a complex experience, Klein's interpretation is just as strongly embedded in the idea that "motivational force is an intrinsic property of pains" (2015b, 1). Grahek's position constitutes a challenge not only to the phenomenological approach I defend here, but also to Klein's motivationalism. After all, if pain sensations as such are devoid of affective and behavioral components, then "the pure juice of pain experience" does not motivate us one way or another, and thus, one loses the grounds to support the biologism that lies at the heart of Klein's motivationalism about pain.[12] If pain lacks representational force, then it does not motivate us.

According to Klein's alternative account, "Asymbolics fail to react to pain because they no longer care about the physical integrity of their bodies" (2015b, 6). According to this proposal, AP is not an instance of a change in the feeling of pain, but rather a matter of a change in the person who feels pain: the person in question is no longer concerned about his body. "Pains motivate because we care about our bodies. Were we to stop caring—something that is ordinarily impossible, for good biological reasons—then pains would not matter. Asymbolics are a realization of this unusual possibility" (Klein 2015b, 8).

I would contend that we face here a counterintuitive thesis, which is grounded in a question-begging strategy. The thesis is counterintuitive because it is just irrelevant whether we care about our bodies or not as far as pains are concerned. Care about your body as much as you wish, or do not care about it—pains will still hurt. One might argue that such a response is contentious in that it overlooks the evidence that underlies Klein's claim. Yet what is this evidence? According to Klein, AP provides us with a clear instance of pain that no longer matters precisely because the patients stopped caring about their bodies. Yet what is the evidence that supports this latter claim, namely, the view that AP is an instance of us no longer caring about our bodies? Supposedly, the evidence lies in the thesis that if we no longer care about our bodies, pains no longer matter to us. In light of such circularity, it remains questionable what evidence underlies the motivationalist conception of AP.

I would like to present an alternative account that is grounded in phenomenological principles. Despite the significant differences between Grahek and Klein, there is one presupposition they both share. According to both, AP provides us with a case in which pain sensations are experienced, although they are not experienced as bothersome. I would contend that this assumption is ungrounded. Appearances to the contrary notwithstanding, there simply is no evidence to suggest that pain asymbolics experience pain sensations. Rather, *what they sense are pain-inducing stimuli, which nonetheless fail to provoke pain sensations*. Arguably, the recognition of this failure is exactly what provokes laughter among AP patients. Thus, in contrast to Grahek, AP is not an instance in which one experiences "the pure juice or essence of pain" (Grahek 2007, 76), just as it is not a case in which the feeling of pain is given in the absence of being in pain. In contrast to Klein, AP is not an instance of the disintegration of care about the integrity of the body. In contrast to both Grahek and Klein, AP provides us with an instance in which pain-inducing stimuli are experienced in the absence of pain sensations; and precisely because the sensory dimension is either severely constrained or entirely missing, one's experience cannot be qualified either in terms of feeling pain or in terms of being in pain.

Have the AP patients truly stopped caring about their bodies, as Klein suggests? It is hard to defend such a view phenomenologically. As Schilder and Stengel hypothesized in their pioneering studies, "that such a common symptom [as AP—SG] has escaped the attention of examiners for so long is probably due to the erroneous opinion that the symptoms are disturbances in attention; our patients, however, were very much interested in pain" (1931, 599). Yet why would these patients be interested in pain if they no longer cared about the integrity of their bodies? Consider also Rubins and Friedman's classical study of AP: when the patient suffering from AP was "told that she would be slapped or struck without any accompanying gesture, she would respond vigorously, saying, 'Don't you slap me, or I'll slap you right back,' or 'Don't you dare punch me,' understanding the unpleasant significance of the act" (1948, 557). It is hard to interpret such proclamations as expressing lack of care for one's body. Consider also the case of the nineteen-year-old youth (case 3 in the same study): "Complete lack of withdrawal was shown to threatening gestures, although he understood verbal menaces and would protest harmful intention" (1948, 561). Protests of this kind are hardly compatible with Klein's contention that pain asymbolics do not care about their bodies.

Is it really true, as Grahek (2007) suggests, that AP patients claim that they sense pain, even though it doesn't bother them? Not really. Consider Schilder and Stengel's observation about two pain asymbolics, who "said that they could remember that the pain had been inflicted, but that they did not feel it" (1931, 599). We can take this to mean that as far as their experience was concerned, what they experienced lacked pain quality, even though they could recognize that the experience in question was provoked by stimuli that normally resulted in a painful experience. Consider also the first case that Rubins and Friedman address in their study. On the first examination for pin-prick sensation, even though the patient had been told that it was going to hurt, "she then answered 'didn't hurt me' when the examiner pricked her to the point of drawing blood" (Rubins and Friedman 1948, 556). Moreover, "after intravenous injection of 1 cc. of histamine phosphate solution (1:1000) sweating and flushing of the face occurred and she complained of warmth but did not complain spontaneously of headache, although she grimaced somewhat" (Rubins and Friedman 1948, 557).

We have the conceptual tools needed to describe the experience these patients live through. In light of Titchener's distinction between different senses that qualify the common use of the concept of sensations, we can say that the patients feel the sensation in the psychophysical sense, yet not in the psychological sense. They experience the stimuli that usually provoke pain experience, yet they do not experience the pain sensation (in the psychological sense)—the kind of sensation that would be stamped with pain quality. AP patients experience the sharp or dull sensation that under usual circumstances gives rise to pain, and thus they proclaim, "Oh, it hurts all right." Yet this sensation—whatever name one were to give it—does not translate into a genuine pain experience—the sensation that is filled with pain quality. Thus, the patients proclaim that the "pain" they feel does not bother them.

In this regard, Hemphill and Stengel's classical study is of great significance. This study provides us with a case of a patient who struggles with word deafness combined with AP. This connection is not unusual either empirically or conceptually. Empirical evidence suggests that in the majority of cases, AP is combined with some form of word deafness.[13] Conceptually, both AP and word deafness share a common feature: "a lack of the ability to make an appropriate response to stimuli reaching the patient from the outer world" (Hemphill and Stengel 1940, 260). They further remark that AP "is the more primitive and more general symptom, while the lack of response in pure word-deafness is confined to one special group of stimuli" (1940, 260).

Phenomenologically, the connection between word deafness and AP is not surprising, since in both cases we face *one and the same defect—the incapacity on the part of the patient to apprehend sense-contents.* Words come, but only as sounds, and the patient is incapable of apprehending the meaning of these sounds. The same holds for pain: pain sensations come, yet only in the form of pain-inducing stimuli, and the sensation of these stimuli fails to trigger a painful experience. Moreover, in both cases, the patients recognize a defect as a defect: they know that they are supposed to experience something more than they experience. With word deafness, this absence is lived as deprivation; with pain, it is experienced as liberation.

Pain asymbolics do not live through pain sensations, insofar as these sensations are filled with pain quality. This means that AP does not provide any evidence against the validity of the fourth qualification of pain experience, which suggests that pain experience is by its very nature aversive. Yet do we have any reason to claim that pain asymbolics live through sensations in the psychophysical sense? We do. Consider Rubins and Friedman's analysis: "Rapid painful stimuli (pinprick) provoked no noticeable changes, but prolonged pinprick produced pupillary dilatation and a rise in blood pressure (20 mm. systolic and 10 mm. diastolic), even when no defense reaction was manifest" (1948, 557). Consider also the Berthier, Starkstein, and Leiguarda study, which shows that the AP patients do not demonstrate primary sensory defects, even though they fail to recognize the pain-inducing stimuli *as painful* or the threat-inducing stimuli *as threatening*. The thorough examination of six cases by Berthier, Starkstein, and Leiguarda led to the conclusion that "while all could recognize pain, none of them reported unpleasant feeling" (1988, 43). The available reports provide all the evidence needed to claim that pain asymbolics do not live through pain sensations in the psychological sense, although they live through them in the psychophysical sense.

Pain asymbolics sense pain in the psychophysical sense of the term, yet they do not sense it in the psychological sense, and, therefore, they identify the sensation they live through as sharp or dull, cold or hot, yet not as disagreeable or unpleasant. This allows us to claim that pain asymbolics do not live through pain sensations in the genuine sense of the term, that the "pure juice of pain" lies beyond their reach, even though they sense pain-inducing stimuli. Arguably, the recognition of the blocked capacity of pain-inducing stimuli is what provokes laughter among these patients.

Thus, in contrast to lobotomized, cingulotomized, and morphinized patients as well as those who suffer from threat hypersymbolia, pain asymbolics neither experience nor intend their pains as painful. However, it is crucial not to overlook (this is where the essential phenomenological difference between AP and CIP lies) that pain asymbolics manifest the same kind of physiological reactions to pain as other patients: tachycardia, hypertension, sweating, mydriasis. Nonetheless, their physiological reactions are not accompanied either with nonintentional or with intentional experiences of pain. Pain asymbolics experience painful sensations, if by this term one means psychophysical sensations; yet they do not live through painful sensations, if by this term one means psychological sensations. It thereby becomes understandable why, when Schilder and Stengel's patient was pricked on her left hand and asked if it hurt, she replied: "It hurts indeed, but I do not know what that really is" (1928, 151). It also becomes understandable how a patient examined by Pötzl and Stengel could remark: "I feel it [pain] indeed . . . but . . . that is nothing" (1937, 180). The very fact that pain asymbolics do not experience pain either pre-intentionally or intentionally, while nonetheless they experience the psychophysical pain sensations, sheds light on the perplexing fact that, as Grahek (2007) points out, almost as a rule, these patients tend to either smile or even laugh during the painful testing (a behavior that comes to an abrupt end as soon as stimulation is discontinued). Their bodies "know" that they should be in pain, yet this bodily knowledge does not resonate in their experience, be this experience pre-intentional or intentional. They feel the pain-inducing stimuli and recognize their sensory qualities (in the psycho-physical sense), such as sharpness or dullness, yet this recognition does not provoke pain experience.

Lobotomized, cingulotomized, and morphinized patients exemplify a conflict between how pain is lived through and how it is intended: they live though pain as a feeling-sensation, although they do not intend pain intentionally. By contrast, threat hypersymbolics and pain asymbolics exemplify a divergence between how their bodies physiologically react to pain-inducing stimuli and how they experience it both pre-intentionally and intentionally. While those who suffer from threat hypersymbolia experience painful sensations in the absence of pain-inducing stimuli, pain asymbolics sense pain-inducing stimuli in the absence of painful sensations. As far as the intentional structure of pain experience is concerned, pain asymbolics cannot intend their pains as painful because they do not live through their pains as painful; there simply are no experiential contents that would lend themselves to a painful apprehension. Pain asymbolics are "liberated" from pain both at the pre-intentional and the intentional levels of experience, and this "liberation" clarifies why their bodily reactions to pain-inducing stimuli are devoid of any biological function that is otherwise characteristic of pain experiences.

It thereby becomes clear that AP does not provide a counterexample to the phenomenological claim that pain is a stratified phenomenon, which rests upon pain sensations, conceived of as feeling-sensations filled with pain quality. AP does not illustrate a case in which pain sensations are experienced in the absence of any negativity and averseness. Rather, it illustrates how pain-inducing stimuli can be experienced in a pain-free way. I would thus contend that AP is an instance of insensitivity to pain, and not indifference to pain, insofar as the concept of pain refers to experience that is stamped with pain quality. Should one wish to preserve the view that AP is a type of indifference, one would have to conceive of it as a form of indifference to pain-inducing stimuli, not pain sensations.

PAIN AFFECT WITHOUT PAIN SENSATION

As we just saw, Grahek's conception of pain without painfulness constitutes a challenge to the view I present here in that it suggests that pain sensations as such should not be conceived of as aversive feelings stamped with a distinct experiential quality that distinguishes pain from other aversive feelings.

Having seen that only insofar as sensations have a distinct aversive quality can they be qualified as pain sensations, let us turn to a different type of dissociation syndrome, which Grahek (2007) identifies as an instance of *painfulness without pain*. If there are cases of painfulness without pain, then pain cannot be conceived of as a stratified phenomenon in the outlined sense: the sensory dimension of pain experience cannot be conceived of as the founding one.

I am in agreement with Grahek when he claims that painfulness of pain must "wear on its sleeve the signature of pain sensation in order to count as genuine pain" (2007, 107). I cannot agree, however, that this realization necessitates one to claim the following: "So, it seems that not only must we allow that pain without painfulness is possible, we must also make room for the opposite possibility: painfulness without pain" (2007, 107). Nothing in Grahek's analysis prepares this transition; it is a non sequitur. Yet let us not dismiss it for formal reasons alone. According to Grahek, "incontestable clinical evidence" supports the view that painfulness without pain exists. The evidence in question concerns the phenomenon that Ploner, Freund, and Schnitzler (1999) have described as pain affect without pain sensation. This is a curious condition, whose discovery occurred during the neurological testing of a patient with selective lesions of the right primary (SI) and secondary (SII) somatosensory cortices. According to Ploner et al. (2002), these cortices of the brain are responsible for the processing of the sensory-discriminative components of pain. By this we are to understand that these areas of the brain enable the precise spatial localization, temporal registration, intensity calibration, and qualitative characterization of pain sensations evoked by pain-inducing stimuli. When cutaneous laser stimulation to the patient's left hand was applied, it did not elicit any pain sensations; yet, nonetheless, it did provoke a feeling the patient described as "clearly unpleasant." Moreover, the patient could not clearly localize this feeling: it extended "somewhere between fingertips and shoulder." It was a feeling the patient wanted to avoid. "The fully cooperative and eloquent patient was completely unable to further describe quality, localization, and intensity of the perceived stimulus. Suggestions from a given word list containing 'warm,' 'hot,' 'cold,' 'touch,' 'burning,' 'pinprick-like,' 'slight pain,' 'moderate pain,' and 'intense pain' were denied nor did the patient report any kind of paraesthesia" (Ploner et al. 2002, 213).

The authors of this study claim that their results for the first time demonstrated "a loss of pain sensation with preserved pain affect" (Ploner et al. 2002, 211). Is their claim justified? I do not think so, and for two reasons. First,

THE PHENOMENOLOGY OF PAIN DISSOCIATION SYNDROMES   95

as Colin Klein has already rightly observed, the patient describes his feeling as "clearly unpleasant" (2015b, 145). Yet, as we know from the introduction, it is not enough to qualify pain as an unpleasant experience. Clearly, there are many other unpleasant feelings besides pain. Why, then, should we conclude that the patient in question felt precisely *pain*? As the quoted passages above demonstrate, the patient himself explicitly denied that he experienced pain, be it slight, moderate, or intense. Second, the patient localized the "clearly unpleasant" feeling "somewhere between fingertips and shoulder." But if so, then the affect the authors describe is not free of sensible components: it is not, as they claim, an affect without sensation. Admittedly, the patient was not capable of localizing unpleasant feeling with precision. Nonetheless, the feeling in question was localized *somewhere* within the body, and thus, it was *sensible*. So also, even though the patient displayed prolonged reaction time to laser stimuli, the clearly unpleasant feeling he lived through had a vague temporal determination. Last but not least, even though the patient had lost the capacity to clearly determine the intensity of the feeling, the feeling in question nonetheless had a vague intensity.

All of this suggests that the selective lesions of the right primary (SI) and secondary (SII) somatosensory cortices affected yet did not annul the patient's sensory-discriminative capacity. Although the patient could no longer spatio-temporally determine his sensations with precision, the feeling he lived through was neither beyond time nor beyond space: the patient still localized it within his body ("somewhere between fingertips and shoulder"); lived through it with some delay in time ("stimulation of the left hand yielded exclusively long-latency responses"); and it was still a feeling with a "'clearly unpleasant' inten-sity," no matter how imprecise this intensity might have been.

On the basis of the foregoing analysis, I would contend that there can be no painfulness without pain, unless, however, one uses the term "painful-ness" in a highly broad sense—either as synonymous with the category of unpleasant feelings in general or as covering a certain group of unpleasant feelings. There can be no painfulness without pain because as soon as the sensory-discriminative capacity is canceled out, one loses the basis to qualify the feeling one lives through as pain. As we will see in chapter 5, as far as human experience is concerned, it is a category mistake to disembody pain, just as it is a category mistake to locate anxiety or depression in one's body.

∾

The phenomenology of dissociation syndromes here presented relies upon three insights developed in chapter 2: (1) pain is a stratified phenomenon;

(2) while at the founding level, pain is lived through as a nonintentional *hyle*, at the founded level, it is marked by intentionality; and (3) the schema "apprehension–content of apprehension" explains the relation between these experiential strata. Building on the basis of these three insights, I have argued here that one can understand many dissociation syndromes as variations of indifference toward pain (threat hypersymbolia is an exception to this rule). Accordingly, CIP patients are neither capable of intending pain as an object of experience, nor living through pain as an experiential content, nor, finally, experiencing pain as a psychophysical sensation. By contrast, lobotomized, cingulotomized, and morphinized patients are indifferent to pain, conceived of as an intentional object of experience, while they nonetheless experience pain "hyletically," as a content of experience. Third, threat hypersymbolics live through pain sensations and intend pain as an object of their experience even in the absence of pain-inducing stimuli. Fourth, pain asymbolics are indifferent to pain conceived both as an experiential content and as an object of experience, yet they continue to experience pain, conceived of as a psychophysical sensation. Finally, according to the perspective presented here, the so-called "pain affect without pain sensation" is a syndrome with an unfortunately confusing name, and it in principle cannot be understood as a case of painfulness without pain.

A phenomenology of these diverse pain syndromes is not an alternative to the explanations we come across in cognitive science. While the task of cognitive science is to clarify the physiological mechanisms that underpin the bewildering types of pain experiences, phenomenology's task is to clarify the structure of these experiences. The recognition that pain is both a nonintentional and an intentional experience, and that this duplicity can be clarified through the apprehension–content of apprehension schema, provides the means needed to supplement the neurological explanations of physiological mechanisms with a phenomenological clarification of the structures of pain experience. Such a clarification enables us to defend the fourth and fifth qualifications of pain experience introduced in this chapter: pain is an aversive feeling with a distinct experiential quality that distinguishes it from other aversive feelings.

CHAPTER 4

· ·

PAIN AND TEMPORALITY

We already know that pain (1) can be given only in firsthand experience; (2) either as a nonintentional feeling-sensation; or (3) as an intentional feeling. Furthermore, we also know that pain is a feeling, (4) which is of an aversive nature; and (5) which has a distinct experiential quality. These qualifications do not yet complete the phenomenological conception of pain; they need to be supplemented with two further characteristics. We still need to see that (6) pain is an *original* experience; and that (7) it is *embodied*. In the present chapter, we will focus on the sixth qualification, and in chapter 5 we will turn to the seventh characteristic.

In phenomenology, one commonly distinguishes original experiences from reproductive experiences. A distinguishing characteristic of reproductive experience is that it intends objects in the mode of the "as if."[1] If I remember, anticipate, or imagine shaking my friend's hand, the experience I undergo is always that of *as if* shaking my friend's hand. Yet pain cannot be lived in the mode of the *as if*, and precisely, therefore, it must be qualified as an original, that is, as a nonderivative experience. Insofar as pains are merely remembered, expected, or phantasized, one does not truly live through them. *Pain inherently resists all modes of reproduction*—this is what it means to claim that pain can be lived only as an original experience.

To claim that pain can be given only in original experience is to suggest that it can be given only in the field of presence, and that in this sense it manifests an inner and uncompromising resistance to any kind of modalization of experience. Yet how exactly is the field of presence to be understood? Far from being sufficient in itself, this characterization calls for further inquiries into the temporality of pain experience. The task of this chapter thereby becomes clear: it must provide an account of the temporal structures of pain experience. Only on the basis of such an account can one determine the meaning of the claim that pain can be given only in *original* experience.

In this chapter, my analysis will take six steps. First, so as to delimit the boundaries of phenomenological reflections on the temporality of pain, I will begin with the fundamental distinction between objective time and subjective temporality. Second, drawing on Husserl's C-Manuscripts, I will single out five fundamental senses in which we can speak of presence in Husserl's phenomenology. Third, building on the basis of some classical as well as contemporary phenomenological analyses of subjective temporality, I will draw a further distinction between implicit and explicit temporality. This will enable us to recognize some characteristic features of pain experience: pain isolates the sufferer within the field of presence, which the sufferer experiences as disconnected from the past and the future. Fourth, I will introduce a distinction between implicit and explicit consciousness of presence. This distinction will enable us to shed some light on the contentious issue concerning the possibility of the so-called "unfelt pains." Fifth, I will supplement the distinction between implicit and explicit presence with the further distinction between implicit and explicit memories. This will allow us to recognize that even though explicit memory appears to play no constitutive role in one's experience of pain, the painfulness of pain is nonetheless heavily determined by implicit memory. Sixth, I will draw an analogous distinction between different forms of anticipation and maintain that the temporality of pain is heavily determined by implicit anticipation. As a result, it will become apparent that the temporality of pain is not merely marked by the expansion of the now ("minutes seem like hours, hours like days"), but also, and much more importantly, that because of the role played by implicit memory and implicit anticipation, the field of presence, no matter how disconnected from past and future it might seem to be, continues to be shaped and affected by the larger temporal horizons of experience.

OBJECTIVE TIME AND SUBJECTIVE TEMPORALITY

In the science of pain one commonly understands the temporality of pain as an objectively measurable and quantifiable duration of pain experience. Consider the distinction between three types of pain, namely, the distinction between transient, acute, and chronic pain. Transient pain is the kind of pain that arises from a mild burn or a stubbed toe. It is of brief duration. One experiences pain for a few seconds or minutes, and then it's gone. Acute pain is the pain one feels when it lingers for as long as the body does not heal.

Despite its perseverance, acute pain contracts and subsequently evaporates when healing is underway. Pain becomes chronic when it persists after healing is complete. This type of pain extends beyond the expected period of healing and refuses to be explained as a mere effect that follows from tissue damage.

The fundamental distinction between these three types of pain concerns temporal determinations. Transient pain is the kind of pain that takes one a couple of seconds, or a couple of minutes, to live through. Acute pain is the pain that lasts longer, although no longer than three months, or six months—the exact length of time depends on the definition one relies on. Finally, chronic pain is the kind of pain that lasts longer than acute pain, that is, longer than three months, or six months—again, depending on the definition. One sees time as invariable and objective, as something that lends itself to quantifiable measurement, and on the basis of such a conception of time, one classifies different types of pain.

In the science of pain, it is quite common to rely on such a quantifiable concept of time while at the same admitting the inevitable deficiencies associated with it. As Sebastian von Peter, among others, has recently maintained, the reliance on clock time while assessing pain entails the danger of bypassing the importance of the individually configured time, which in its own turn carries profoundly negative therapeutic consequences (see Peter 2010, 14–15). In light of these circumstances, the phenomenology of time obtains not only theoretical but also therapeutic significance.

The phenomenology of time begins with the distinction between objective time, as addressed in the previous paragraphs, and subjective temporality, the time of experience. Objective time is inflexible and unyielding: it can neither expand nor contract. By contrast, subjective temporality is not fixed externally and commonly is experienced in a more or less extended or contracted way. When viewed from the perspective of lived temporality, the five minutes one waits in the doctor's office to hear the results of a medical test, or the five minutes one spends looking through the morning press, are experienced as incomparably different lengths of time. So also, "the now of the pain I live through may appear to me to be endless, while the procedure inflicting it may by the clock take only 45 seconds" (Brough 2001, 43). For as long as pain lasts, we experience it as a disturbance or a disorder, whose lived duration cannot be measured in terms of objective time.

According to one of the fundamental claims in the phenomenology of pain, we cannot understand the lived temporality of pain insofar as we rely on clock time. Following the method of the phenomenological epoché, we can bracket the conception of objective and measurable time. Such a methodological procedure is highly needed in the philosophy of pain, which would aim to give an account of the temporal structures of pain experience. The phenomenological epoché that suspends objective time (that is, places it out of consideration) provides the researcher with the methodological means to focus on lived temporality and to understand it in its own terms. In our subsequent reflections on the temporality of pain, let us employ this methodological procedure.

THE DIFFERENT SENSES OF PRESENCE:
THE FUNDAMENTAL LEVELS OF TIME-CONSTITUTION

What does it mean to claim that pain is given in the field of presence? With this question, let us turn to Husserl's so-called C-Manuscripts (see Husserl 2006), where presence (*Gegenwart*) is one of the main themes. Following Husserl's analysis, I would like to single out five fundamental senses in which we can speak of presence in Husserl's phenomenology. Once we have a taxonomy of presence, we will be able to ask again: What does it mean to claim that pain can be experienced only in the field of presence? With a more precise answer to this question, we will obtain a deeper understanding of what it means to qualify pain as an original experience.

In the C-Manuscripts, Husserl couples the phenomenological epoché with a specific type of a reduction, which ultimately leads to the living present (*lebendige Gegenwart*), conceived of as the origin of all time determinations and meaning configurations. Despite its obvious centrality, the exact meaning of the living present is by no means unambiguously determined in these manuscripts.[2] In the manuscripts collected in the C 2 group, Husserl identifies the living present with the original stream of consciousness. In Text Nr. 2, he writes: "The primal stream of the living present is the primal temporalization, in which lies the final origin of spatio-temporal world and its spatiotemporal form" (Husserl 2006, 4; my translation—SG). As he further adds, "Times, objects, worlds in every sense originate in the primal streaming of the living present" (2006, 4; my translation—SG). This is crucial not to overlook: according to Husserl, *time itself has its origins in the temporalizing consciousness*. This means that, strictly speaking, *the living present is not a temporal category, it does not belong to time*; rather, time is constituted in the living present. We see how ambiguous the concept of presence

(*Gegenwart*) is. On the one hand, we all know that this concept can refer to the midpoint between past and future. Yet, on the other hand, we now see that it also refers to the living present of the streaming consciousness. When Husserl speaks of the living present, he has in mind the original stream of presencing, the originally streaming present, which is given in the mode of presence, and only presence (see Husserl 2006, Text Nr. 3).

Husserl identifies the streaming consciousness as the primal phenomenon (*Urphänomenon*) and often refers to it as the "phenomenon of all phenomena." By this we are to understand that everything that is given, is given only insofar as it gives itself in the streaming consciousness. Everything that has meaning for me, has its meaning in the streaming consciousness. Indeed, everything that is, is a unity of meaning in this stream, which Husserl further qualifies as *anonymous*. This stream is the temporalizing consciousness: that consciousness in which all time modalities are constituted. This constituting stream, conceived of as the living present, is to be conceived of as a closer determination of the *sum* of the *cogito ergo sum*. As Husserl has it, "I am, I live, and my life is an unbroken unity of primal streaming temporalization" (2006, 3; my translation—SG). Such, then, is the first sense of presence that we come across in Husserl's C-Manuscripts.

In what other senses can we speak of presence? In the C-Manuscripts (and not only there), Husserl draws a distinction between time-constituting consciousness (conceived of as the living present) and immanent time, or subjective temporality. According to Husserl, immanent time is constituted in the temporalizing stream. How are we to understand this process of constitution?

The streaming consciousness of the living present is the terminus ad quem of the reduction, as it is thematized in the C-Manuscripts. Husserl argues that the living present entails two essential structural moments. On the one hand, this streaming consciousness has its own center point, the *original ego* (*Ur-Ich*). On the other hand, the stream of consciousness is intentional: something is always given in the stream; what is given to it is the "not I" (*das Ich-Fremde*), which, at the lowest levels of constitution, Husserl identifies as the original *hyle* (*Ur-Hyle*).

The constitution of any sense unities would not be possible if the streaming consciousness were nothing more than originally impressional consciousness, which could grasp the original hyletic data only in the momentary now. Any sense unity whatsoever is an achievement, a synthesis, and, first and foremost, it is a temporal synthesis. It is therefore crucial to stress that the consciousness of the living present is not merely a consciousness of a succession of impressional data; it is not merely a stream in which new hyletic data replace earlier data. As Husserl puts it in Text Nr. 5, "The streaming present is also the present of the movements of flowing, of having flown, and of having yet to flow. The now, the continuity of the past, and the living protentional horizon are conscious 'at the same time,' and this 'at the same time' is an 'at the same time' that flows" (2006, 12; my translation—SG). We can take this to mean that the consciousness of the living present has a *fixed form*, namely, it is a streaming unity of impressions, retentions, and protensions. The streaming consciousness impressionally apprehends the pure hyle as given in the momentary now; retentionally, it grasps the hyletic moments as slipping into the past and retains those moments in the stream; protentionally, it grasps the not-yet and the movement from the not-yet into the now.

In short, impressional consciousness is the phenomenological origin of the consciousness of the now; retentional consciousness is the phenomenological origin of the consciousness of the past; protentional consciousness is the origin of the consciousness of the future. Consciousness is a time-constituting consciousness insofar as it can intend the past, present, and future; and it intends these temporal modalities precisely because, as the living present, it is at one and the same time a consciousness of the streaming, the streaming by, and the streaming in.

Within such a framework, we grasp a second sense in which we can speak of presence. We can identify presence as the impressionally given momentary now that lies between the retentionally intended "just gone" and the protentionally anticipated "not yet." Both in the C-Manuscripts and elsewhere, Husserl identifies such a conception of presence as abstract and specious. This conception is abstract even though, as Husserl maintains in the C-Manuscripts, what is given impressionally is not just a datum, but an impressional field. While recognizing that impressional consciousness is already a synthesizing consciousness, Husserl distinguishes such a conception of an abstract present from a third sense in which we can speak of presence, namely, from concretely experienced presence, which is given as a unity intended in impressional, retentional, and protentional consciousness.

Yet even such a conception of concretely lived presence has its limits. So far, we do not yet know how to distinguish such a concretely lived presence from the past and the future, conceived of as independent temporal fields. How does the consciousness of the past and the future, conceived of as independent temporal fields, originate?

PAIN AND TEMPORALITY

In the C-Manuscripts, Husserl conceptualizes this process employing such metaphorical terms as "darkening" (*Verdunkelung*); "sleep" (*Schlaf*); "the sphere of the 'unconscious'" (*die Sphäre des "Unbewussten"*); and "wakening" (*Weckung*). He conceptualizes the retentional process as a process of "concealment that still shines through" (*"Verdeckung unter 'Durchscheinen'"* [2006, 81]). This is a striking and, to my mind, highly fitting characterization of the retentional process. This phraseology suggests that what consciousness retains still shines through in the present consciousness, but what shines through is given as covered up, and in a gradually lower level of vivacity. As the rays of the sun are covered up by the approaching clouds that get darker and darker, the retentional moments continuously lose their levels of brightness, until night sets in and they enter complete darkness. When this occurs, consciousness no longer holds them in grasp; and when the retentional moments no longer coexist with the present impressional consciousness, they can no longer be qualified as retentional. What we face here is a gradual process of *darkening* (*Verdunkelung*), which ultimately terminates in full darkness, or—to use another of Husserl's metaphors—dreamless sleep. However, any moment of retentional consciousness that has sunk into dreamless sleep can be *reawakened*. This reawakening takes the form of recollection (*Wiedererinnerung*). In contrast to retention, which always follows *and* coexists with the present consciousness, a recollection for principle reasons is separated from the present consciousness by darkness, or sleep. *"I can only retain what I still haven't lost; I can only remember what I have forgotten."*

More is to be said about the distinction between the rententional process and recollection. For the moment, I wish to stress only that insofar as a gap separates the living present from the remembered past, recollection (*Wiedererinnerung*) must be conceived of as a form of reproductive consciousness. Recollection reproduces the past present in the living present. It provides consciousness with access to the past, conceived of as an independent temporal field. In general lines, what has just been said about the constitution of the past can also be said about the constitution of the future, although, admittedly, some significant modifications would be needed. A detailed analysis of this issue in the present context would take us too far afield.

With the constitution of the past and of the future as independent temporal fields, we transition from the constitution of subjective presence to the constitution of subjective temporality, conceived of as a synthetic unity of subjectively lived past, present, and future. To be conscious of time, it is not enough to be aware of the difference that divides the present from the past and the future. Besides separating these temporal fields from each other, one must also establish a relation of sequence between them. How do I know how to order my own recollections in a certain order of sequence? How do I know which of my recollections precede or follow other recollections? Arguably, consciousness obtains this kind of knowledge on the basis of other syntheses. While the syntheses I have addressed above are largely passive and prereflective, the new syntheses to which I now appeal are active and reflective. More recently, Thomas Fuchs (2013, 80) has addressed these syntheses in some of his writings, where he argues that these syntheses for the first time occur in the second year of human life. These new syntheses give rise to extended, personal, and narrative consciousness. The performance of these active syntheses marks the birth of autobiographical memory and autobiographical time.

Still in the framework of the living present, I am conscious of the field of presence, conceived of as a synthetic unity of the present, the not-yet, and the not-anymore. While the present is given through primary impressions, the not-yet is intended by means of protentions, and the not-anymore is given through retentions. By means of recollections and anticipations, I constitute the fields of the past and the future, conceived of as independent temporal fields. By means of yet further active and reflective syntheses, I establish an order of sequence between the remembered moments and thereby procure a sense of subjective temporality, conceived of as an unbreakable continuity. Taking all these syntheses into account, we still do not reach the level of objective time. Suffice it to say that the constitution of objective time is not an egoic but an intersubjective achievement. We have to limit ourselves to the following observation: in the framework of each of these constitutive achievements, the concept of the present gains a different and enriched sense.

Now we can say that the present can be conceived of in five fundamental ways: (1) as the presence of the streaming consciousness, conceived of as the *Urphänomen*; (2) as the abstract presence intended in impressional consciousness and situated between the retentional past and the protentional future; (3) as the extended and concrete presence intended in the impressional, retentional, and protentional consciousness, and conceived of as a synthetic unity of the now, the not-yet, and the not-anymore; (4) as the presence, conceived of as the meeting point between the experienced past and the future; and, finally, (5) as the objective presence in the objectively measurable and intersubjectively constituted objective time.

At this point, we can return to our guiding question: What does it mean to claim that pain is lived in the field of presence? It is quite obvious that the first, second, and fifth determinations are inappropriate for determining the temporal nature of pain experience. We can therefore easily set them aside from our considerations.[3] Out of all the senses here distinguished, the third determination appears to be most fitting. To claim that pain is given in the field of presence is first and foremost to suggest that pain is experienced as a temporally extended phenomenon, which is intended not only impressionally but also retentionally and protentionally, and which therefore is constituted as a synthetic unity of the now, the not-yet, and the not-anymore. To claim that pain is lived in the field of presence is to suggest that pain is given as a temporal *duration*, or as an *extended* presence (that is, as a unity of the now, the not-anymore, and the almost-now). Yet even if we accept such a view—and I do not see on what possible phenomenological grounds it could be overruled—we are still left with the open question that concerns the suitability of the fourth determination. Are we to say that this determination, which suggests that pain is lived in the field of presence, conceived of as the point of intersection between the experienced past and the experienced future, further enriches our understanding of the temporal nature of pain experience? Or are we, on the contrary, to assert that such a view is ill-suited, since we live our pains as cut off from all past and future? We still do not have the conceptual basis to address this issue in sufficient detail. To do so, we must first supplement the foregoing analysis with the fundamental distinction between implicit and explicit temporality in all three temporal modalities (present, past, and future). Let us begin with the distinction between implicit and explicit presence.

IMPLICIT AND EXPLICIT PRESENCE

In Eugene A. Kaplan's study of pain and hypnosis, we come across the following account of a twenty-year-old college student who had been "developed" as a hypnotic subject. This patient was unusually susceptible to hypnotic treatment, and, during the fourth visit, automatic writing had developed: "His right hand achieved the ability 'to write anything it wanted to, not subject to the control or restrictions of the 'conscious' personality" (Kaplan 1960, 567). The patient was informed ahead of time that he would be pricked in his arm several times with a hypodermic needle and that he would be asked to report if he felt anything.

> A hypnotic analgesia for the left arm was suggested, and the subject was pricked in the left arm four times, with sufficient force to puncture the skin and subcutaneous tissues. After a minute or two, the subject asked the experimenter, "When are you going to begin?," apparently not having felt any pain. However from the moment that the pricking began, the subject's right hand had begun to write: "Ouch, damn it, you're hurting me!" (Kaplan 1960, 567–68)

What sense are we to make of this odd case, in which the patient both asserted and denied that he was in pain? One possibility would be to claim that one of those assertions was not sincere. As Roger Trigg remarks, a "philosopher who wishes to preserve the incorrigibility of avowals might suggest, in this case, that the spoken avowal . . . was not in fact sincere" (1970, 67). Following this line of interpretation, one could argue that the patient felt pain, yet the effect of hypnosis was such that it inhibited his capacity to articulate this fact verbally. That is, the patient denied that he was in pain, yet not because he did not feel any pain. His denial derived from the inhibited capacity to verbally articulate his feelings. The patient could not help but be insincere as far as his verbal expressions were concerned.

However, one should not too quickly dismiss the possibility that the patient might have been sincere when making both avowals, despite the contradiction between them. Confronted with odd cases such as this one, it is of course interpretively convenient to proclaim that one of the contradictory avowals is insincere. Nonetheless, Roger Trigg is right when he observes that such an interpretation begs the question in that it does nothing more than assert that sincere avowals are incorrigible.

The distinction drawn above between implicit and explicit temporality provides us with the basis for an alternative interpretation, which would stay true to the patient's verbal and written avowals. According to this interpretation, here we face an instance of a conflict between the patient's implicit and explicit experiences of the present. The patient was implicitly aware that he was in pain, while nonetheless he did not know this explicitly. In fact, this comes close to how Kaplan interprets the effects of hypnosis upon pain: "The subject's speaking voice seemed to be the organ of communication for that part of the personality (conscious?) which did not seem to perceive the pain, but the arm via automatic writing 'spoke' for the portion of the personality which did perceive the pain" (1960, 568). On this basis, Kaplan further articulated his reservations concerning the use of

PAIN AND TEMPORALITY

hypnosis for pain relief. The patient's case shows that even when one is unusually susceptible to hypnosis, one nonetheless continues to feel pain, even though its conscious articulation is repressed. We face here an instance in which a person was implicitly aware of something that he did not integrate into explicit consciousness.

The self-distantiation that lies at the heart of pain experience clarifies how,[4] under some highly unusual circumstances, pain can be felt implicitly, although one might not be aware of this explicitly. At least in this case, hypnosis did not liberate the patient from pain, but only blocked the patient's capacity to integrate his feelings at the level of explicit experiences. The patient did not know what he felt, which does not mean—Roger Trigg's argument to the contrary notwithstanding—that the patient's pain was unfelt.[5] We thus face here a conflict between implicit and explicit sense of the present, a conflict that demonstrates that pain can be felt and only felt, without becoming explicit or thematic.

The strange quasi-indifference to pain characteristic of various types of depressive patients can also be clarified in terms of a conflict between implicit and explicit temporality in general, and implicit and explicit experience of the present in particular. This conflict between implicit and explicit temporality is made possible by the inner split that characterizes pain experience. Consider the report by K. R. L. Hall and E. Stride, which is based on experiments measuring the intensity of pain by means of thermal radiation:

> One patient . . . did not report pain even at the maximum intensity, but, on being asked to describe the nature of the sensation, he said: "Well, it was like a lighted cigarette-end being held against my forehead." This type of patient will frequently describe a sensation as "burning" or "very hot" without, however, making any admission that it was at all what they meant by pain. (1954, 48)

Just as in the case of a hypnotic patient, so in this case, too, we are faced with a circumstance in which a patient both asserts and denies that he is in pain. Yet, despite the contradiction, with the aim of determining whether or not the patient is in pain, one does not need to sacrifice either assertion and to explain it away as an insincere avowal. Just as in the previous case, so in this case, too, what the patient experiences implicitly, he does not know explicitly. It is the conflict between the implicit and the explicit experiences of the present that renders these cases comprehensible.

What are the conditions that need to be met if one is to be capable not only of feeling pain, but also of knowing that one is in pain? This basic capacity rests on a synthesis of the two modes of consciousness of presence. For consciousness to know explicitly what it feels, it must unify its implicit and explicit ways of intending presence.[6] While implicit and explicit modes of consciousness of presence often overlap with each other, in some odd cases, such as those addressed above, we face a breakdown in the congruence that is supposed to join these two forms of awareness to each other. How common are these breakdowns? Clinical evidence suggests that they are rare. However, if one is justified in thinking of the experiences of pain on the part of the depressives as instances of such breakdowns, then by the same token one is further invited to conjecture that not so rarely a gap separates explicit and implicit forms of consciousness of presence, and, therefore, it is not uncommon at all to feel pain, yet not to know explicitly that one is in pain.

We thereby obtain the conceptual basis to readdress the polemical issue concerning the possibility of "unfelt pain" (see Palmer 1975). On the one hand, it is phenomenologically highly dubious to speak of such pain, if only because, as I argued in chapter 2, pain is an aversive bodily feeling that has a distinct experiential quality. Yet what exactly does one mean when one speaks of the *feeling* of pain? We are all familiar with instances of being woken up by pain. When this happens, we recognize pain as something that was already there in the past, even though in the past we did not notice it. Consider also the "pain-in-the-eyes" of which Jean-Paul Sartre speaks in *Being and Nothingness* and which we already addressed in chapter 2. One can certainly be fully absorbed in objects of interest, so much so that only subsequently one would admit to oneself that one was in pain. Finally, what exactly happens at the moment we recognize that we are in pain? Is not every recognition a belated act? When we recognize that we are in pain, does the act of recognition not indicate that the pain we feel is an ongoing experience, whose beginnings by necessity stretch beyond the field of presence into the past? Do these undeniable facts of experience not provide us with phenomenological counterevidence, which confirms the existence of unfelt pains?

I do not think so. The distinction drawn between implicit and explicit modes of consciousness of presence suggests that here we face instances in which implicit awareness of pain is lived in the absence of the corresponding explicit acknowledgment of this awareness. Since pains can be lived in the absence of explicit consciousness of pain, it is hard to agree with Gilbert Ryle (2009) when he contends that "unnoticed pain" is an absurd expression.[7]

PAIN AND TEMPORALITY

Although we certainly are familiar with unnoticed pain, I would nonetheless contend that *there are no unfelt pains*. To have a feeling is one thing; to be explicitly conscious of having this feeling is a different matter. For the most part, having a feeling and being conscious of having a feeling go hand in hand. Nonetheless, in some rare instances, this unity can be interrupted. When this occurs, pain is felt in the absence of a corresponding consciousness of having the feeling.

In a recent study Serrano de Haro (2017) has provided a strong phenomenological basis to clarify the structure of noticed and unnoticed pains. In *Ideas I*, Husserl introduced a fundamental distinction between three modes of attention, which, he argued, accompany each conscious experience: attentional focus, co-attention, and inattention. Drawing on this distinctly noetic distinction, Serrano de Haro contends that, on the noematic level, attentional focus is correlated with what is experienced thematically, and co-attention is correlated with co-presence, while inattention is correlated with the peripheral horizon. Of what significance are these distinctions for the phenomenology of pain? According to Serrano de Haro, they provide us with the basis to contend that as far as pain experience is concerned, pain can be lived on three different experiential levels. We thus need to draw a distinction between focal, co-attended, and unattended pain:

> There are, on the one hand, frightful physical pains that occupy the foreground of consciousness and violently monopolize the center of interest. Other painful occurrences, on the other hand, do not dominate the attentional focus and still allow some free co-attention; finally, there are still other physical pains that due to their weakness, familiarity or lack of relevance do not even dominate co-interest and may pass by in the mode of inattention, scarcely interfering with present interests. (Serrano de Haro 2017, 168)

For the most part, the distinction between focal, co-attended, and unattended pain can be clarified in terms of different degrees of intensity. In this regard one could say: while all pain, *without any exception*, must have some kind of intensity,[8] one of the ways in which pains differ from each other concerns their different intensities. *For the most part*, the more intense the pain, the greater the likelihood that it will be experienced as focal pain; and contrariwise, the less intense it is, the greater the probability that it will be either co-attended or unattended. We should not take this to mean, however, that by necessity the intensification of pain transforms pain into a focally lived-experience. The manner in which pain is lived by the hypnotic patients and depressed patients provides clear evidence that at least in some cases, even unbearable pains can remain unattended, that is, unnoticed: one is aware of them only implicitly, not explicitly. More generally, one could also claim that when intense pains are lived alongside other highly disturbing forms of psychological suffering, their relevance diminishes, and, therefore, they often remain either co-attended or unattended, despite their intensity.

Such a tripartite distinction between focal, co-attended, and unattended pain makes clear that, contra Ryle, unnoticed pain is *not* an absurd expression. Not all pain is focal, and thus, not all pain absorbs and, as Serrano de Haro aptly puts it, monopolizes our attention. To strengthen this view, one could further draw an analogy between pain and other sensations. Over the last few hours, I have been sitting at my desk, in front of my laptop, immersed in my thoughts about the temporality of pain. I have had various visual, auditory, tactile, gustatory, olfactory, kinaesthetic, vestibular, and organic sensations. I was not, however, explicitly aware of having these sensations as I felt them. I became conscious of having them only after reflecting on my past experience. Almost as a rule, we live through various sensations without being explicitly conscious of living through them.

At least in some cases, we can live through pain sensations without the accompanying explicit consciousness of living through them, just as we normally live through tactile and visual sensations without being thematically conscious of having them. From the mere fact that we are not explicitly conscious of our visual and tactile sensations, it does not follow that we are not living through these sensations. So also, from the mere fact that we are not explicitly conscious of being in pain, it does not follow that we do not feel any pain. The distinction drawn between implicit and explicit consciousness of presence suggests that the split between implicit and explicit consciousness of sensations has its root in subjective temporality.[9]

THE FIELD OF PRESENCE AS THE HORIZON
OF PAIN EXPERIENCE

Of what significance is the distinction between implicit and explicit temporality for our understanding of pain experience? Three points call for a special emphasis. The first point concerns implicit temporality. As far as the basic temporal synthesis of impressions, retentions, and protentions is concerned, the temporality of pain is no different from any other kind of temporal consciousness. Like all other experiences, the pain one lives through is also given as temporally extended, as a unity of the now, the not-anymore, and the almost-now. This concerns all three types of pains singled out in the last section—focal, co-attended, and unattended pains. The second point concerns explicit temporality and focal pains. Since, by definition, unattended and co-attended pains cannot be lived focally but only implicitly, they cannot be experienced at the level of explicit temporality. Thus, as soon as we turn to reflect on the explicit temporality of pain, we must concentrate exclusively on focal pain.[10] The emergence of focal pains is often experienced as a breach that secedes different temporal fields: focal pain does not fulfill any past intentions, but places them in suspense. Due to the disruptive nature of pain experience, the field of painful presence is experienced as disconnected from the painless past and the painless future.[11] The third point also concerns focal pain and the way in which it is lived at the level of explicit temporality. We can further say that focal pain continues to be lived for as long as the sufferer does not find the resources needed to reestablish the experiential order of sequence between the temporal moments and does not accomplish anew what I identified above as the active and reflective synthesis that gives rise to the extended, personal, and narrative consciousness. These three points call for further elucidation.

Regarding the first point: as mentioned above, *all* experiences are lived as temporally extended. How, then, does the experience of pain differ from other experiences at the level of implicit temporality? These differences become especially conspicuous when we turn our attention to focal pain. On the one hand, any kind of pain can be experienced only in original first-person experience, which means that it can be lived only in the now. On the other hand, when it comes to focal pain, the sufferer experiences this now as a field of stagnating presence, a time that has come to a standstill. To be sure, pain has its own future, just as it has its own past. Yet the past and the future belong to the field of presence, which is now lived as the time of infinite sameness.[12] To suffer from pain is to be stranded in the field of presence, which, at the level of explicit temporality, is lived as infinite sameness in that it is cut adrift from other temporal fields. Such, indeed, is the way that those who suffer from pain (and especially chronic pain) qualify their experience. In the words of one, "Constant, can't never get comfortable. Can't never rest. Can't do anything." "Wake up with it, go to bed with it, every time I move, something hurts" (Thomas and Johnson 2000, 693).

As David B. Morris once put it, "Pain obliterates ordinary time" (2010, 55). This brings us to the second point. Arguably, ordinary time is marked by the difference between the before, the now, and the after, a difference that consciousness reabsorbs within a unified biographical whole. By contrast, the more intense and focal the experience of pain, the harder it is for consciousness to synthesize these three temporal fields. One commonly experiences them as disconnected from each other. To be sure, the sufferer does not lose all awareness of painless experiences. And yet, painless recollections and anticipations commonly appear as irreal, that is, as characteristics of an alien life. Thus, especially those who suffer from chronic pain soon call into question the expectation that pain will come to an end. So also, as time goes by, they commonly forget what it was like not to be in pain.

It thereby becomes understandable why those who suffer long-lasting unbearable pain often tend to think of their pain as an alien power that overwhelms them by robbing them of all distinctly personal characteristics. What we face here are pain's *depersonalizing* effects, which pain patients commonly have in mind when they describe their pain as an alien force they cannot resist or as a monster that cannot be tamed.[13] Insofar as one suffers pain's *depersonalizing* effects, one cannot regain the past as one's *personal* past, just as one cannot retain one's future as one's *personal* future.

To clarify what is at stake in the third point made above, it is necessary to address the role that memory and anticipation play in pain experience. The next two sections are focused on these themes.

MEMORY AND PAIN

Let us turn back yet again to our guiding question: What exactly does it mean to claim that pain can be lived only in the field of presence? In the last two sections, I have aimed to clarify the meaning of this claim while focusing on the third determination of the living present, which conceives of presence as an extended duration, which is intended in the impressional, retentional, and protentional consciousness and conceived of as a synthetic unity of the now, the not-yet, and the not-anymore. We can now return to the question that we raised earlier, which still remains without an answer. Does this mean that the experience of pain is fundamentally cut off from the past and the future? Does this mean that our memories and anticipations do not affect the way we live our pains? In other words, is the fourth determination of the living present (namely, the view that conceives of presence as the meeting point between the experienced past and the future) of any relevance for our understanding of the temporal structures of pain experience? It is crucial to supplement the foregoing analysis with further reflections, which would demonstrate that even though the field of presence constitutes the exhaustive horizon of pain experience, this experience is nonetheless largely shaped by our memories and anticipations.

Although pain can be lived only in the present, and although those in pain view their past lives as alien lives, our pain is heavily determined by our memories.[14] To recognize that such is the case, alongside the above-mentioned distinction between implicit and explicit consciousness of presence, we need to draw a similar distinction between implicit and explicit memory. While explicit memory functions as a specific kind of objectification, implicit memory marks how, in the absence of any objectification, consciousness of the past can nonetheless determine the present.[15] Put differently, while explicit memory exemplifies how the present reaches into the past, implicit memory exemplifies how the past reaches into the present.

In 1911, the Swiss neurologist Édouard Claparède (1911, 79–90) offered an intriguing description of the effects of implicit memory on pain experience in a paper on recognition, which was based on the study of a patient suffering from amnesia.[16] The patient could never remember her physician, although she used to meet him regularly. One day, during an early meeting, Claparède hid a pin in his hand with which he shook the patient's hand. Due to the unexpected outburst of pain, the patient withdrew her hand quickly. Curiously, when Claparède tried to reintroduce himself to the patient on another occasion soon afterward, the patient refused to shake the physician's hand. Even more curiously, despite such caution, the patient could not consciously remember either shaking the physician's hand or having been stuck by the pin.

Here we face an instance in which the patient's body associated the physician's presence with danger in the absence of any conscious recollection. The patient's body knew implicitly what she did not know explicitly. This anecdote thereby illustrates how the experience of pain sinks into one's memory and affects one's subsequent experiences. Indeed, as Nietzsche's *On the Genealogy of Morals* demonstrates especially forcefully, no other experience is as edifying as pain: "'If something is to stay in the memory it must be burned in: only that which never ceases to *hurt* stays in memory'—this is a main clause of the oldest (unhappily also the most enduring) psychology on earth" (2000, 497). Moreover, as research conducted on implicit memory amply demonstrates, it is not just that pain forms our memories ("pain is the most powerful aid to mnemonics" [Nietzsche 2000, 497]); the reverse also holds: memories form our pain (see Schacter 1987). Indeed, according to some researchers, implicit memory can already be detected in organisms that belong to low biological levels (such as *aplysia*), and this memory largely determines the experience of pain. Moreover, in the case of mammals, and especially human beings, implicit memory is more complex, and the role it plays in the experience of pain is even more overwhelming. For instance, if painful stimuli are applied repeatedly to a body part of a human being, even a gentle stimulus applied to the same body part in the future will suffice to provoke a painful reaction (Fuchs 2008, 66–67).

The recognition that our pains are largely shaped by our implicit memories invites us to admit that pain has distinctly personal characteristics. Our pains are shaped by our own personal histories, even though, for the most part, this fact escapes us, especially when we are in pain. Yet does this realization not cancel out my earlier contention that pain is a depersonalizing experience? I will address this issue in much greater detail in chapter 6. In the present context, I will limit myself to a general clarification.

What is the evidence that supports the claim that at least some forms of pain can be qualified as depersonalizing experiences? The evidence in question concerns two points: (1) the person suffering from pain can find it difficult to resynthesize the breach between different temporal fields; and (2) insofar as the ongoing experience of pain is characterized in terms of reality, it can irrealize the painless past and the painless future, which up to a large degree make up one's personal identity. Insofar as pain cuts off the ties that bind one to one's past and future, pain takes one hostage and robs one of personal characteristics. Yet such a characterization of the depersonalizing effects of pain does not stand opposed to my claim that in a significantly different sense, pain is also a deeply personal experience. The personal characteristics of pain are constituted by implicit memory, which continues to function despite pain's depersonalizing effects.

One could raise another objection and maintain that my current emphasis on the role of memory stands opposed to my foregoing insistence that the experience of pain unfolds in the field of presence. In this regard, I should stress once again that the memory of which I speak here is implicit, nonthematic, and nonobjectifying. In contrast to explicit memory, which commences in the present and terminates in the past, implicit memory performs the reverse movement: it resonates from the past and colors what is given in the present. In light of implicit memory, although one cannot help but be in the present, one continues to have one's foot in the past.

ANTICIPATION AND PAIN

In their notable study, *The Challenge of Pain*, Melzack and Wall (2008) have addressed the role that anticipation plays in pain experience while focusing on anxiety. They argue that the intensity of pain experience largely rests on the person's attention directed at a potentially painful experience. "The mere anticipation of pain is sufficient to raise the level of anxiety and thereby the intensity of perceived pain" (Melzack and Wall 2008, 22). In a similar vein, Harris E. Hill et al. (1952) have also argued that if anxiety is dispelled, a certain level of electric shock or burning heat is perceived as significantly less painful than it is perceived under conditions of high anxiety. To obtain a more precise understanding of the role that anticipation plays in pain experience, consider CRPS/RSD—a chronic neuroinflammatory disorder. This pain syndrome was discovered in the nineteenth century by Silas Weir Mitchell, an American physician and writer who was considered by many contemporaries a genius on a par with Benjamin Franklin. Mitchell, who is often considered to be the father of neurology, identified this pain syndrome as causalgia. Causalgia typically appears after a wound caused by an object such as a bullet or a knife has damaged a nerve in the limb. It should therefore come as small surprise that this pain syndrome was discovered by Mitchell, who, during the Civil War, was treating soldiers suffering from nervous injuries and maladies at Turner's Lane Hospital in Philadelphia. As Mitchell put it in 1872,

> Perhaps few persons who are not physicians can realize the influence which long-continued and unendurable pain may have on both body and mind. . . . Under such torments the temper changes, the most amiable grow irritable, the bravest soldier becomes coward, and the strongest man is scarcely less nervous than the most hysterical. . . . Nothing can better illustrate the extent to which these statements may be true than the case of burning pain, or, as I prefer to term it, causalgia, the most terrible of all tortures which a nerve wound may inflict. (1872, 196)

Patients suffering from this syndrome experience excruciating pain when touched by a feather or the bedsheets, or even when not touched by any object at all. "Minor events like a cry of a child, the rattling of a newspaper, or watching a television program can provoke intense pain" (Chapman, Nakamura, and Flores 2000, 17). Recall also threat hypersymbolia—a pain syndrome addressed in detail in chapter 3. In some cases, visual stimuli suffice to trigger agonizing pain. Recall the case of a patient who had lost all sensations in the left side of his body. "On seeing that the left part of his body was approached for sensory testing, the patient invariably made a brisk withdrawal movement; at the same time he felt a burning pain" (Hoogenraad, Ramos, and Van Gijn 1994, 851). Of what significance are such syndromes as causalgia and threat hypersymbolia for our understanding of the temporality of chronic pain?

Nikola Grahek (2007) provides a neurological explanation of both syndromes, highlighting the fact that the patients had suffered brain damage in the right parietal cortex populated by polymodal neurons.[17] These syndromes, however, are instructive not only from a neurological but also from a phenomenological point of view. A phenomenological analysis of these syndromes brings to light the significant role that *anticipation* plays in the experience of pain. In the case of threat hypersymbolia, it is telling that the patient could not feel the sensation of pain with his eyes closed. The sight of the approaching object, that is, *the anticipation of the pain to come*, was what triggered his pain.

The situation we are faced with here is not as mysterious as it might seem. As mentioned, a repeated application of noxious stimuli to a body part will result in the patient's bodily anticipation that similar stimuli will give rise to similar feeling-responses in the future. It thereby becomes understandable that even a touch of a feather on the bodily area that has been subjected to repeated noxious stimulation in the past can, at least on some occasions, provoke a painful response. Or consider the role that emotions such as fear and anger play in the experience of pain. Think of the knot in the stomach that comes with fear, or the blushing that accompanies anger. It is by far not uncommon for physical pain to accompany emotional outbursts. In such circumstances we are faced with pain experiences provoked by anticipation.

So as to determine the role of anticipation with greater precision, alongside the distinction drawn between implicit and explicit memory, one also needs to distinguish between implicit and explicit anticipation. We are faced here with structures of experience analogous to the ones addressed in the previous section. While implicit memory could be called "memory without conscious remembering," implicit anticipation can be termed "anticipation without conscious expectation." Moreover, just as in the case of memory, so also in the case of anticipation we can distinguish between its implicit and explicit forms by saying that while explicit anticipation is perspicuous and self-reflexive, merely implicit anticipation is the anticipation that is felt only in and by the body. While explicit anticipation has its terminus a quo in the present and its terminus ad quem in the future, implicit anticipation proceeds in the opposite direction: it originates in the future and culminates in the present. The distressing occurrence one anticipates in the future is transferred into the field of presence and lived as bodily pain. Whether we are dealing with highly unusual cases, such as those exemplified by threat hypersymbolia, or with much more common cases as described above, we are faced with the effects of implicit anticipation—a nonconscious expectation that is transferred from the field of the future into the field of presence and experienced as pain.

We are thereby led to the realization that pain cannot be qualified either as a personal or as a depersonalizing experience in an unqualified way. Pain is depersonalizing insofar as it imprisons the sufferer within the field of presence, which is marked by the expansion of the now and the contraction of the past and the future, and which, in severe cases, isolates the sufferer within presence. Nonetheless, implicit memory and implicit anticipation compel us to admit that even in such extreme scenarios, pain continues to be lived as a deeply personal experience.

~

Let us sum up the results of the analysis undertaken in this chapter. To claim that pain can be given only in *original* experience is to suggest that it can be lived only in the field of presence, conceived of as the exhaustive horizon of experience. More precisely, pain is experienced as a temporal duration, which unfolds in an extended temporal horizon, yet this horizon is experienced as cut off from all past and future. The more intense and focal pain becomes, the more it is experienced as the waxing of the present and the waning of the past and the future. In the case of excruciating pain, it imprisons the sufferer in the field of presence, which is experienced as disconnected from other temporal modalities. Due to this disconnection, either the past and the future appear irreal, or, by contrast, the field of presence is marked by irreality. Yet, even though the subject in pain is locked in the field of presence and thus incapable of resynthesizing this field with the past and the future, these other temporal modalities covertly shape the ways one suffers pain. Implicit consciousness of presence, implicit memory, and implicit anticipation, despite their camouflaged manifestations, individualize the pain of the sufferer. In this regard, despite its depersonalizing effects, pain is lived as *principium individuationis*. Implicit consciousness of presence, implicit memory, and implicit anticipation are indicative of the underlying continuity of one's personal life, which serves as the ground that underlies the ruptures, which in extraordinary circumstances overwhelm us. Even in the case of highly disruptive experiences such as excruciating pain, what is given in the field of presence continues to be surrounded by the horizons of the past and the future.

Are there any therapeutic implications one could draw from such a phenomenology of the temporal structures of pain experience? Recall the conceptual gap that separates the objective conception of time, which is paradigmatic of modern medicine, and the subjective temporality characteristic of pain experience. Partly due to this gap, in the patient-physician encounter, those who suffer from chronic pain are forced to reconceptualize the temporal structures of their experience in quantifiable terms. This shift in perspective, necessary as it is, brings about a growing sense of alienation from experience. As S. Kay Toombs has argued, "The further one moves from the lived-experience, the greater is the sense of alienation from one's body" (1990, 239). Moreover, the greater the alienation from one's body, the stronger the feeling that pain is an alien force that invades one's body from without, as though there were no inner ties that bind it to one's past and future. The paradigmatic conception of chronicity in modern medicine exacerbates pain's depersonalizing effects while simultaneously disregarding its distinctly personal characteristics.

Within such a framework, the phenomenological analysis of the temporal structures of pain experience obtains therapeutic relevance. The phenomenological recognition of the role that implicit consciousness of presence, implicit memory, and implicit anticipation play in pain experience leads to the realization, which is difficult to accept from the medical as well as from the everyday standpoint. Both the patient and the physician, although for different reasons, want to believe that pain comes from the outside, not from the inside. The health practitioner's reasons are methodological, while the patient's are psychological.[18] This deep and seemingly unbending belief is a form of what Sartre (1956) calls *bad faith*, and no matter how methodologically and psychologically understandable it might be, it limits our capacity to counteract the effects of pain upon the sufferer. If it is true that chronic pain

PAIN AND TEMPORALITY

is nested in the implicit consciousness of presence, implicit memories, and implicit anticipations, then one also has to admit that one must transform their effects if one is to be liberated from pain. A necessary (although not necessarily sufficient) condition for this is the recognition that chronic pain is an irreducibly temporal phenomenon and that implicit consciousness of presence, implicit memory, and implicit anticipation play a vital role in one's pain experience.

Abraham Olivier remarks that "one of the major problems of pain management . . . is that doctors do not actually realize the role that the 'psyche' plays. For instance, only 10% of the cases of chronic back pain have serious 'physical' causes . . . 90% of cases are thought to be the consequences of the psychological attitude" (2007, 163). The analysis undertaken in this chapter strongly suggests that what is usually referred to as the "psychological attitude" is in truth a bodily phenomenon. The "psychological attitude" is rooted in the person's bodily sense of presence, bodily memory, and bodily anticipation, which mark pain as an irreducibly temporal phenomenon. It is here, at the heart of temporality, that emancipation is to be sought, and not only because the mere recognition of the roles of memory and anticipation diminishes their adverse effects. By recognizing their effects, one can transform their meaning and dissipate their significance.

Although at different points of our analysis we have been drawn repeatedly to the realization that pain is a bodily phenomenon, we have so far left this matter largely unexplored. This is a gap that the next chapter is meant to fill: we have to supplement the foregoing analysis with explicit reflections on the embodied nature of pain experience. Addressing this issue will enable us to complete our conceptual analysis: by the end of chapter 5, we will have justified the novel conception of pain that was presented in the introduction.

CHAPTER 5

THE BODY IN PAIN

Leib and *Körper*

Our clarification of the new phenomenological conception of pain is not yet complete. On the basis of the phenomenological analysis offered in the last chapters, we can say: *pain is an aversive bodily feeling with a distinct experiential quality, which can be given only in original firsthand experience, either as a feeling-sensation or as an emotion.* Such a conception of pain remains deficient. It is undeniable that pain can be felt only in one's body. The goal of this chapter thereby becomes clear: it must clarify what it means to qualify pain as an embodied feeling. The account I will offer will rely heavily on Husserl's phenomenology of the body, and especially as it was developed in *Ideas II* (see Husserl 1989). To some, such a strategy will sound highly dubious: all too often, Husserl's phenomenology is conceived of as a preamble to subsequent phenomenologies of the body that we come across in the works of Maurice Merleau-Ponty, Jean-Paul Sartre, Michel Henry, and others. While admitting that these thinkers have significantly expanded the boundaries of phenomenology, I nonetheless consider such a view too dismissive. This view all too easily overlooks not only the groundbreaking contribution that Husserl has made to the phenomenology of embodiment, but also the unique significance of Husserl's phenomenology of the body for the phenomenology of pain. In this chapter, my goal is to demonstrate that Husserl's phenomenology of the body provides highly useful resources to address certain philosophical problems that continue to plague the philosophy of pain. My central attention will be directed at two puzzles: (1) the relation between pain's *indubitability* and its bodily *localizability*; and (2) the issue concerning the determination of *the subject of pain*.[1] As we will see, these two themes are closely related to each other.

My analysis will unfold in five steps. I will begin with what I consider to be an uncontroversial issue: pain is given in experience as an *indubitable* and a *bodily localizable* experience. Second, I will contend that these two charac-

THE BODY IN PAIN

teristics appear to be incompatible with each other and that, therefore, the experience of pain is a seemingly paradoxical phenomenon. Third, I will show that the paradox in question has not escaped attention in the philosophy of pain. We can reconstruct at least six ways to resolve this paradox: *semiological*, *causal*, *associationist*, *representational*, *perceptual*, and *phenomenological*. Fourth, after sketching the first five approaches, my central goal will be to develop the phenomenological resolution and to show that it culminates in the realization that the subject of pain is neither the disembodied consciousness nor the physiological body, but the *lived-body*, conceived of as *the field of sensings*. Fifth, I will show in which way the phenomenological approach taken here sheds light on the structure of pain experience. The analysis offered will lead to the conclusion that pain is the already appropriated body's inner protest against its constitutive appropriation.

PAIN'S INDUBITABILITY AND BODILY LOCALIZABILITY

Admitting that a phenomenological theory of pain should not distort our actual experience of pain but rather accept this experience as its foundation, we need to return once again to the fundamental question: How exactly is pain given in experience?[2] We can supplement the analysis offered in the earlier chapters with the following observation: insofar as we are conscious of our pain, it is given as an *indubitable* and *bodily localizable* experience.

We face here two eidetic insights into pain experience. First, insofar as one is conscious of one's pain, its experience cannot raise any doubt. This does not mean, however, that all pain must be conscious. Our analysis of waking up from sleep and recognizing that we are in pain has demonstrated that such is certainly not the case (see chapter 2). Moreover, the distinction we drew between noticed and unnoticed pain provided further confirmation that not all pain is lived thematically (see chapter 4). With these qualifications in mind, we can say that *noticed* pain is experienced indubitably. To provide this claim with further support, we can also recall the analysis, offered in chapter 3, of the CIP patient who came to the conclusion that she could experience pain. As we saw, insofar as pain experience is based on an inference, that is, insofar as pain experience entails any doubt, it is not a genuine pain experience. Such being the case, one can say that while one can suspect that one is suffering from depression or struggling with other forms of suffering, one cannot just suspect that one is in pain.

Second, one can experience pain only as localized within one's body. I would contend that the fundamental difference between pain and suffering hinges upon this very issue. While pain has a bodily location, suffering does not: while the migraine lies in one's head and the abdominal pain in one's stomach, one would be committing a category mistake if one were to provide one's depression or anxiety with a bodily location. To be sure, we sometimes draw associations between anxiety and heart palpitations, or depression and specific headaches, or stress and back pain. Still, these bodily manifestations of different forms of psychological suffering should not be misconceived of as their bodily localizability.[3]

We can now ask: How can pain be *both* an embodied feeling and an indubitable experience? We have to admit that, at least at first glance, these two characteristics appear to be irreconcilable with each other. We could clarify the problem as follows: On the one hand, only what is given through *inner* rather than *outer* perception, only something *mental* rather than *physical*, can be given indubitably. If so, then reflection on pain's indubitability suggests that pain is a psychological content of experience.[4] On the other hand, and in contrast to all forms of the cogito, we experience pain as necessarily localized within the body, which suggests that pain experience is not psychological, at least in the sense in which thoughts or pure emotions are said to be psychological. Thus, in contrast to pain's indubitability, which suggests that pain (much like joy and sorrow, elation and grief, or happiness and unhappiness) is a psychological experience, pain's bodily localizability intimates that pain (much like the sensations of heat or cold, of tickling or of bodily pleasure) must be in some sense physical.

Before working out a phenomenological resolution to this apparent paradox, let us turn to other philosophical approaches to pain, which provide us with alternative resources to address this dilemma. We can single out at least six ways to reconcile pain's indubitability with its bodily localizability.

1. A *semiological account* suggests that pain is a *sensation* and that sensations are inherently *nonspatial*. This means that in its core, pain is given to us as an indubitable, although not as a localizable, experience. But if so, what sense are we to make of the undeniable fact that we feel pain as localized in our bodies? According to the semiological account, pain's localizability is an offshoot matter that derives from the peculiar way in which consciousness *reacts* to its own pains. Supposedly, it is through reactions that consciousness transforms its own pains into *signs* that indicate malfunctions in the body. Due to such semiological apprehensions, pains obtain a bodily location.

According to the semiological theory, the migraine is not originally in the head, just as abdominal pain is not originally in the stomach. Rather, I apprehend pain in the mind, yet I apprehend it as a sign that allows me to interpret my pains as indications of bodily lesions or tissue damage with different bodily locations.

Thus, according to the semiological account, insofar as pain is a pure sensation, it lacks bodily localizability. Insofar as we treat our pains as expressions of physiological malfunctions, however, we can indirectly assign pains bodily location. According to this theory, the content of pain is something psychological, not physical, which means that the subject of pain is consciousness, not the body. Hermann Lotze (2011) in the nineteenth century and Gilbert Ryle (2009) in the twentieth are important representatives of the semiological account, also known as "the local sign theory."

2. A *causal account* suggests that a solution to the apparent contradiction between pain's indubitability and its bodily localizability should be derived from the realization that pain is an *effect* that follows from *physiological causes*. According to this account, what we usually consider as pain's location is nothing other than the place we assign to the *cause* of pain. Thus, much like the semiological account, the causal account also suggests that the content of pain is not something physical but something psychological, which further means that the subject of pain is not the body but consciousness. Presumably, when we assign pain bodily location, what we in effect capture is not the sensation of pain, but the cause that triggers the sensation of pain. Thus, when I claim that my foot is in pain, the true meaning of my claim is: some damage in my foot is the cause of the nonspatial sensation of pain. D. M. Taylor's (1965) account in "The Location of Pain" is a good illustration of the causal solution to the problem at hand.

3. An *associationist account* shares a number of assumptions that underlie both the semiological and the causal theories. This account also grants primacy to pain's indubitability over pain's bodily localizability; it suggests as well that insofar as we consider pain pure and simple, it lacks bodily localizability. Moreover, all three theories suggest that pain's localizability derives from specific conscious acts. However, in contrast to the semiological account, which interprets the relation between the sensation of pain and its bodily location as the relation between the signifier and the signified, and in contrast to the causal account, which asserts that the sensation of pain relates to its bodily location as an effect relates to its cause, the associationist account suggests that through an associative apprehension, consciousness

fuses two distinct phenomena into one—the sensation of pain, on the one hand, and tissue damage, on the other.

By replacing semiological and causal apprehension with an associative apprehension, the associationist account overcomes a significant shortcoming that lies at the heart of the semiological and causal theories. What exactly does it mean to conceive of pain semiologically? As mentioned above, it means to interpret the sensation of pain as a signifier and a physiological malfunction as the signified. However, a sign functions properly only when it *diverts* attention away from itself to other objects of experience. Wthout occupying a different spatial location from the signified, the alleged signifier would absorb attention and therefore could not perform its semiological function. The semiological account therefore fails to explain what it tries to explain: it fails to clarify how pain could be both an indubitable and a bodily localizable experience.

A similar shortcoming affects the causal explanation. This account leaves unexplained why consciousness would confuse the cause with its effect and be tricked into believing that pain itself, rather than its cause, is localizable in the body. The replacement of the semiological and causal apprehensions with an associative apprehension provides a solution to the problem at hand. One can now argue that in virtue of such an apprehension, the sensation of pain and the physiological malfunction are fused into one as "bone of its bone and flesh of its flesh." William James (1980, vol. 2, chap. 20) is the most significant representative of this third account.

4. Much like the semiological and the causal accounts, a *representationalist account* also suggests that the experience of pain is a purely psychic phenomenon and that in the strict sense, the content of pain is also something purely psychological. This means that according to this account, too, the subject of pain is consciousness, not the body. Representationalists contend, however, that the experience of pain entails not only pain sensations but also, in a curious way, what these sensations represent, namely, the representative contents of physical reality. Supposedly, our willingness to assign pain a bodily location derives from the conflation of representative contents that are present in experience with physical phenomena that they represent. Michael Tye's (2005) "Another Look at Representationalism about Pain" is arguably the most forceful illustration of such a theoretical attempt to reconcile pain's indubitability with its bodily localizability.

5. In contrast to the four accounts mentioned so far, the *perceptual account* suggests that to solve the problem at hand, one needs to recognize that

the notion of pain is *equivocal*. Such an account invites one to conceive of pain according to the model of perceptual consciousness. Just as in the case of visual sensations, we distinguish between the seeing and the seen, and just as in the case of tactile sensations, we draw a distinction between the touching and the touched, so also, when it comes to pain, we need to distinguish between the "sensing of pain" and "pain as an object of experience." According to the perceptual account, while the sensing of pain is a psychological experience, the pain as sensed is a physical phenomenon. According to the perceptual account, when we claim that pain is an indubitable experience, we mean that *the sensing of pain* is given indubitably. By contrast, when we assign our pain a bodily location, we mean that *the object of this sensing* is tissue damage. Christopher S. Hill's (2005) "Ow! The Paradox of Pain" provides one of the best illustrations of the perceptual account.

6. The sixth account is phenomenological, and it is the account that I will aim to develop in the subsequent sections of this chapter. Before turning to this issue, I would like to address what I consider to be a serious drawback of all five accounts. These accounts have been in regular dialogue with one another and each has aimed to justify its own superiority over others on two grounds: logical consistency and compatibility with the naturalistic assumptions. However, the fundamental concern of a philosophical analysis of pain should not be that of establishing consistency within the proposed context of analysis. What we face here is not a logical puzzle whose solution is satisfactory as long as it is coherent, but a paradox that lies at the heart of the experience of pain. Such being the case, the success or failure of a philosophical clarification of this paradox is to be measured in accordance with the evidence of experience. Therefore, before deciding whether pain fits within a naturalistic framework or not, one needs to clarify the structure of pain experience.

Leaving the controversies between the indicated positions aside, let us stress that none of these accounts live up to the evidence of experience. With an eye on the semiological, causal, associationist, and representationalist accounts, one should emphasize that experience contradicts their fundamental assumption: *never do we experience pain in midair*. As far as experience is concerned, the migraine *is* in my head, just as the abdominal pain *is* in my stomach. In this regard, the perceptual account seems to be in a better position, since it has found a way to demonstrate that the experience of pain is both indubitable and localizable. However, this account suffers from another deficiency in that its founding assumption also contradicts the evidence of experience. Experience does not corroborate the supposition that the structure of pain is analogous to the structure of perceptual consciousness. Experience suggests that while perception can establish a bond with objects only *from without*, the sensation of pain provides us with a sense of the body *from within*. We do not perceive our pains through sensations; rather, we *sense* our pains, that is, we live through our pains *as* sensations. To clarify this point, we will need to address pain as an *Empfindnis*. Yet before we do so, we first need to address with much greater precision what it means to qualify pain as an embodied feeling.

THE PHENOMENOLOGICAL ACCOUNT

In the 1960s, in the context of a rather extensive debate concerning the location of pain, Godfrey N. A. Vesey introduced what he identified as "the Sartre-type account" of pain's location. According to this account, our understanding of pain's location will remain inaccurate for as long as we do not draw a distinction between two fundamentally different concepts of the body. "A person may say that he feels a pain in his foot, but it is obvious that he does not feel it as he might feel a pin in his foot" (Vesey 1961, 30). So as to recognize that a pin is in my foot, I need to consider my own body as a perceptual object among other objects, that is, I need to relate to my own body *outwardly*. By contrast, I can experience pain only in my own body because the body-in-pain is given to me *inwardly*. With a reference to Sartre's distinction between the body *in the midst of the world* and the body *as it is for me*, Vesey introduces the fundamental distinction between the *sensitive body* and the *sensible body*. According to Vesey, when we locate pains in the body, we have in mind the "body *qua* sensitive" (as it is for me), not the "body *qua* sensible" (as it is in the midst of the world). In Vesey's view, important implications follow from such a theory: "To understand what is meant by talk of 'one's body *qua* sensitive' is to appreciate how misleading is talk of 'feeling' bodily sensations. It misleads one into thinking that a person is somehow divorced from his body, a disembodied observer of it" (1961, 33). However, as Vesey himself was later to admit, his analysis of "the Sartre-type account" was not without shortcomings. In his response to Kurt Baier's critique in 1965, Vesey remarked: "I introduced the 'body *qua* sensitive/body *qua* sensible' terminology in my *Mind* paper. . . . The drawback to the use of this terminology is that while it suggests the question 'What is the relation of the body *qua* sensitive to the body *qua* sensible?,' it does nothing to suggest an answer" (1965, 64).

This is an ambiguous observation in that it remains unclear whether, in Vesey's view, the indicated question cannot be answered on the basis of "the Sartre-type account," or whether Vesey's development of this account did not generate a clear answer. No matter which is the case, in what follows, my goal is to develop "the Sartre-type account" in a way that would generate an answer to this question. As is well known, Sartre's (1956, 279–336) distinction between the body *as it is for me* and the body *in the midst of the world* is a critical appropriation of the distinction between the subject-body (*Leib*) and the object-body (*Körper*) that we come across in Husserl's phenomenology. In what follows, I will attempt to show how the position of which Vesey gave only a blueprint could be further developed on the basis of the insights expressed in Husserl's phenomenology.

THE LIVED-BODY AS THE SUBJECT OF PAIN

As Kurt Baier puts it in "The Place of a Pain," the question concerning the location of pain might appear trivial at the outset, yet a closer look reveals that its solution could throw light on highly significant matters for philosophy, "in particular the problem of the relation of a person's mind to his body" (1964, 139). As mentioned above, one of the fundamental shortcomings of the five approaches sketched earlier lies in the unjustified assumption that there are only two ways in which the content of pain experience could be determined: as either psychological or physical. We have already seen the phenomenological difficulty involved in either solution: if this issue is to be determined in accordance with the evidence of experience, and if this principle demands one to acknowledge that pain is both an indubitable and an embodied experience, then the content of pain experience cannot be either purely psychological or purely physical. Is it in any way possible for any experiential content to be lived as simultaneously indubitable and embodied? Husserlian phenomenology of the body provides us with a much-needed solution. It enables us to claim that pain is neither purely psychological nor purely physical. Rather, it is an experience that affects the *lived-body*. Such, then, is the resolution that phenomenology offers to the apparent paradox we address here: pain is neither purely psychological nor purely physical; rather, it is an *embodied feeling* that affects the *embodied consciousness*. Insofar as pain is a feeling, it is given indubitably; insofar as this feeling is embodied, it is given as localized within the body. In its own turn, such a realization provides us with the further basis to answer the question concerning the subject of pain. In the proposition, "I am in pain," what does the word "I" refer to? Husserlian phenomenology of the body invites us to claim that it refers neither to the disembodied consciousness nor to the physiological body, but to the *lived-body*, conceived of as the field of sensings. So as to clarify the meaning entailed in these observations, it is necessary to determine the phenomenological notion of the lived-body with some precision.

1. The lived-body is the *zero point of orientation*: it is the *absolute here* to which the relative *here* and *there* relate (see Husserl 1989, §41a). Such a conception highlights the sense of the lived-body as a perceptual organ: "The 'far' is far from me, from my Body [*Leib*]; the 'to the right' refers back to the right side of my Body. . . . . I have all things over and against me; they are all 'there'—with the exception of one and only one, namely the Body, which is always 'here'" (Husserl 1989, 166).

Insofar as pain affects the lived-body, it must affect it in a different sense than this one. Insofar as my body is the *zero* point of orientation, insofar as it is the *absolute* here, it lies beyond the scope of my thematic consciousness: my body largely remains an *absent body* (see Leder 1990), through which I relate to other objects of consciousness. Yet if I recognize that my body is in pain, my body is no longer absent. Pain captures and absorbs our attention; it objectifies the body, which we start recognizing as a mediating entity between our perceptual, evaluative, and cognitive acts, on the one hand, and all possible correlates of these acts, on the other hand.

2. The lived-body is *the organ of my will and the seat of free movement*. While extra-Bodily things are moveable only mechanically, the lived-body is "the *one and only Object* which, for the will of my pure Ego, is *moveable immediately and spontaneously*" (Husserl 1989, 159). Just as the first determination, so the second one, too, does not fix the original sense in which pain could be said to affect the lived-body. The experience of pain is to be understood as *the lived-body's protest against the will*, as its *resistance* that takes the form of freezing the lived-body's free movement. With a reference to Heidegger's analysis of *Zuhandenheit*, one could liken the experience of pain to the lived-body's *unreadiness-to-hand*: just as a piece of equipment becomes noticeable when it no longer functions properly, so the lived-body becomes thematic when it is no longer an obedient servant of the will.

THE BODY IN PAIN   129

3. A third central determination suggests that the lived-body is *the expression of the spirit (Ausdruck des Geistes):*[5] "The Body is not only in general a thing but is indeed expression of the spirit and *is at once organ of the spirit*" (Husserl 1989, 102). In this regard, the lived-body differs from "extra-Bodily things" in that it is *animated* by the spirit; thus, the body has not only psychological but also *spiritual* significance. Husserl's own reflections on this determination of the lived-body are scarce, which is deeply unfortunate, for, arguably, this conception provides us with the fundamental philosophical condition that underlies the analyses of pain undertaken in human sciences (*Geisteswissenschaften*). Without a bond that would tie the lived-body to spirit (*Geist*), it would remain incomprehensible how, as Ernst Jünger once put it, pain could be one of the keys to unlock man's innermost being as well as the world: "Man's relation to pain changes with every significant shift in fundamental belief. This relation is in no way set; rather, it eludes our knowledge, and yet is the best benchmark by which to discern a culture" (2008, 1–2).

Nonetheless, I would contend that it is not the body-in-pain but rather our *reactions* to pain, our *confrontations* with it as well as the diverse ways in which we *suffer* from it that take on diverse forms of spiritual expression. To be sure, these reactions to and confrontations with pain are irreducible components of what in chapter 3 I call the "whole pain experience." Nonetheless, the very fact that these reactions are conceivable only as reactions *to* pain, and that these confrontations can be understood only as confrontation *with* pain, provides sufficient evidence to contend that the identification of the lived-body with the expression of the spirit does not fix the *original* sense in which pain could be said to affect the lived-body. The involuntary passivity characteristic of the experience of pain, the immediacy of pain due to which pain so often catches us off guard, is more fundamental than all the spiritual expressions that accompany it *almost* immediately.

4. Besides the above-mentioned ways, Husserl (1989, §§36, 40) also addresses the lived-body as the *bearer of localized sensations*. With this determination of the lived-body, we finally come across the original sense in which the lived-body could be identified as the subject of pain. Consider the determination of the lived-body as the *zero point of orientation*. As mentioned above, the body-in-pain can no longer be conceived of as an *absolute here*, but it becomes an *absolute there*—in the extreme case, it becomes the "living wall" that blocks my access to all other objects around me. Nonetheless, this body-in-pain, despite its resistance, retains the sense of being my

lived-body, precisely because it retains the sense of being *my field of sensings*. Consider also the conception of the lived-body as the *organ of the will*: when our lived-bodies approach the limits of physical exhaustion, they can hardly be conceived of as subservient organs that produce spontaneous movements. Nonetheless, even under such circumstances, our bodies remain the bearers of localized sensations. Finally, with regard to the lived-body conceived of as the *expression of the spirit*, one could point out that when the dentist's drill hits the nerve and the person "sees stars," the experienced pain "brackets" the person's spiritual world while accentuating the overwhelming presence of the lived-body as the bearer of localized sensations.

Two implications follow from the foregoing analysis. The first concerns the subject of pain: now it is clear why the two most common determinations of the subject of pain—the identification of this subject either with the disembodied consciousness or with the physiological body—remain misleading. Neither the disembodied consciousness nor the physiological body can be determined as the bearer of localized sensations such as pain. The second implication concerns the tension between pain's indubitability and its bodily localizability: the determination of the lived-body as the bearer of localized sensations alleviates this tension by bringing to light that the problem in question appears irresolvable only for as long as one assumes that there is just one conception of the body, namely, the naturalistic conception, which conceives of the body as an object given through outer perception. *Conceived of as a field of sensings, the lived-body is a self-conscious body*: insofar as it is self-conscious, pain is given to it indubitably; insofar as it is a body, it experiences pain as a localized sensation.

PAIN AS *EMPFINDNIS*

In our foregoing reflections, we have qualified pain as a sensation. Such a qualification, however, remains too general: pain is a peculiar kind of sensation, which, borrowing Husserl's neologism, we will try here to conceptualize as *Empfindnis* (sensing). With the help of this concept, Husserl aims to describe the unique way in which we experience our own lived-bodies. On the one hand, I can *see* my own body, or at least parts of it, just as I see all objects in front of me. So also, I can *hear* my own footsteps or my own breathing. In some exceptional circumstances, I can even hear the beating of my heart, just as I hear the other sounds around me. In this regard, my relation to my own body relies upon the same kind of sensations (*Empfindungen*) and their apprehension as my relation to all other objects around me. Yet, on the other hand, it is crucial to stress that the self-givenness of my own lived-body is not reducible to this kind of seeing and hearing. The self-givenness of my own lived-body is unique, and so as to capture its uniqueness, Husserl introduces the concept of *Empfindnis*, suggesting thereby that we grasp our own lived bodies through special sensations.

Sensings (*Empfindnisse*) differ from other kind of sensations in that they are those sensations that have immediate bodily localization (see Husserl 1989, §39). When we live through visual sensations (such as color sensations) or audible sensations (such as tone sensations), we do not experience them as localized within our own bodies. Therefore, when we apprehend these sensations, we immediately ascribe them to objects of experience. Thus, by means of specific acts of objective apprehension, the sky appears as blue, the melody as beautiful. Here there is no place for confusion: to claim that the sky is blue is not the same as to claim that one's eyes are blue; so also, to claim that the melody is beautiful is not the same as to claim that one's ears are beautiful. Yet the situation proves fundamentally different when we turn our attention to tactual sensations. My fingers now touch the table and I feel its cold and rough surface. To be sure, I can apprehend the rough and cold sensations that I now live through as qualities of the table, just as I apprehend the color-sensations as the blueness of the sky, or the audible sensations as the beauty of the melody. What we said about audible and visible sensations, we can also say about tactual sensations: through peculiar acts of objectifying apprehension, we can ascribe them to objects of experience. However, this should not overshadow an important difference between the sensations under consideration. *Only tactual sensations are localized within our bodies.* Therefore, when we feel the cold and rough surface of the table, we cannot help but at the same time feel it *in our own bodies*, say, in our fingertips. On the one hand, when I see blood, my eyes don't turn red. So also, when I hear the sound of thunder, it does not literally crash in my eardrums. By contrast, when my fingers touch the hot stove, the sensation-appearance of the burning heat is at the same time a feeling-sensation localized in my fingertips. So also, when I step on broken glass, I feel its sharpness in my own feet. Such localizations need not be precise. They can also spread over larger areas of my lived-body, or even my whole body, as happens when I sense, extended over my body, the pressure and pull of my clothes (see Husserl 1989, §36), or when the water of the sea cools my body on a hot and humid day. "An eye does not appear to one's own vision" (Husserl 1989, 155), just as an ear does not hear itself. By contrast, the touching body experiences a *double sensation*: it feels itself touching. The phenomenological concept of *Empfindnis* is designed to capture this unique double-sidedness of tactual sensations. Sensings (*Empfindnisse*) are at one and the same time touch-sensations and touch-appearances. Besides being objectifying, they are also *self-reflexive*, and thus, besides apprehending them as properties of objects of experience, we also sense them as embodied feelings—as feelings that are localized within our own bodies. Such, then, is the fundamental difference between sensible and audible sensations, on the one hand, and tactual sensations, on the other. Only tactual feelings are *somatesthetic*—embodied sensory feelings, which are by their nature both self-reflexive and objectifying.

What does it mean to qualify sensings (*Empfindnisse*) as localized sensations? Here we are on the brink of another misunderstanding. The localization of sensings is fundamentally different from the localization of things in objective space (see Husserl 1989, §37). Following Husserl's lead, we can clarify this difference with the help of the phenomenological concept of *adumbrations* (*Abschattungen*). To claim that spatial things are localized in space through adumbrations is to suggest that they can manifest their different sides and that they can be given to us from different perspectives. Thus, the table with the cold and rough surface can be seen from the left and from the right, from above and from below. So also, as I keep running my fingers over its surface, its sensuous qualities, such as roughness, coldness, and so on, are continuously experienced as qualitatively different sensations. Nonetheless, despite the plurality of manners of givenness, I recognize the object for what it is, namely, as an object of experience that is constituted through the sensuous schema and manifolds of adumbrations. By contrast, sensings cannot be given to us by means of adumbrations. The feeling of the cold-sensation that I have in my fingertips when I touch this table is not something that I can either distance myself from or come closer to, at least in the literal sense of the term. The sensings thus have nothing to do with the manifold of adumbrations. Insofar as *Empfindnisse* are given to me, they are just what they are.

Pain is an *Empfindnis*, and as such, it belongs to the group of those unique sensations that are fundamental to the lived-body's self-constitution. When Husserl writes that "*a subject whose only sense was the sense of vision could not at all have an appearing Body*" (Husserl 1989, 158), he means thereby

THE BODY IN PAIN

that the lived-body, conceived of as *my own* body, can be constituted only by means of *Empfindnisse* (sensings), conceived of as self-reflexive localized sensations. In this regard, tactual sensations are more fundamental than all other sensations: "The Body as such can be constituted originarily only in tactuality and in everything that is localized with the sensations of touch: for example, warmth, coldness, pain, etc." (Husserl 1989, 158). Only a consciousness that is capable of double apprehension, and thus of localized sensations, can constitute itself as an embodied consciousness.

PAIN'S TWOFOLD LOCALIZABILITY

What sense are we to make of the common experience that concerns the misidentification of pain's location? In the dentist's office, I point at the tooth that hurts, yet soon I find out that a different tooth has triggered my pain. This common experience invites us to address the following question, which Vesey left unanswered: "What is the relation of the body *qua* sensitive to the body *qua* sensible?"

Husserl's phenomenology provides us with helpful resources to address this question, especially because his analyses of *Empfindnisse* are part of a larger project of *transcendental constitution*. Of central importance is Husserl's claim that *the body is constituted as a twofold unity*. On the one hand, insofar as the lived-body is the bearer of sensations, it is constituted as a *referential unity of sensings*. On the other hand, insofar as the body is a perceptual object, it is constituted as a *perceptual unity of appearances*. Husserl's analysis of *Empfindnisse*, and especially as they are exemplified by one hand touching the other (see Husserl 1989, §37), is an account of how the lived-body, conceived of as the referential unity of sensings, identifies itself as the body, conceived of as the perceptual unity of appearances.

Insofar as my lived-body is the subject of tactual sensations, it is given as a field of *sensings*. Insofar as my body is the object that I touch, it is constituted on the basis of tactual *presentations*. Therefore, one could qualify the body as a *founded phenomenon*, whose full-scale constitution rests on the congruence (*Deckung*) of two separate unities of sense. Only due to this congruence can the body be not only the bearer of localized sensations, but also a material object among other objects. Only because of this congruence can the body be viewed not only *from within*, but also *from without* (see Husserl 1989, §42).

One might be tempted to assert that the possibility of bodily localization of sensations rests upon such a twofold constitution of the lived-body. Yet, arguably, even at the basic constitutive level that marks the givenness of the lived-body as nothing more than the bearer of sensations, bodily sensations are experienced as localized.[6] Indeed, it is crucial not to overlook the sui generis nature of the localizability of bodily sensations.[7] On the one hand, at the merely sensory level, the exact locality of sensations is only *sensed*. On the other hand, when I find myself in the dentist's office and I *point* at the hurting tooth, I refer to my body not merely as a field of sensings, but also as a perceptual unity of sense: I no longer feel my body inwardly, but I see it outwardly. This basic capacity to point at the hurting tooth already rests on a twofold constitution of the body, conceived of as the unity of sensings and as the unity of appearances. This basic capacity is already a *complex act*, which rests on the congruence of the *sensory and perceptual localization of pain*.

On the one hand, insofar as my lived-body is given to me as the bearer of sensations, I can only *sense* the location of my pain. On the other hand, insofar as it is constituted as a material object "from without," I can *perceive* the location of my pain. The full-scale localization of my pain is built upon a peculiar *congruence* between the lived-body as a field of sensings and the body as a material object.

A careful look at the experience of pain makes clear why *the congruence in question is rarely, if ever, precise*. In the earlier chapters I have observed that there is no language appropriate to pain and that most of the terms we use are metaphorical descriptions. Hence, we speak of sharp pains or cutting pains, burning, stabbing, drilling, pinching, and gnawing pains, thereby transferring the sense of the terms designed to characterize material objects to the domain of sensations (see Scarry 1985, 7–8). With this in mind, one could say, metaphorically, that insofar as pain is given as a sensation, it announces the swelling up of the body and the simultaneous contraction of the world. By contrast, insofar as pain is given to me as a perceptual object, it announces the reverse movement of the compression of the swollen body and the simultaneous revival of the contracted world. It is these "ebbs and flows" of experience that stand at the bottom of the misidentification of pain's location.

Such, then, is the answer that one can offer to the question regarding the relation of the body *qua* sensitive to the body *qua* sensible—a question that Vesey's analyses left unanswered.

PAIN AND THE CONSTITUTION OF THE LIVED-BODY

Some doubts continue to linger. Why do we find it difficult to reconcile pain's indubitability with its bodily localizability? Insofar as it is indubitable, pain is immanent, and thus I myself am the subject of pain. By contrast, insofar as it is localizable, pain transcends me, and thus, strictly speaking, it is not *I myself*, but only my body that is in pain. If pain indeed has these two characteristics—indubitability and localizability—its possibility must rest on a curious self-distantiation of the ego: *I must be both myself and something other than myself if I am to be capable of experiencing pain*. What sense are we to make of this self-distantiation?

In the context of phenomenological reflections on the lived-body, the distinctive nature of Husserl's analysis lies in the fact that Husserl conceives of our lived-bodies as our own constitutive accomplishments. In contrast to thinkers like Merleau-Ponty, who identify the body as the place of origin of both consciousness and reality, Husserl contends that from a transcendental standpoint, the lived-body is a constitutive achievement of absolute consciousness. For this reason, Husserl has often been accused of "residual metaphysical dualism" that allegedly haunts his phenomenology. For instance, Taylor Carman suggests that

> notwithstanding Husserl's professed ontological neutrality, there is an undeniable spirit of dualism animating his phenomenology. . . . It is precisely this conceptual dualism, this idea that consciousness and reality are separated by an "abyss of meaning," that prevents Husserl from acknowledging the body as the original locus of intentional phenomena in perceptual experience. . . . It is only in light of this residual phenomenological dualism, then, that we can hope to understand Husserl's account of the intentional constitution of the body and its role in perception. (1999, 208–10)

To call the fundamental distinction between consciousness and reality "metaphysical dualism" is, among other things, to suggest that it lacks phenomenological justification. To my mind, such a claim is too dismissive.[8] Arguably, the peculiar self-distantiation that lies at the heart of the experience of pain provides this fundamental Husserlian distinction with a much-needed phenomenological confirmation. In the remaining parts of this chapter, I would like to highlight some phenomenological reasons that lend support to the Husserlian standpoint. I would like to show that the peculiar self-distantiation we have already started to address highlights a curious split in the embodied subjectivity that can be clarified on the basis of those resources that derive from Husserlian phenomenology. Such is the basis that will underlie my suggestion that self-distantiation inscribed in the experience of pain provides experiential support to the alleged "metaphysical dualism" in Husserl's phenomenology.

How are our lived-bodies given to us? They are given as real unities, or specific fusions, of the body and what Husserl calls "soul." Such a fusion is absent in the case of inanimate objects, which, as Husserl points out, might very well obtain spiritual meaning, yet they have no soul.[9] The houses we live in, the pictures that hang on the walls, and the furniture we associate with various functions are not merely naturalistically determined material things, but objects with a distinctly spiritual meaning; in a good sense, just like the lived-bodies, these material things are expressions of the spirit. However, unlike all these cultural objects that are suffused in ample valuations, the lived-body is an animated thing, a real fusion of the body and soul.

Arguably, this two-sided nature of the lived-body provides us with a transcendental clarification of our perplexity over indubitability and bodily localizability characteristic of pain experience. The experience of pain carries such contradictory determinations because the subject of pain is a *founded reality*. In light of this circumstance, one has to assert that the constitutive framework that envelops Husserl's reflections on the lived-body is not a matter of a "residual metaphysical dualism." Quite on the contrary, this framework proves to be supremely well suited to capture, describe, and clarify the tensions that lie at the heart of pain experience.

Within the context of the constitution of our bodies, the sensation of pain performs a crucial role. As we saw above, pain is an *Empfindnis*. Therefore, like King Midas, who transforms any object he touches into gold, the experience of pain transforms any object it touches into my own lived-body. For this reason, if, by impossibility, I would experience the other person's pain, *this would have to be conceived of as the most egoistic act imaginable*, for it would envelop the other's body within the field of my own sensings and transform the other's body into my own. *Pain delivers to consciousness a body as its lived-body*: the experience of pain carries with it the awareness that the body-in-pain is precisely my own lived-body.

Precisely because pain is an *Empfindnis*, it belongs to the group of those tactual sensations through which the lived-body is constituted. Even more, as

THE BODY IN PAIN

Husserl argues in §39 of *Ideas II*, all higher objectivities remain bound to my lived-body as their foundation. Highlighting each and every word, Husserl writes: "*A human being's total consciousness is in a certain sense, by means of its hyletic substrate, bound to the Body*" (1989, 160). Thus, despite the marginal role that the problematic of pain plays in Husserl's phenomenology, its constitutive function is overwhelming: as the transcendental basis that underlies the lived-body's constitution, pain belongs to the group of those feeling-sensations that underlie the constitution of all objectivities (see Husserl 1989, §§37–39).

Admittedly, all I have said about the constitutive function of pain could also be said about other *Empfindnisse*. Whether one thinks of itches, tickles, or the sensation of warmth or cold, all these bodily sensations also play a role in the constitution of the lived-body, which in its own turn underlies the constitution of higher objectivities. Moreover, all *Empfindnisse*, and not just pain, can be qualified as embodied bodily feelings, which can be given only in original first-hand experience. So also, one could further hypothesize that all *Empfindnisse* can be experienced either as nonintentional feeling-sensations or apperceived as intentional feelings. What distinguishes pain from these other *Empfindnisse*? The analysis undertaken in chapter 3 provides us with an answer: pain's distinguishing characteristic lies in its inherently aversive nature and its distinct experiential quality that distinguishes pain from other aversive feelings.

THE STRUCTURE OF PAIN EXPERIENCE

With an eye on Husserl's claim that the lived-body is a constituted unity of sense, one could further suggest that the experience of pain is the experience of an inner cleavage, in which my lived-body unwillingly becomes the one and only *object* of experience, while still retaining the sense of being the subject of experience. *The body-in-pain splits into two, while still remaining one.* On the one hand, even though I can distance myself from any object of experience, I cannot distance myself from pain, which further means that I myself am this lived-body that is in pain. On the other hand, I can feel pain only *in* my body (in the head, back, abdomen, etc.), which in its own turn suggests that, in a curious way, pain is necessarily lived *at a distance*.[10] Insofar as it is both subject and object, the body-in-pain is to be identified with me and distinguished from me. *Could this paradoxical self-distantiation not be the fundamental reason why pain is both indubitable and localizable?*

The experience of pain is not the only experience, which entails a sense of my body as both subject and object. Husserl's analysis of one hand touching the other provides another illustration of the body as a twofold unity of sense. However, when one hand touches the other, my lived-body is not subject and object *at one and the same time*, or *in one and the same respect*. Rather, my consciousness fluctuates between these two senses, identifying my hand at one moment as subject, and at another moment as object. *Insofar as my body is a unity of sensings, it is not a tactual unity of appearances, and vice versa*. By contrast, severe pain marks my body as both subject and object *at one and the same time* and *in one and the same respect*. I sense pain in the body, which in a certain sense is no longer mine. Here we stumble against the depersonalizing nature of pain experience, which is a theme we will continue to address in the remaining chapters of this study. Not unlike the click of a camera, pain freezes the body, objectifies it, and distances it from the subject of experience; yet, unlike such a click, the experience of pain announces that I myself have become this frozen body, objectified and distantiated from the center of my stream of experiences. In a curious way, the experience of pain is an experience of *sensing at a distance*. This experience marks the lived-body as both something that I am and something that I no longer am. How are we to understand such a paradoxical structure of pain experience?

This is where Husserlian phenomenology proves highly resourceful. As we saw, the lived-body can be conceived of as the *zero point of orientation*, the *organ of the will*, the *expression of the spirit*, and as the *field of sensings*. With these determinations in mind, one could characterize the normally functioning body as the body in which these four characteristics coincide. By contrast, the experience of pain is anomalous in that it announces an inner split between these determinations. The experience of pain brings into question the determination of the body as the *absolute here* from which the world unfolds; so also, it brings into question its determination as the subservient *organ of my will*; last but not least, it also makes one wonder if one still has the right to qualify the body as the *expression of the spirit*. Nonetheless, although these three qualifications become questionable, the body-in-pain still retains the sense of being the *field of sensings*.

In this regard one could qualify the experience of pain as *the lived-body's resistance to its constitutive appropriation*. This resistance takes the form of a refusal on the part of the lived-body to be the *zero point of orientation*, the *organ of the will*, as well as the *expression of the spirit*. The experience of pain unsettles these three determinations of the lived-body. When experienced

THE BODY IN PAIN   139

in its moderate forms, the experience of pain could be described as the lived-body's insubordination to such a threefold determination. When pain becomes excruciating, we come to experience the heavy presence of such a threefold privation. Still, whichever form it takes, it manifests itself as a tendency that strives to reverse these three functions of the body. Instead of being the *absolute here*, the body-in-pain tends toward becoming the *absolute there*, which limits my capacities and absorbs my attention. In this regard, to experience pain is to experience the lived-body's attempts to transform itself into an object of experience that would block my free access to everything else around me. The body in pain is a body that strives to become the one and only object from which I cannot distance myself for as long as pain lasts.[11] So also, instead of being a subservient *organ of the will*, the body-in-pain is experienced as a rebellious object that actively resists my will, and it does this more or less explicitly and more or less successfully. Thus, when suffering from a migraine, I can no longer entertain free thoughts about an arbitrary subject matter. So also, if I have a broken foot that hurts me, I can no longer use the steps, and so on. The more uncontrollable one's pain, the more excruciating is its nature. Finally, instead of being the *expression of the spirit*, the experience of pain is experienced as the negativity that is inherently set against spiritual expressions; it announces, more or less explicitly, the fragility of the spiritual world.

Such a threefold reversal of the lived-body's inner determinations provides us with three fundamental reasons why pain is a depersonalizing experience. Yet, as I will argue in the next chapter, besides being depersonalizing, pain is, or at least can be, also repersonalizing. In this regard, one should stress the following: the subject in pain is well aware that in order to regain access to other objects and the world, it must find the means to overcome the otherness of its body and to reconstitute its sense as the *absolute here*. By announcing the withdrawal of the world and its sense unities, the experience of pain highlights their dependence upon the lived-body. In the case of excruciating pain, by bringing about the inner dissolution at the foundations of sense, by transforming this body into the "last object of experience," the experience of pain returns consciousness back to its constitutive beginnings—to the fundamental need to appropriate this recalcitrant body and render it once again one's own. In this regard, one can conceive of the tension between pain's indubitability and its bodily localizability as a direct and forceful experience of the *paradox of subjectivity* that Husserl addressed in a number of his works (see especially Husserl 1970/1976, §53): *I am not this body, yet I must be it, if this world of mine is to be.*[12]

My central goal in this chapter has been to clarify what it means to claim that pain is an embodied experience. While hardly anyone would reject the claim itself, its meaning remains clouded in ambiguities. Building on the basis of Husserl's phenomenology of the body, I argued that the phenomenological distinction between the lived-body (*Leib*) and the physical body (*Körper*) is of fundamental importance in such a framework. The realization that the subject of pain is neither the disembodied consciousness nor the physical body, but the lived-body, conceived of as the field of sensings, led to the further apprehension that pain itself is a peculiar kind of sensation, namely, a type of *sensing* (*Empfindnis*). The analysis of this theme in its own turn has led to the realization that insofar as we think of pain in the constitutive framework of Husserl's analysis, pain is to be conceived of as the lived-body's resistance to its constitutive appropriation.

On the basis of the analysis undertaken here, I would like to put forth two closely interrelated theses. First, our theoretical approaches to pain largely depend on how we understand the content of pain experience. Although in the philosophy of pain, this determination often remains nonthematic, it largely shapes the theoretical contours of pain apprehension. This content is most commonly determined either psychologically or physiologically. One of my goals in this chapter was to show that pain can also be conceived of as *Empfindnis* and that such a conception carries far-reaching implications. This realization leads to the second thesis. Much like Aristotle's being, pain can be said in many ways. It can be said in four fundamental ways, each of which depends on how we answer the fundamental question: When I say that I am in pain, what does the word "I" refer to? This question largely overlaps with the question concerning pain's location, although not entirely. (1) One could say that we feel pain in the body, and when one says this, one could uncritically accept the physiological conception of the body. If we follow this path, we conceive of pain as a physiological phenomenon and we apprehend the subject of pain as the physiological body. Such is the dominant approach to pain in the contemporary science of pain as well as in the nowadays-dominant philosophy of pain. (2) One could argue that we feel pain not in the body (after all, a physiological body cannot feel anything), but in consciousness. Should we conceive of consciousness as the subject of pain, we will also conceive of pain as a psychological phenomenon. Such is the approach to pain that Franz Brentano takes in his investigations. Such is also the dominant standpoint in the contemporary psychology of pain. (3)

We could also identify the lived-body as the subject of pain. In its own turn, such identification suggests that we identify the subject of pain as the embodied consciousness. Such an apprehension of the subject of pain invites us to conceptualize pain phenomenologically. There is one more possibility, which so far remains unexplored. At least as far as human experience of pain is concerned, one could say that the subject of pain is neither consciousness, conceived of psychologically, nor the body, conceived of either physiologically or phenomenologically, but rather the person. To develop such an approach, one must conceptualize pain personalistically, and the account of pain one would thereby offer would fall into the framework of philosophical anthropology. We will develop such an approach in the next chapter.

As I argued in the introduction and in chapter 1, the established definition of pain that was offered by the International Association for the Study of Pain (IASP) cannot be justified in accordance with the fundamental phenomenological principles, and, therefore, it cannot be relied upon in phenomenologically oriented pain research. In the last four chapters, I have aimed to develop an alternative conception of pain, and the current chapter has completed this task. At this point, we have clarified what it means to claim that *pain is an aversive bodily feeling with a distinct experiential quality, which can be given only in original firsthand experience, either as a nonintentional feeling-sensation or as an intentional feeling.*

CHAPTER 6

··

THE PHENOMENOLOGY OF EMBODIED PERSONHOOD

Depersonalization and Repersonalization

This study is guided by three fundamental tasks. It aims to (1) spell out the fundamental methodological principles that must underlie phenomenologically oriented studies of pain; (2) offer a novel conception of pain on the basis of such methodological principles; and (3) demonstrate what contribution the phenomenology of pain can make to philosophical anthropology. We are now ready to turn to the third task.

In the last chapter, while focusing on the embodied nature of pain experience, I argued that the subject of pain is not the body (*Körper*), conceived of neurophysiologically, but the lived-body (*Leib*), conceived of phenomenologically. When pain is addressed in the framework of philosophical anthropology, it is crucial to supplement this claim with a further qualification. When the discussion turns to human pain, no matter how one conceives of the lived-body—(1) as the zero-point of orientation; (2) as the organ of the will and the seat of free movement; (3) as the expression of the spirit; or, finally, (4) as the bearer of localized sensations—the lived-body itself cannot be the subject of experience, but must belong to such a subject. *As far as human pain is concerned, the lived-body belongs to the person.*[1] Accordingly, in the framework of philosophical anthropology, the person, rather than the lived-body, must be conceived of as the subject of pain. This supplementation might appear trivial, yet a closer look will show that it is highly fruitful: once the person is identified as the subject of pain, it becomes possible to address the *depersonalizing* and *repersonalizing* nature of pain experience.

Not all pains are depersonalizing and repersonalizing. Recall the distinction between transient, acute, and chronic pain that was introduced in chapter 4. Transient pains are felt only in the lived-bodies, and they are devoid of genuinely

THE PHENOMENOLOGY OF EMBODIED PERSONHOOD

personal significance. Pains are "just pains" when they unfold at a safe distance from the subject of experience (see Moran 2010; Serrano de Haro 2017).[2] By contrast, some intense and long-lasting acute pains affect not only our lived-bodies, but resonate at the very core of our existence. They are depersonalizing in that they modify our relation to our bodies, to others, to the environment, and even to ourselves. Chronic pains *as a rule* are depersonalizing in the above-mentioned ways. They rob us of those characteristics that make up our personalities: *all* chronic pains are depersonalizing.[3] What, then, distinguishes chronic pains from other types of pain? In contrast to both transient and acute pains, chronic pains are not only depersonalizing but also repersonalizing.[4]

In light of these differences, in this chapter I will focus on chronic pain, although by implication, much of what will be said here is also of significance for our understanding of long-lasting and intense acute pain as well as other forms of psychological suffering, such as depression. My central goal is to show that the concept of the person designates the subject of chronic pain and that the processes of depersonalization and repersonalization make up the essential characteristics of intense chronic pain experience. *There is no intense chronic pain that is not depersonalizing and repersonalizing.*

I will take five steps in my analysis. I will begin by clarifying the meaning of the claim that the subject of pain is the person, conceived of phenomenologically. Second, I will argue that chronic pain is a depersonalizing experience in that it unsettles the fundamental relations that bind the person to his body, surroundings, others, and himself. Third, I will argue that chronic pain is also a repersonalizing experience in that, due to its temporal nature, it forces the person to reconstitute those fundamental relations that pain disrupts. Fourth, I will show how such a conception of chronic pain invites one to reconceptualize some entrenched distinctions in the phenomenology of medicine: the distinction between psychogenic and organic pain, as well as the illness/disease and healing/curing distinctions. Fifth, on the basis of the foregoing analysis, I will revisit the widely spread view that suggests pain is neither sharable nor expressible. I will conclude with some reflections on the therapeutic significance of dialogue and offer a brief propaedeutic to the phenomenology of listening.

THE PHENOMENOLOGY OF EMBODIED PERSONHOOD

The phenomenological concept of the person designates the subject of chronic pain.[5] To clarify the meaning of this claim, let us first provide it with a negative determination. The identification of the person as the subject of pain should be understood as an alternative to the nowadays dominant view, which identifies the subject of pain with the brain, conceived in accordance with the fundamental principles of neurophysiology (see Thacker 2015). Instead of entering into a detailed analysis of such a standpoint, let me briefly indicate three fundamental reasons why the neurophysiological identification of the brain as the subject of pain cannot be accepted in phenomenologically oriented pain research. First, this view is incoherent. Insofar as the brain is conceived exclusively neurophysiologically, it cannot be conceived of as the subject of any feelings; and if it is incapable of feelings, it is incapable of experiencing pain. Second, assuming that all possible causes of pain are organic, this view proscribes both the recognition and the treatment of psychogenic pain—the kind of pain that derives not from organic but rather from purely psychological causes (see Szasz 1975, 93–99). Third, this view underestimates pain's deeper effects upon the person. Frederik J. J. Buytendijk emphasized this point especially strongly. Against Max Scheler, who in his *Formalism in Ethics and the Non-Formal Ethics of Values* maintained that pain is nothing other than a feeling-state and that, therefore, the subject of pain is not the self (that is, the person) but the body, Buytendijk insisted that pain has its effects on the deepest levels of personality: "The more violent a pain, the deeper it penetrates, affecting not merely the 'body-self,' but our actual personality as well" (1962, 114). Mick Thacker has recently reiterated the significance of this insight: "I remain unconvinced that brains are sufficient for pain. . . . I believe that the only entity sufficient for the experience and perception of pain is the person" (2015, 3).

What are we to understand by the concept of the person? As far as philosophical literature on medicine and medical practice are concerned, it is worthwhile recalling Eric Cassell's observation that they both systematically suppress what is specifically personal, and thus, at least in the framework that concerns health care, "we still do not know how to define a person" (1978, 96). More recently, Dermot Moran reiterated this claim, when he contended that "the health sciences (person-centered medicine, nursing, personalistic psychiatry, geriatrics, end-of-life care) recognize the importance of persons, but with little theoretical underpinning" (2014, 37). The regrettable situation of which both authors speak can be remedied by turning back to Husserl's phenomenology and, specifically, to his phenomenology of personhood, as presented in *Ideas II*. In the remaining part of this section, I would like to take a detour to Husserl's analysis of the person as presented in this work.

Husserl's analysis of personhood relies on the methodological insight that our ontological commitments, whatever they might be, are correlated with corresponding attitudes of consciousness. Insofar as our absorption in a particular attitude is concerned, seeing and blindness walk hand in hand; insofar as we inhabit a particular attitude, we are blind to what is given in other attitudes. Still, we are not imprisoned within the confines of any attitude; the possibility remains always open to transition from one attitude to another. Some of the attitudes that we take on (such as the arithmetic or the aesthetic attitudes) are devised artificially; we are the ones who have crafted them. In this regard, Husserl's thesis is uncontroversial: for numbers to exist, consciousness must take on a certain attitude—the arithmetical attitude. Numbers, conceived of as objects of consciousness, exist only insofar as consciousness inhabits this attitude. What holds for numbers also holds for geometrical forms, logical principles, or fictive entities. Following Husserl's (1983, §49) notorious experiment concerning the world's annihilation, one can say that if a universal plague swept through this world and annihilated all beings capable of taking on a mathematical or an aesthetic attitude, this event would nullify all mathematical and aesthetic objectivities. This does not mean, however, that *all* attitudes are artificial. In contrast to the artificial attitudes we have designed ourselves, there is also a natural attitude—that attitude in which we always already find ourselves.

The concept of the natural attitude is dangerously equivocal: it can be understood in two fundamentally different ways—either naturalistically or personalistically. Although in the earlier chapters of this study we juxtaposed phenomenological analysis to naturalistic explanations, we haven't found it necessary to discuss the personalistic attitude. According to a central thesis in Husserl's phenomenology, the naturalistic attitude arises as a modification of a more basic, personalistic attitude. Husserl contends that what is given in the personalistic attitude is not nature, but something fundamentally contrary to nature. As Dermot Moran fittingly puts it, the personalistic attitude is "the default mode of experiencing for all human subjects" (2009, 96).[6] Husserl invites us to treat the naturalistic attitude as secondary when compared with the attitude that guides us when we are immersed in the affairs of our lives: "The naturalistic attitude is subordinated to the personalistic" (Husserl 1989, 193). It is only in virtue of a certain self-forgetfulness that the naturalistic attitude establishes its own relative autonomy vis-à-vis the personalistic attitude. In this regard, phenomenology is meant to perform a mnemonic function: it is meant to disclose the personalistic background that underlies all our activities.[7]

With the distinction between the personalistic and the naturalistic attitudes in mind, one could say that the category of the person refers to the subject of experience who sees the world personalistically. The person is the subject capable of taking on the first-person perspective (see Baker 2000, by which we are to understand that the person is the subject to whom things matter. The person is the subject of sensations, affections, and thoughts and a concrete agent in the sociohistorical world. The person not only perceives the world, but also is emotively touched by the world as well as cognitive of it. The person is moved by affective tendencies, instincts, and a large variety of strivings, wishes, and volitions (see Peucker 2008, 319). The person is an embodied, self-conscious, social, historical, and engaged self.

Husserl himself often spoke of the person in terms of a large variety of dependencies: the person is "dependent on others, and not merely on individual persons, but on communities of persons, social institutions, the state, morals, the law, the church, etc." (1989, 148). Husserl even contends that "the apprehension of man as a real personality is determined throughout by such dependencies" (148). Nonetheless, the person is not only a recipient, but also an active, meaning-making being (see Moran 2009); and the meanings the person produces often become part and parcel of the intersubjective and sociohistorical world. This means that the intersubjective worlds persons inhabit are irreducibly cultural-historical and that the configurations of sense that make up these worlds are built upon acts that are distinctly personal. No less importantly, the person is a being who can intend values and who can orient his or her life in accordance with these values. Furthermore, the person is also actively engaged in the world, which means that the person is the subject of action—a concrete agent in the sociocultural world. For Husserl, the person is the subject capable of acting in accordance with his or her choices and decisions, capable of acting responsibly. In Husserl's writings, the link that binds persons and intersubjective worlds is so strong that, in his *Kaizo* articles from the early 1920s, he broadens his concept of the person so as to include social groups and peoples, conceived of as "personalities of the higher order" (1988, 22). Nonetheless, no matter how strong this intentional link might be, the person is also a subject who is free from the world and who can enter the "worlds" of phantasy, memory, and anticipation, or conceptually "resettle," at least temporarily, in distant cultural and historical worlds.

On the basis of the phenomenological description of personhood offered here, I would contend that the naturalistic conceptions of the human subject are severely limited, and that even though they have their legitimacy, they become inappropriate insofar as one either "forgets" or denies that they are modifications of a more basic, personalistic conception. Husserl does not deny that we have the capacity to treat a human being theoretically "as a thing," that is, "as mere annex of natural Objects which are mere things and consequently take him as a mere thing" (1989, 200). He further claims, "Within certain limits this is legitimate," yet to this he adds a crucial remark: such a mode of theorizing "becomes an injustice if we do not acknowledge at all that the naturalizing of persons and souls can allow us to recognize only certain relations of dependency" (1989, 200). The distinction between naturalistic and personalistic attitudes invites us to acknowledge that persons have "a being properly their own" (1989, 200). From here Husserl is led to the conclusion that is of great relevance in the framework of the phenomenology of pain: "He who sees everywhere only nature, nature in the sense of, and, as it were, through the eyes of natural science, is precisely blind to the spiritual sphere, the special domain of the human sciences. Such a one does not see persons" (1989, 201).

By now it must be clear that the question concerning what it means to be human lies at the heart of the distinction between the personalistic and the naturalistic attitudes. While recognizing the importance of the naturalistic attitude for various forms of theoretical reason, Husserl nonetheless invites us to concede that, as Maria Villela-Petit emphasizes especially strongly, "only the personalistic attitude is capable of preserving humanity as such" (2007, 216). To be a person is to be an embodied subject of perceptual, cognitive, emotive, and practical acts. To be a person is to stand in an intentional relation to the surrounding world and in a communicative relation to others. The various acts that the person lives through build up the person's unique history, which up to a large degree "determines" the person's style of existence. This history, taken along with the cognitive, emotive, and practical acts, colors the subject's intentional relation to the world in a particular atmosphere, which *motivates* the person to project particular plans into the future. As Edith Stein once put it in a heavily Husserlian spirit, "Motivation is the lawfulness of spiritual life" (1989, 96).[8]

Having taken the detour to Husserlian phenomenology of personhood, we are in the position to understand what it means to claim that the person is the subject of pain experience. However, even though the meaning of this claim by now must be clear, its philosophical relevance still continues to elude us. We need to see that the phenomenology of personhood outlined above is of philosophical importance for the philosophy of pain first and foremost because it enables us to conceptualize the depersonalizing and repersonalizing nature of chronic pain experience.

CHRONIC PAIN AS DEPERSONALIZATION

In psychiatry, the concept of depersonalization refers to the *depersonalization syndrome*, which *DSM IV* conceptualizes as a "feeling of detachment or estrangement from one's self." This syndrome is described as follows:

> The individual may feel like an automaton or as if he or she is living in a dream or a movie. There may be a sensation of being an outside observer of one's mental processes, one's body, or parts of one's body. Various types of sensory anaesthesia, lack of affective response, and a sensation of lacking control of one's actions, including speech, are often present. (*American Psychiatric Association* 2000, sec. 300.6)

Not everything we find present in this description is characteristic of how chronic pain is lived. Neither sensory anaesthesia nor lack of affective responses is a feature of chronic pain experience. In the present context, I employ the concept of depersonalization (and, correspondingly, repersonalization) in a different way. To borrow an expression from Matthew Ratcliffe, one could say that depersonalization and repersonalization are phenomenological experiences "united by a distinctive experiential role," which they play "regardless of what their neurobiological underpinnings might be" (2008, 122). What is this role? It is my thesis that chronic pain emerges in the field of experience as a rupture at the core of our personal existence, and it is this rupture that justifies the characterization of chronic pain as depersonalization.[9] Chronic pain is lived not merely as an assault on our bodies, but as an *assault on our personalities*—in the words of Edmund Pellegrino and David Thomasma, as a *wounding of our humanity* (1981, 157). To determine this notion of pain as a rupture with greater precision, it is important to distinguish between four essential characteristics of chronic pain experience.

First, chronic pain disrupts the usual relation between the self and the body, a relation that in a painless body is marked by the body's subservience to the self. As we saw in chapter 5, in the normal flow of experience, I first and foremost experience my body not as a material thing (*Körper*) but as a lived-body (*Leib*). While itself remaining nonthematic and nonobjective, my lived-body is that very "thing" that enables me to access all other material things around me. Even acute pain (along with such feelings as excessive heat or excessive cold, bodily repulsion and exhaustion, as well as fatigue and vertigo) belongs to the group of those bodily feelings, which are marked by *negativity* and which *stand out* from the normal flow of experience, thereby unsettling the normal relation between the lived-body and the self. As I argued in chapter 5, pain marks the body's inner protest against its constitutive appropriation. In the present context, let us couple this claim with the insight, substantiated by the reports of many chronic pain patients, that chronic pain marks the body's refusal to be identified with the self.[10] Chronic pain patients often experience their own lived-bodies with what the phenomenologically oriented anthropologist Byron Good has so appropriately called an "irrational sense of betrayal" (1994b, 127): "I think it's against me, that I have an enemy," some patients with chronic pain have proclaimed.[11] The body-in-pain is experienced as *paradoxical*: it certainly retains the sense of being *my own* body; and yet (as patients struggling with chronic pain so often point out) it has also become something alien, something that resists the self.[12]

Second, by disrupting the usual relation between the self and the body, chronic pain also transforms the person's *self-relation*. Pain takes away from the person the capacity to accomplish some of the most basic activities, thereby robbing the person of self-confidence and self-reliance. If you wonder why one needs a sense of bodily self-reliance, consider how its absence would affect the most basic daily activities, such as walking down the steps, carrying a cup of coffee to the table, or shaking someone's hand. As Eric Cassell puts it, "We need to soar above our bodies . . . to be whole and to grow" (1978, 30). Having lost self-confidence and self-reliance, one feels crippled.

Third, chronic pain disrupts the person's perceptual, affective, and conceptual relation to the world. Blepharitis blinds us, the migraine makes it hard to contemplate our thoughts; an asthma attack forces us to forget our affective relation to others. Chronic pain transforms the body into a living wall that stands between the self and the surrounding world: in extreme cases, the body-in-pain becomes the one and only perceptual, affective, and conceptual object, whose sheer magnitude blocks the person's access to any other object (see Sartre 1956, 404–45 and 460–71).

Fourth and finally, chronic pain unsettles the person's relation with others. This must be understood in three ways. First, one must stress the isolating nature of pain experience. Being in principle nonshareable, pain introduces a breach between the person in pain and everyone else. Second, the experience of pain lies at the limits of understanding. This point has been forcefully stressed in anthropological studies of chronic pain. As Arthur Kleinman has famously put it, "If there is a single experience shared by virtually all chronic pain patients it is that at some point those around them . . . come to question the authenticity of the patient's experience of pain" (1988, 57). In the words of Jean Jackson, "After a while, no-one believes you" (1994, 138).[13] Third, the person suffering from chronic pain becomes dependent upon others. Thus, the relation between the one in pain and others is fundamentally asymmetrical: the other—the very one who cannot understand me—is the only one who can help me overcome my pain.

We can thus say that chronic pain is a rupture that unsettles four of our most fundamental relations: (1) the relation between the self and body; (2) the person's self-relation; (3) the relation between the self and the surrounding world; and (4) the relation between the self and others.[14] Pain is a depersonalizing experience in these four fundamental ways.

CHRONIC PAIN AS REPERSONALIZATION

Despite its depersonalizing nature, chronic pain is also a deeply personal experience. As Drew Leder has insightfully remarked, "Pain *reorganizes* our lived space and time, our relations with others and with ourselves" (1990, 73; emphasis added—SG). The concept of *reorganization* is key in this context: besides disorganizing, pain also reorganizes lived spatiotemporality and the fundamental relations that make up the core of our personal lives.

Although in his reflections on pain and suffering Max Scheler interpreted pain as "death in miniature" (1992, 89), there is a significant difference between the two, and this difference has been especially forcefully described by Viktor von Weizsäcker (2011). According to Weizsäcker, it is a fundamental error to think of pain as though it were a mere sensation. Pain, and especially chronic pain, is not something that we merely live through. Rather, pain, and especially chronic pain, is something that we cannot help but respond

THE PHENOMENOLOGY OF EMBODIED PERSONHOOD   151

to. Weizsäcker qualified the experience of pain as the human exposure to evil. When faced with such afflictions as chronic pain, we cannot help but respond, and the way we respond will prove to be constitutive in a twofold way. How shall I respond to pain? I cannot help but choose a way; and the way I will choose will not only codetermine my experience of pain, but also form the person I will be.[15]

Following Eric Cassell, I would argue that responses to pain are essentially of three different types: *bodily*, *emotive*, and *cognitive*.

1. With regard to bodily responses, consider how our muscles tighten and our posture changes in response to both chronic and acute pain. Almost immediately, such bodily responses become part and parcel of pain experience.[16]

2. With regard to emotive responses, consider how fear, panic, or anger can aggravate the experience of pain. For instance, consider the patient who interprets the pain in his chest as an impending heart attack. The emotions that accompany this interpretation significantly exacerbate his pain experience. Or consider the patient who had an expanding metastatic lesion of the femur (from cancer of the lung). "It was only when the patient was reassured that his leg was not going to be amputated . . . that his pain became controllable" (Cassell 2001, 381).

3. With regard to cognitive responses, consider a patient diagnosed with metastatic carcinoma of the prostate in the lumbar spine. This diagnosis triggered severe pain attacks, which only worsened with time and which led the doctors to diagnose the patient as chronically ill. However, the reason for such severe attacks of pain could not be explained by the disease. These reasons were triggered by the patient's independent discovery that survival is shortest when the metastatic disease affects young men and that metastatic disease has no cure. Clearly, the patient suffered the pain in his body; yet it seems that his pain was of cognitive and not physiological origin. More generally, if I interpret my pain as an expression of an incurable disease, as a test or punishment, my cognitive responses affect the manner in which I live my pain, thereby modifying my experience of pain. Thus, bodily, emotive, and cognitive responses largely make up the painfulness of pain.

These diverse responses to pain are not only co-constitutive of pain experience; these responses also repersonalize the self. While the depersonalizing nature of pain and illness has been addressed in phenomenological literature quite extensively, their repersonalizing dimensions are hardly touched upon either in phenomenology or in pain research in general. Elaine Scarry's (1985) classical study, *The Body in Pain*, provides us with a paradigmatic example of how the emphasis placed on pain's depersonalizing dimensions leads one to overlook its repersonalizing characteristics. According to the central claim put forth in Scarry's study, while pain unmakes the world, work remakes it. That is, while pain is depersonalizing and only depersonalizing, work is, fundamentally, repersonalizing. Insofar as Scarry's analysis is focused on torture, her claim makes good sense. Yet, as Serrano de Haro (2017) has convincingly shown in his recent study, we would be committing a serious mistake if we were to presume that *all* pain has the structure of torture. The distinction Scarry draws between the unmaking of the world and its remaking does not so much indicate a fundamental difference between pain and work, but rather highlights two essential characteristics of chronic pain experience.

In this regard, Viktor von Weizsäcker's writings on pain prove to be remarkably helpful. Weizsäcker distinguishes between three fundamental forms of pain management, identifying them as different forms of the "work of pain" (*Schmerzarbeit*). First, he speaks of a stoic objectification of pain, an objectification that is marked by indifference. Second, he speaks of a battle that one can enter into against one's pain, which ends either in victory or in loss. Third, he also refers to the patient's free capacity to either produce pain in oneself and love it, or bring it to a stop and eliminate it (see Weizsäcker 2011, 273). How exhaustive is this typology? I take it to be indisputable that there are also other ways to confront one's own pain.[17] The fundamental lesson to be learned here concerns the idea that *the way we choose to react to our pain will form the person we will be.*

In Weizsäcker's words, the goal of pain management lies in the overcoming of a separation (*Ent-Scheidung*) between the self and the body; it lies in the reestablishment of a lost unity between myself and my own embodied existence.[18] Yet, as Weizsäcker goes on to say, "Wherever pain passes by, it leaves an inerasable trace *how* it passed by" (2011, 273). This trace of pain is the effect its management has upon our own selfhood: the manner in which I respond to pain is formative of my own personhood.

Recall my earlier claim that pain is depersonalizing in that it unsettles four fundamental relations: (1) the relation between the self and the body; (2) the person's self-relation; (3) the relation between the self and the environment; and (4) the relation between the self and others. The particular emotive and cognitive reactions to pain enable the subject of experience to form anew these four fundamental relations. Thus, if one "gives oneself up" to pain, or

THE PHENOMENOLOGY OF EMBODIED PERSONHOOD 153

"pits oneself against" it; if one "endures," "tolerates," or "enjoys" pain; if one seeks pain or makes efforts to escape it; if one interprets it as a penalty or an atonement, or as a means of purification or correction—these diverse responses to pain enable one to establish a particular kind of relation to one's body, one's self, one's environment, and other selves. By constituting these four fundamental relations, the responses to pain form the person one becomes.

So far, I have emphasized the projective nature of pain experience: the manner in which I respond to pain will form the person I will be. However, the responses to pain are also expressive of the person's past: as addressed in chapter 5, these responses also rely upon the person I already am. In this regard, Thomas Fuchs's (2008) research into the bodily memory of pain (*Schmerzgedächtnis*) is highly informative. According to Fuchs, a bodily reaction, which at first glance seems to be nothing more than a merely mechanical reflex, once subjected to a phenomenological analysis proves to be a response determined by the body's prereflective memory. The body's past experiences largely determine the way the body responds to similar experiences in the future. Our bodily, emotive, and cognitive responses to pain rely upon our past experiences. Moreover, these responses are also formed by our specific interpretation of our experience, which in its own turn often relies upon the experiences of others.

In the literature on chronic pain, Emily Dickinson stressed the forgetfulness of pain especially forcefully:

> Pain has an element of blank;
> It cannot recollect
> When it began, or if there was
> A time when it was not.
>
> *It has no future but itself,*
> *Its infinite realms contain*
> *Its past, enlightened to perceive*
> *New periods of pain.* (1960, 323–24)

In Dickinson's famous lines, everything is presented from pain's point of view, with no reference to the person suffering pain. Although such a characterization of pain highlights pain's dominating nature, the price one thereby pays for pain's personification is a radical depersonalization of the subject of pain. However, it is undeniable that the manner in which one suffers one's pain is largely determined by one's involuntary and unconscious recollection of the past and involuntary and unconscious anticipation of the future. Despite the overwhelming *timelessness* of pain, which Dickinson expresses so powerfully, it would be phenomenologically illegitimate to confine pain within one temporal dimension, namely, that of presence. Largely due to the temporality of pain (due to the manner in which memory and anticipation affect pain experience), the subject of pain should be conceived neither as disembodied consciousness nor as a physiological body, but as the person, as embodied subjectivity.

Pain, and especially chronic pain, is a highly complex phenomenon. Our understanding of pain is significantly enriched if, besides taking into account the physical body's neurophysiological structure, we also pay attention to the person's immersion in the life-world (*Lebenswelt*)—the world of everyday experience, filled with perceived, affective, and practical properties.[19] Without understanding the person's history, self-understanding, relations to others, and lifelong goals; without recognizing the significance of the person's bodily, emotive, and cognitive responses to pain, one can have only a severely limited understanding of pain experience.

IMPLICATIONS FOR THE PHENOMENOLOGY OF MEDICINE

Of what significance is such a phenomenology of embodied personhood for the phenomenology of medicine? The foregoing analysis invites us to reconceptualize the fundamental distinctions entrenched in this field of research: the distinctions between psychogenic and organic pain, between illness and disease, and between healing and curing.

Let us begin with the distinction between psychogenic and organic pain. I argued earlier that one of the chief limitations of the exclusively neurophysiological approach to pain concerns its failure to recognize the existence of psychogenic pain. Such a form of resistance to the neurophysiological approach can easily lead to misunderstandings. To be sure, chronic pain can be triggered by either organic or psychogenic causes. Yet to this it is crucial to add that chronic pain, which derives from organic causes, is never only organic, just as chronic pain, which is psychogenic, is never only psychological. Put otherwise, it is crucial not to misinterpret the distinction between organic and psychogenic pain as a distinction between physiological

THE PHENOMENOLOGY OF EMBODIED PERSONHOOD   155

and psychological pain—a misinterpretation that would immediately re-introduce the schism between body (the subject of physiological pain) and mind (the subject of psychological pain), while leaving it unexplained how these presumed "subjects of pain" (that is, body and mind) relate to each other. The phenomenological identification of the person as the subject of pain is meant to recapture the living unity that binds the mind to the body as well as to denounce the tendency to treat them as independent entities. Thus, first, to claim that the person is the subject of pain is to suggest that this subject is also *embodied*, *ensouled*, and *encultured*. If so, then, second, when it comes to chronic pain, there is no such thing as purely physiological pain or purely psychological pain. Rather, purely physiological, just as purely psychological accounts address only parts of a larger whole, and this larger whole—namely, the person—is not reducible to the sum of its parts. No matter what the causes of pain might be, the concrete bodily, emotive, and cognitive responses enable the person to invest the physiological tissue damage and psychological traumata with a sense, through which the person's unique experience of pain is formed.

The temporality of chronic pain proscribes the possibility of explaining such a complex phenomenon as chronic pain in terms of its origin. Just as chronic pain is not reducible to its origin, so its treatment cannot be reduced to its origin's treatment. If one agrees that responses to pain—bodily, emotive, and cognitive—are part and parcel of the very experience of pain, then one also has to concede that chronic pain is never purely physiological or purely psychological. This established distinction conceals the personal meaning with which the sufferer has invested her pain.

Let us turn to the other two distinctions mentioned above: illness/disease and healing/curing. According to these established distinctions, which are deeply entrenched in the phenomenology of medicine, while the concept of disease stands for actual pathology and pathophysiology, the concept of illness refers to the patient's experience. Correlated with this distinction, there is another established distinction between healing and curing: just as one cannot cure illness, but only the disease, so one cannot heal disease, but only illness.

The phenomenological analysis offered in this chapter brings into question the validity of these distinctions.[20] Why are these distinctions so important? Arguably, their introduction was meant to provide the phenomenology of medicine with its raison d'être. While disease constitutes the subject matter of neurophysiology, illness is a distinctly phenomenological concept; so also, while healing is correlated with illness, curing is correlated with disease. Yet I would argue that these distinctions have outlived their function and that, presently, they leave phenomenology with an artificially confined domain that it sooner or later must transgress.

Consider Eric Cassell's description of how the patient personalizes the disease. A patient who develops a life-threatening disease will soon know the worst that can happen. Normally, those who know the worst expect the worst. Moreover, those who expect the worst act in a way that brings the worst. Cassell (2001, 382) is right to maintain that we face here a self-fulfilling prophecy, brought about by the person's reaction to the disease. But this means that through the bodily, emotive, and cognitive responses, the person transforms not only the illness, but also the actual disease. Just as the person's bodily, emotive, and cognitive responses to pain change the course of pain experience, so these responses also affect the disease. As Cassell puts it, "By virtue of their behavior—for example, the doctors they see, medications they take, changes in life pattern from sleep to food—they change the expression of the pathology and the behavior of the disease, as a result of the person they are" (2001, 382).

If the person's bodily, emotive, and cognitive responses have pathophysiological consequences, then the phenomenology of medicine cannot be limited to the analysis of illness, but must also address the disease. Moreover, if the person's feelings, thoughts, and behavior modify the behavior of the disease, then to change the course of the disease, one must directly confront the patient's bodily, emotive, and cognitive responses to pain and illness. To do so, one must supplement curing with healing.

In the phenomenology of medicine, one often comes across the view that runs along the following lines: "In order to heal the patient, it is not enough to cure the disease. The medical establishment must also take the necessary precautions that the process of curing the disease does not have adverse consequences to the patient." Phenomenologically informed studies of illness expressed this thesis with the help of the distinctions between illness and disease as well as healing and curing. When I claim that the recognition of the person as the subject of pain brings these distinctions into question, I mean thereby that just as curing the disease constitutes a part of the process of healing the patient, so healing the patient constitutes a part of curing the disease.

PAIN AS AN EXPRESSIBLE PHENOMENON: THE BASIC ELEMENTS OF A PHENOMENOLOGY OF LISTENING

According to one of the most established claims put forth in phenomenologically oriented literature on pain, pain is a fundamentally nonshareable experience. This insight, whose phenomenological origins lead back to Stumpf's reflections, also played a central role in Scheler's writings, specifically in the context of his stratification of the emotional life (see Scheler 1973, 328–44). According to Scheler, it is precisely the nonshareable nature of pain that allows us to distinguish it from other related phenomena, such as grief and despair. This insight also played an important role in Viktor von Weizsäcker's famous lecture from 1926, "Die Schmerzen" (2011, 265). More recently, we also come across this insight in Elaine Scarry's (1985) study *The Body in Pain*, where pain's nonshareability is equated with its nonexpressibility. Still more recently, Drew Leder has argued for this thesis in *The Absent Body*: "But pain strikes one alone. Unlike the feel of the cool wind, pain is marked by an interiority that another cannot share" (1990, 74). This insight is deeply rooted not only in phenomenologically oriented studies of pain. As John Updike elegantly puts it,

> [Pain] shows us, too, how those around us
> do not, and cannot share
> our being; though men talk animatedly
> and challenge silence with laughter
> and women bring their engendering smiles
> and eyes of famous mercy,
> these kind things slide away like rain beating on a filthy window
> when pain interposes. (1983, 34)

There is indeed a good sense in which the *experience* of pain is nonshareable: I cannot live through your pain, just as you cannot live through mine. Pain introduces a breach between what is my own and what is not my own. As I argued in chapter 5, if, by impossibility, I were to experience your pain, this would prove to be the most egoistic act imaginable, for it would amount to appropriating your body and rendering it my own. The experience of pain delivers the body-in-pain as *my* body; *pain individualizes*. However, while the *experience* of pain is nonshareable, it nonetheless is always possible (although by no means easy) to bring this experience to expression. By saying this, I am arguing against one of Elaine Scarry's (1985) central claims in *The Body in Pain*, where she took pain's nonshareability to mean that the experience of pain shatters language and is in principle nonexpressible. Scarry's arguments to the contrary notwithstanding,[21] it is important to emphasize that we do have at our disposal various languages of pain—autobiographic, medical, literary, and scientific, to mention the four most significant categories. Let us not overlook that Scarry's own book is one particular way of bringing pain experience to expression.

The experience of pain *is* expressible. The explicit recognition of this matter is of profound importance for those who suffer from chronic pain, for the discursive process in which one comes to terms with one's own pain experience is of therapeutic significance. Borrowing an expression from Daniel Benveniste (2015), one could qualify chronic pain experience as a cap covering untold or unelaborated stories. When these stories are told, examined, and retold, this very process of bringing one's experience to expression has a curative effect. This is not just a matter of getting things off one's chest, but of coming to terms with one's own experience, which means that bringing pain to expression fulfills not just a mimetic but also a disclosive function. These untold stories are not there ready-made, waiting to be told. In a sense, they need to be created, yet only in a sense, since their creation cannot be arbitrary. To have a curative effect, these stories must be disclosive: they must highlight what one for the most part overlooks and ignores; they must be both eye-opening and faithful to one's own experience.

Let us supplement our analysis of pain's depersonalizing and repersonalizing characteristics with further reflections on the therapeutic significance of *dialogue* and *listening*. As S. Kay Toombs (1993) has argued in *The Meaning of Illness*, the patient and the physician experience and conceptualize the patient's affliction in fundamentally different ways. While the patient conceives of pain as a lived-experience that affects her lived-body (*Leib*), the physician thematizes it as a collection of physical signs and symptoms that disrupt the normal functioning of the patient's physical body (*Körper*). For this reason, far from representing the same reality, for the patient and the physician, the phenomenon of pain represents two distinct realities, which, in light of the foregoing analysis, we could characterize as a personalistic and a naturalistic reality. So as to overcome this ontological gap, it is necessary that "the physician explicitly attend to the lived experience when devising therapeutic goals" (Toombs 1993, xvi). Both the patient and the physician, besides inhabiting different realities, are also motivated to overcome the ontological gap that separates them. The patient, besides living through pain at the level of immediate experience, is also aware that the biomedical explanation of pain holds the promise of liberating her from affliction, and thus is motivated to trust pain's biomedical treatments. So also, the physician is motivated to understand the patient's pain not only as a symptom of disease, but also as a depersonalizing and repersonalizing experience, for the liberation of the patient from pain's dehumanizing effects constitutes one of the central goals of his professional praxis.

Only through dialogue can the patient and the physician overcome the ontological gap that separates them. Especially in the context of such afflictions as chronic pain, which typically is experienced in the absence of any detectable tissue damage, living dialogue between physician and patient obtains preeminent therapeutic significance. A meaningful dialogue, however, rests on the shoulders of *listening*.[22] In the present context, I employ the concept of listening in a very broad sense: it refers to attentiveness, which is by no means reducible to listening to words alone. Just as important is the listening to silences, visual appearances, changes in posture, and a whole variety of other forms of nonverbal communication. Listening is not just a matter of hearing the patient's words, but also recognizing the values that inform those words, as well as the value with which the person has invested her pain. It is not just a matter of identifying the symptoms, but also recognizing the specific meaning they have for the patient, the specific relation the person has toward her pain. It is not just a matter of understanding the person's relation to her pain, but also how it affects the person's relation to others, and to her own future plans. It is not just a matter of understanding the person's current condition, but also understanding how her understanding of this condition is formed by her past. Without understanding the person's history, her insertion in the life-world, and her relation to others, as well as her orientation toward her future, one cannot understand pain's personal significance.

One can single out narrative medicine (see esp. Charon 2006) and psychoanalysis (Akhtar 2012; and Benveniste 2015) as the two fields of research that pay special attention to the function of listening in the framework of a medical encounter between the patient and the physician. What can phenomenology contribute in such a framework? There are at least five fundamental contributions it can make. First, phenomenology can serve the function of clarifying the philosophical presuppositions that underlie these mostly empirically oriented analyses into the function and significance of listening. Such, in fact, has been the goal of this chapter. The philosophical presuppositions that have been addressed here concern the recognition of the primacy of the personalistic attitude over the naturalistic. Moreover, they concern the clarification of what it means to claim that the patient is a person and what it means to recognize that chronic pain is both a depersonalizing and a repersonalizing experience. Second, phenomenology can also provide a philosophical clarification of the fundamental goals that must guide the concrete analyses of listening in the empirical fields of research. One can characterize these goals as the overcoming of the depersonalizing tendency that we have come across in pain experience and that of enabling the patient to reconstitute the four fundamental relations (relation to oneself, one's body, others, and the world) that make up the patient's personal existence. Building on the basis of S. Kay Toombs's (1987) analysis, one could further say that the goal is to close the ontological gap that has opened between the worlds of the patient and the physician. The goal is to show that the transition from the personalistic to the naturalistic attitude was a necessary detour that one had to take so as to confront the patient's affliction not only naturalistically but also personalistically.

Third, it is crucial to recognize that the available discussions of the therapeutic role of listening are of a limited scope. Both in narrative medicine and in psychoanalysis, listening is addressed as a capacity of the physician and the analyst. For this reason, much of the discussion in these fields centers on the methodological issues surrounding different types and functions of listening. One has to stress, however, that the encounter between the patient and the physician constitutes neither the only nor even the privileged framework within which listening can have therapeutic significance. In this regard, phenomenology can perform the crucial function of broadening the analytic framework. The capacity to listen on the part of the patient's family and friends may also have a curative effect upon the patient. If listening is called for due to pain's depersonalizing nature, then insofar as listening is conceived of as the function of the physician or the analyst alone, its curative effects will be only limited.

Fourth, phenomenology also requires that we direct our attention not only to the physician but also to the patient, and supplement listening to others with listening to ourselves. In narrative medicine and psychoanalysis, listening is for the most part addressed as a capacity of the physician or the analyst at the expense of focusing on the patient's own need for listening. Presumably, the medical establishment robs the patient of his voice, even though he has a burning need to speak; it also methodologically proscribes the physician's capacity to hear the patient, even though he cannot fulfill his medical obligations without listening. Having identified the problem in such a fashion, one proceeds to argue that to remedy the situation, one needs to enable the patient to tell his story and one needs to teach the physician how to listen. Paradoxically, such a way of resolving the problem can have adverse effects upon the patient. By enabling the patient to speak and the physician to listen, the prevailing accounts of listening inadvertently reduce the patient to a witness of the case, who is compelled to tell a story but is not in the position to understand it. In this way, paradoxically, the dominant accounts of listening do not diminish but rather exacerbate pain's depersonalizing effects. We need to find a way to counteract this adverse tendency, and in this regard, phenomenology can perform a highly helpful function. It can bring to light that listening is able to perform a curative role if, and only if, it results in the patient's own capacity to listen to experience. For listening to have a therapeutic effect, the patient must be capable not only of telling a disclosive story, but also of deciphering what the story means. Listening is therapeutic if, and only if, it enables the sufferer to come to terms with his own experience.

In this regard, phenomenology contests the objectivistic prejudice that is deeply rooted in many fields. By objectivistic prejudice, one is to understand the established view that listening to oneself is unavoidably arbitrary and subjective and that it therefore needs to be replaced with listening to others, for only the latter can be methodologically reliable and result in intersubjectively verifiable clarifications.[23] Resisting such a deeply rooted bias toward third-person accounts of experience, phenomenology invites us to grant listening-to-oneself incontestable phenomenological priority over listening-to-others, taken in all the diverse forms addressed above.

Fifth, this insight leads to the further realization that to understand one's own long-lasting and depersonalizing chronic pain personalistically and not naturalistically, an inner dialogue is called for and that listening-to-oneself is one of its fundamental components. Within such a framework, we stumble across the fifth contribution that phenomenology can make to the ongoing discussions of listening. Let us stress that not all listening, just as not all dialogue, is meaningful per se. Dialogue is not meaningful when someone repeats something ad nauseam, or when one does all that is in one's power to deceive the listener, or, finally, when dialogue serves only the function of an instinctual and emotional discharge (see Akhtar 2012, 125–43). Phenomenology provides an exceptionally refined and sophisticated methodological apparatus to open up an inner dialogue in a meaningful and promising way. Especially due to its methods of the epoché and the phenomenological reduction, it enables one to liberate one's experience from its naturalistic misconceptions. In light of its fundamental methodological distinction between the personalistic and the naturalistic attitudes, it enables one to recapture the manifold ways in which pain affects the sufferer.

~

In the earlier chapters of this study, my goal was to clarify the fundamental methodological principles that must underlie phenomenologically oriented pain research, and, on the basis of these principles, to work out a novel conception of pain. In the present chapter, I have aimed to supplement the foregoing analysis with a further investigation into what the phenomenology of pain can contribute to philosophical anthropology. Within such a framework, it is not enough to raise the question concerning the specific ways in which human beings experience pain. More importantly, it is necessary to ask, What can a phenomenologically oriented study of pain contribute to the philosophical understanding of those beings we identify as human?[24] Such a switch in thematic focus was coupled with a shift in methodological orientation. While in my foregoing analysis I mainly relied on the principles of static phenomenology (epoché, the reduction, eidetic and factual variation), in this chapter my reflections have been based primarily on the methodological guidelines of genetic methodology.

Along with Donn Welton (2003b), one can conceive of the transition from static to genetic phenomenology as the overcoming of a number of abstractions that we come across in static phenomenology. One of the most fundamental of these abstractions concerns the phenomenological understanding of *subjectivity*. While static phenomenology conceptualizes subjectivity as the pure ego, genetic phenomenology conceives of the pure ego as an abstract structure of the concrete ego, which is further conceptualized as a *person*. My goal in the present chapter has been to clarify what the phenomenological concept of personhood means, which in its own turn provided the phenomenological basis to demonstrate that the processes of depersonalization and repersonalization constitute the essential characteristics of chronic pain experience. In its own turn, the analyses of these essential features have enabled us to revisit some fundamental distinctions that are deeply entrenched in the phenomenology of medicine. Last but not least, the phenomenology of personhood here offered has enabled us to reevaluate the presumably nonshareable nature of pain experience and to further address the therapeutic significance of dialogue in general, and listening in particular.

The overcoming of the abstract conception of subjectivity does not constitute the only transformation with which the transition from static to genetic phenomenology is associated. Rather, the novel conception of the person that we come across in genetic phenomenology proves to be inseparable from a novel conception of the *world*. In static phenomenology the world is conceived of as the correlate of certain experience-patterns (see Husserl 1983, 93). Conceived in such a fashion, the world can be brought to a hypothetical annihilation, which in its own turn would not result in the hypothetical annihilation of consciousness. For this reason, Husserl (1983, §49) notoriously argues that transcendental consciousness is the residuum after the nullifying of the world. By contrast, in genetic phenomenology the world is conceptualized not as a correlate of experience, but as a *horizon* and as *a life-world*. These two transformations (the transformation in the phenomenological concept of subjectivity and in the phenomenological concept of the world) make up the thematic basis that underlies the distinction between static and genetic phenomenology. It remains to be seen in the next chapter that the concrete ways in which one lives one's pain are tied to the concrete ways in which one's existence is rooted in the life-world. While focusing on this theme, we will continue our inquiry into what the phenomenology of pain can contribute to philosophical anthropology.

CHAPTER 7

· ·

PAIN AND THE LIFE-WORLD

SOMATIZATION AND PSYCHOLOGIZATION

In this study, pain has been conceptualized as *an aversive bodily feeling with a distinct experiential quality, which can be given only in original firsthand experience, either as a feeling-sensation or as an emotion*. I have argued that this definition, which entails seven constitutive features, is grounded in phenomenological evidence; and in different chapters of this study, I have clarified each of these features. However, one might still find the last characterization questionable and one might be willing to ask: *What does it mean to claim that pain is experienced as an emotion?*

The claim is not self-evident. As we know from chapter 2, especially in phenomenology, it is common to distinguish between different kinds of feelings. On the one hand, there are those feelings that Stumpf has labeled as feeling-sensations (*Gefühlsempfindungen*), whose distinctive characteristic is that they are nonintentional. On the other hand, there are those feelings we identify as emotions, and the essential feature of those feelings is that they are intentional. One thus commonly claims: fear is fear of x, love is love of y, anger is anger over z. By contrast, it seems that pain is not of, for, or over anything. It seems that pain is a feeling-sensation that belongs to a different category than emotions.

As I have already argued in chapter 2, this typology of feelings is not convincing. Admittedly, we are all familiar with the experience of pain that is lived as a mere feeling-sensation, free of emotional components. This is especially true of transient pain. Yet we are also familiar with different kinds of pain, namely, those that are filled with emotive dimensions. We cannot understand what these pains are—and such pains are most common—when we draw such a sharp distinction between nonintentional feeling-sensations and intentional feelings, which include emotions. Our philosophical understanding of pain is artificially constrained when we subscribe to the view that partitions feelings into different categories, as though the feelings belonging to these categories had nothing in common with each other. To show that this is the case, in this chapter I will focus on somatization and psychologization, which bring to light to what astonishing degree, and in what curious ways, pain is an emotionally charged experience.

Cultural anthropology, cultural psychopathology, psychoanalysis, and psychosomatic medicine are the main fields of research that concern themselves with somatization and psychologization. A phenomenological analysis of pain provides us with a possibility to open a dialogue between phenomenology and these disciplines. This can be done in two ways. First, one can demonstrate how phenomenological analyses of the body, the person, and the life-world underpin concrete empirical investigations that we come across in these fields of research. In this regard, the significance of phenomenological analysis consists in its capacity to broaden the analytic field of pain research. It is not enough to conceptualize pain physiologically, since pain concerns not only the objective body (*Körper*), but also the *lived-body* (*Leib*); not only the lived-body, but also the *person*; not only the person, but also the *life-world*. It is this latter qualification that will be my focus here: *pain unfolds in the horizon of the life-world*. I will contend that it is precisely the rootedness of our experiences in the life-world that renders such processes as somatization and psychologization philosophically intelligible. Second, besides inquiring into the significance of phenomenological analysis of the life-world for our understanding of somatization and psychologization, I will also inquire into how the concrete analysis of these processes can enrich the phenomenological conception of the life-world. I will contend that a philosophical inquiry into the conditions that underlie these processes brings to light that it is not enough to speak of the life-world as a home-world. In an important sense, the life-world is also a world in which the sufferer feels homeless. With reference to the analysis of pain and embodiment that was offered in chapter 4, we could qualify our relation to the life-world analogously to our relation to our own bodies. The body-in-pain is my own, yet it demonstrates resistance to being appropriated as my own (as we saw, it resists being the zero point of orientation, the organ of my will, and the expression of the spirit, while it nonetheless remains the field of sensings). So also, the sufferer's life-world is his home, yet at the same time, he finds himself homeless in his homeworld.

SOMATIZATION AND PSYCHOLOGIZATION

"Somatization" is an umbrella term that covers multiple expressions of personal and social distress in an idiom of bodily complaints. It embraces a large variety of ways in which the sufferer transforms nonbodily modes of distress into embodied feelings. By contrast, psychologization denotes the expression of bodily distress in an idiom of psychological complaints. It refers to a variety of ways in which somatic suffering gets to be refashioned into various forms of psychological distress. Thus, a person suffering from depression will, as a rule, manifest a whole array of somatic complaints, such as bodily fatigue and various forms of bodily pain. So also, a cancer victim will develop various forms of psychic complaints, which will add another dimension to his somatic suffering.

Just as the concept of feelings, and just as the concept of pain, so also the concepts of somatization and psychologization are ambiguous. With reference to Mark Sullivan and Wayne Katon's (1993) study of somatization, one could distinguish between three forms of somatization and psychologization: *acute*, *subacute*, and *chronic*. Acute somatization and psychologization are related to traumatic situations the person finds herself in or stressful experiences the person has to go through; subacute somatization and psychologization arise due to acute psychiatric and somatic disorders; and, finally, chronic somatization and psychologization are linked to chronic psychiatric and chronic somatic disorders. A typology such as this one enables us to avoid a common error of reducing somatization and psychologization to chronic forms of suffering. Thinking of chronic somatization and psychologization either as the only form or as the most common form of somatization and psychologization has led to the regrettable supposition that they both derive from an inherent, and possibly genetic, property of individuals, which can be addressed only at the level of organic pathology. Resisting this line of thought, which reduces somatization and psychologization to rare occurrences and overlooks the overwhelming role played by the cultural environment, one must stress that chronic forms of somatization and psychologization are rare instances of somatization and psychologization. As Sullivan and Katon put it, "Somatization is the rule, not the exception"; it is "among the most common of medical phenomena" (1993, 147). It should therefore not surprise us that, as Laurence J. Kirmayer has it, "somatization has been found wherever it has been sought" (1984a, 161).

The fact that somatization and psychologization are ubiquitous phenomena brings into question the common view that pain is a feeling-sensation, not an emotion. Admittedly, pain is in many ways unlike emotions, such as fear, anger, or love. It does not intentionally bind us to objects of value, at least directly. However, pain does entail emotional characteristics, and research on somatization and psychologization suggests that this happens almost as a rule. In the case of somatization, pain turns out to be a somatic expression of various forms of emotional distress; in the case of psychologization, pain manifests itself as a somatic disturbance that underlies and gives rise to emotions. With this in mind, we could say that just as our understanding of various forms of pain remains curtailed for as long as we do not establish a bond that ties pain to emotions, so also, our understanding of emotions remains deficient for as long as we do not link them to bodily feelings.

So far, we are still operating on the basis of a preliminary understanding of somatization and psychologization. It is clear that our understanding of these processes relies on a certain conception of how *soma* and *psyche* relate to each other. It remains unclear, however, how exactly this interrelationship is to be understood. It can be understood in at least five ways: in terms of *emphasis, expression, interpretation, transformation*, and *denial*. First, somatization and psychologization can be understood as tendencies to *emphasize* somatic or psychological symptoms when presenting psychopathology.[1] Second, somatization can be understood as the *expression* of personal and social distress in physical ways; by contrast, psychologization can be understood as the *expression* of bodily distress in psychological ways. Third, somatization could be qualified as a *reinterpretation* of personal, psychological, or social problems as somatic problems. Analogously, psychologization can be said to be a *reinterpretation* of somatic problems as personal, psychological, or social problems. Fourth, somatization can also be understood as the *transformation* of the body into a metaphor of emotional and social experiences. So also, psychologization can be understood as the *transformation* of the psyche into a metaphor of somatic feelings. Fifth, somatization could be determined as a *denial* that one's suffering is psychological, while psychologization could be qualified as a *denial* of the somatic nature of one's suffering. As forms of denial, the processes of somatization could be further interpreted in two ways: either as a *lack of awareness* or as a *form of self-delusion*.

Following Kirmayer's (1984a, 1984b) outstanding studies of somatization, one can complement such a typology with a further threefold distinction (1984a, 159–60). First, somatization can be understood as the presentation of physical symptoms *in the absence of* organic pathology. Correlatively, psychologization could be said to be a presentation of psychological symptoms *in the absence of* psychological pathology. Second, one could also conceive of somatization as the presentation of somatic symptoms *in place of* a personal or social problem. So also, one can think of psychologization as the presentation of psychological symptoms *in place of* somatic problems. Third, one can also think of somatization as a *pattern of mechanisms* by which emotions give rise to somatic signs and symptoms. So also, one can conceive of psychologization as a *pattern of mechanisms* by which somatic feelings of distress provoke psychological signs and symptoms.

These different ways of typologizing somatization and psychologization share a common feature: they all involve an *element of divergence* between what the sufferer experiences and how he understands, interprets, or qualifies his experience. In the case of somatization, the sufferer identifies his suffering as organic, although his suffering derives from either interpersonal relations or emotional distress. In the case of psychologization, the psychological distress that affects the sufferer is of organic origins.

The discrepancy in question can be interpreted in two ways. First, one could argue that the processes of somatization and psychologization are instances of reflective misunderstanding and confusion. By confusing the nature of her distress, the sufferer misrepresents the nature of her experience. Second, one could also interpret somatization and psychologization as defense mechanisms. On such a view, the sufferer either explicitly or implicitly knows that she qualifies her suffering incorrectly, yet, despite this knowledge, she chooses to distort the nature of her experience. As we will still see, the reasons for such a deliberate distortion pertain to political and social pressure as well as stigmatization.

SOMATIZATION, PSYCHOLOGIZATION, AND THEIR ORIGINS IN EXPERIENCE

Somatization and psychologization do not just open a gap between actual experience, on the one hand, and the sufferer's understanding of experience, on the other. Rather, through these processes, experience itself undergoes a transformation, as it mutates into something other than it previously was. Somatization and psychologization are such processes that bring psychic and somatic experiences into fusion with each other. We can now ask: How can somatic pain and psychic suffering fuse with each other and become inseparable?

Such a fusion occurs either when a purely somatic reaction to a somatic rupture, or when a purely psychological reaction to a psychic rupture, proves ineffective. When exactly do we experience the ineffectiveness of such seemingly appropriate responses to somatic pain and psychic suffering? This occurs when, despite such "appropriate" reactions, pain and suffering continue to linger and refuse to cease. When "appropriate" responses (somatic responses to somatic pain and psychological responses to psychological suffering) prove ineffective, the sufferer obtains the motivation to supplement them with "inappropriate" responses (psychological responses to somatic pain or somatic responses to psychological suffering). Under such circumstances, which are by no means unusual, pain and suffering join hands with each other.

However, psychological responses to somatic rupture and somatic responses to psychological rupture are not yet instances of somatization and psychologization. Somatization is not just a matter of a somatic response to psychological rupture, but the expression, reinterpretation, and transformation of psychic trauma as though it were somatic. Analogously, psychologization is not reducible to a psychological response to somatic trauma, but rather is the expression, reinterpretation, and transformation of somatic trauma as though it were psychic. We thus need to ask: What could motivate the somatizing and psychologizing sufferer to play hide-and-seek with himself and reinterpret the phenomenal nature of his lived-experience? The research we come across in cultural anthropology, cultural psychopathology, psychoanalysis, and psychosomatic medicine demonstrates that the reasons are numerous and highly diverse. Such transformative and reinterpretive acts can be triggered both internally and externally. They can derive from the sufferer's traumatic past, or his incapacity to express his lived-experience, or the sociopolitical frameworks that delegitimize direct expression of his lived-experience.

In this regard, the research we come across in medical anthropology is quite telling. First and foremost, I have in mind the work of Arthur Kleinman and Joan Kleinman (2007, 468–74), who conducted research on the widespread outbursts of neurasthenia in China after the Cultural Revolution, and argued that these outbursts were widespread instances of somatization. Since the political framework did not legitimize critical discourse on the cultural revolution, forms of bodily complaint provided the only safe way to express the personal meaning that the revolution had for the sufferers.

During the Great Proletarian Cultural Revolution, all mental illness, including, most notably, depression, had been called into question by the Maoists as wrong political thinking. . . . Indeed, neurasthenia is a much safer, and more readily accessible and widely shared, public idiom of frustration and demoralization. . . . Though most demoralization relates to local issues in work and family, for some this is a dual discourse (overt physical complaints, covert political ones) to express dissatisfaction with the broader political situation. . . . Our analysis suggests that in spite of the undoubtedly great international professional pressures on Chinese psychiatry to recast neurasthenia as depression, neurasthenia and depression have a much more complex relationship, and the former, not the latter, is a more socially suitable and culturally approved diagnostic category in Chinese society. (Kleinman and Kleinman 2007, 471–72)

Other anthropologists have offered studies of nerve-related illnesses in the Mediterranean and South America, and in a similar fashion argued that under particular regimes, physical and mental illness provided the only safe way to express the effects of poverty and hunger.[2] In her study of hunger and its complex relation to the diseases of the nerves in Northeast Brazil, Nancy Scheper-Hughes writes:

There was a time, even at the start of the politically repressive years of the mid-1960s, when the people of the Alto spoke freely of fainting from hunger. Today one hears of people fainting from "weakness of nerves" or nerves, a presumed personal deficiency. There was a time not long ago when people of the Alto understood nervousness (and rage) as a primary symptom of hunger, as the *delírio da fome*. Today hunger (like racism) is a disallowed discourse in the shantytowns of Bom Jesus da Mata, and the rage and the dangerous madness of hunger have been metaphorized. (2007, 460)

For our purposes, these few references to anthropological studies of somatization will suffice. They provide ample evidence to support the claim that more often than not, pain is neither purely physiological nor purely psychological. Almost as a rule, pain is a mosaic of physiological, psychic, cultural, historical, and social factors, unified in the framework of the personal meaning.

THE PHENOMENOLOGY OF SOMATIZATION
AND PSYCHOLOGIZATION

Having identified different senses in which we can speak of somatization and psychologization, and having accounted for the common reasons that motivate the sufferer to become a somatizing or a psychologizing agent, we can now turn to the question that is of central importance for us: *What contribution can phenomenology make in this field of research?*[3]

The main disciplines that study somatization and psychologization—cultural anthropology, cultural psychopathology, psychoanalysis, and psychosomatic medicine—are largely preoccupied with two sets of issues: they strive to identify different *motivations* that underlie somatization and psychologization; they also strive to depict the different *mechanisms* of somatization and psychologization. We nonetheless need to ask: *What are the conditions that need to be met for such processes as somatization and psychologization to be possible?* To formulate this question more precisely: *What must a human being be like if he is to be capable of somatizing and psychologizing his experiences?* While it is not the task of these disciplines to answer this question, phenomenology provides us with the conceptual tools to address it.

It is clear that somatization and psychologization rely on a curious interconnection between organic pathology and psychosocial distress. However, neither cultural anthropology, nor cultural psychopathology, nor psychoanalysis, nor, finally, psychosomatic medicine strives to clarify those conditions that make such an interconnection possible. What is more, these disciplines sometimes rely on imprecise conceptions of *psyche* and *soma*, which make such interaction quite impossible. I would contend that such phenomenological concepts as the *lived-body* and *embodied personhood* are the fundamental theoretical presuppositions that underpin concrete empirical analyses of these processes. With the help of these phenomenological concepts, we can make good sense of the interaction of *soma* and *psyche* without any need of clarifying this interaction on the basis of questionable presuppositions. Building on the basis of these phenomenological concepts, one no longer needs to clarify how *soma* and *psyche* relate to each other: once interpreted phenomenologically, they prove to be abstract parts that belong to a concrete whole.

In the foregoing chapters, we have had plenty of opportunities to see that we misunderstand various forms of pain when we conceive of pain in exclusively physiological terms. *Pain is not a physiological phenomenon.* It affects not the physical body (*Körper*), but the lived-body (*Leib*). As we further saw, one cannot stop with this realization. Pain does not affect only the lived-body; rather, the subject of pain is the embodied subjectivity. Yet even this realization determines the field of pain research too narrowly. To this one can further add that *pain unfolds in the horizon of the life-world*. I would contend that these phenomenological themes constitute the fundamental conditions that underlie empirical research on somatization and psychologization. Insofar as pain affects the embodied subjectivity, conceived of as the person in the life-world, it becomes not only understandable how such disciplines as cultural anthropology, cultural psychopathology, psychoanalysis, and psychosomatic medicine can enrich our understanding of pain, but also, and more specifically, how organic pathology can be a symptom of psychosocial distress, and vice versa.

THE LIFE-WORLD AS THE *WHEREFROM, WHEREIN,* AND *WHERETO* OF EXPERIENCE

What could it possibly mean to claim that pain unfolds in the horizon of the life-world? Husserl designates the life-world as "the only real world, the one that is actually given through perception"; he further describes it as "the original ground of theoretical and practical life" (1970, 49). These qualifications highlight the phenomenological primacy of the world conceived of as the life-world over the world conceived of as nature, and, correlatively, the phenomenological fact that the naturalistic conception of the world is derived from the personalistic. Conceived of as the life-world, the world is the practical horizon in which we act, judge, and live our everyday lives. The life-world is the realm of original self-evidences, the universe of what is intuitable.[4] The life-world is the world of actions and affections, of plans, feelings, and evaluations. It is a pretheoretical world, a perceptual and practical world, in which persons live and act.

The life-world is the world to which the person, conceived of as the subject of actions, feelings, and thoughts, is passively exposed and in which he is actively engaged. It is a world that is transformed by the person's actions, just as it itself transforms the person. Not only is the life-world the "grounding soil" (*gründende Boden*) of the scientifically determined nature. Besides functioning as the ground, the life-world also functions as the universal horizon that encompasses all activities, including the scientific ones (see Husserl

1970, 131). The life-world, taken in its concreteness, is fundamentally and irreducibly intersubjective, sociocultural, and historical. This is important for our purposes, since different forms of distress derive from personal interrelations, which include not only face-to-face encounters with others, but also far less direct relations—personal, cultural, historical, and institutional—which ultimately constitute the social, historical, cultural, and political frameworks of our everyday worlds. On the one hand, these forms of distress, taken in their unrestrictive generality, are the sources of somatization. On the other hand, somatic pain can also be translated into these forms of distress, and when this happens, we are confronted with psychologization.

The qualification of the life-world as a horizon is ambiguous. On the one hand, the life-world, conceived of as a surrounding world, is a horizon that is marked by familiarity. In this regard, Husserl speaks of the life-world as a *homeworld* (*Heimwelt*). He qualifies the homeworld as a world that is shared by a historical community, and he further argues that the homeworld is constituted by means of *concordant* experience (*einstimmige Erfahrung*).[5] We are to distinguish the homeworld from the alien-worlds (*Fremdwelten*), the worlds of other historical communities that are characterized by other practices, traditions, and worldviews. In this regard, we can speak of the life-world as a horizon of unfamiliarity, of a life-world that stretches beyond the reach of our own concordant experience.

We will still have reasons to come back to Husserl's conception of the homeworld. Before we do so, we can ask: Of what significance is the phenomenological thematization of the life-world for our understanding of somatization and psychologization? We can say that somatization and psychologization are possible if, and only if, the subject of pain is the person, conceived of as the acting, feeling, and thinking subject in the life-world, conceived of as a particular homeworld. The rootedness of the person in the life-world, conceived of as the intersubjective world and, more precisely, as the historical and sociopolitical homeworld, constitutes the fundamental presupposition of concrete empirical research on somatization and psychologization. Empirical investigations of these processes presuppose that pain is a human experience, which at one and the same time is physiological, psychological, cultural, historical, social, and personal. So also, they presuppose that pain is a sociocultural phenomenon, for only so can we conceive of certain types of pain as forms of indirect expression of social conflicts, as a defense mechanism against stigmatization, or as a help-seeking behavior. The conception of pain as a human experience and as a sociocultural phenomenon presupposes that the subject of pain is a person in the life-world.

One can conceive of the life-world in three complementary ways: as the *wherefrom*, the *wherein*, and the *whereto* of experience. The world-horizon is the ultimate ground from which experience arises; it is the fundamental framework within which experience unfolds; it undergoes an enrichment of sense itself in virtue of the historicity of experience. More precisely, the life-world is the *wherefrom* of experience insofar as through customs and traditions it has always already been structured as a homeworld. So also, the life-world is the *wherein* of experience in that it is constituted as a set of sense configurations within which the things we encounter in our experience obtain their meaning and significance. The life-world is the *whereto* of experience in the sense that the personal presence in the life-world transfigures the configurations of sense that make the life-world into what it is.[6]

With the threefold determination of the life-world in mind, we can clarify with greater precision what it means to claim that the person's rootedness in the life-world constitutes the fundamental basis that underlies the processes of somatization and psychologization. While somatization is intelligible only insofar as pain unfolds within the life-world, conceived of as the *wherefrom* and the *wherein* of experience, psychologization is intelligible only insofar as pain is lived in the life-world, conceived of as the *wherein* and the *whereto* of experience. This thesis calls for a further clarification.

Somatization is possible if, and only if, such experiences as pain can themselves be *reactions* to essentially nonsomatic dilemmas that the sufferer comes across in the life-world. In the case of somatization, the conflicts of various kinds that the person has to confront are translated into and expressed as somatic complaints. The body in pain manifests itself as a metaphor of nonsomatic obstructions. Therefore, the understanding of pain that arises through somatization calls for sophisticated hermeneutics,[7] which would be capable of decoding experience and clarifying its metaphorical nature. The success or failure of such hermeneutics would ultimately depend upon its capacity to disclose those essentially nonsomatic dilemmas, which the sufferer, consciously or unconsciously, experiences and presents somatically. But if so, then the person's rootedness in the life-world, his exposure to the multifaceted and often conflicting configurations of sense in the pregiven historical and sociocultural world, constitutes the fundamental presupposition of somatization. Only by placing the subject of experience back into the life-world, conceived of as the *wherefrom* and the *wherein* of experience, can one render somatization intelligible.[8]

The process of psychologization follows the opposite trajectory: although its origins are organic, it does not manifest itself organically but as a psychic phenomenon. When pain is psychologized, it manifests itself as somatic distress, as a metaphor that simultaneously conceals and expresses somatic disturbances and presents them as social, political, or interpersonal problems. Pain thereby reveals itself as a multifaceted phenomenon with organic roots and a psychic face—as a concealed expression of somatic complaints. Being uprooted from the organic level and lived as a psychological emotion, pain proves to be an experience, which, at the phenomenal level, has little if anything to do with specifically somatic ruptures or traumas. At the phenomenal level, pain manifests itself as a psychic phenomenon, which, supposedly, is itself triggered by events unfolding in the life-world. Such a reinterpretation of one's own experience, brought about through the process of psychologization, transforms the person's presence in the life-world. The life-world, conceived of as the world of experience taken in all its factual concreteness, obtains new configurations of sense when the subject of experience reinterprets organic phenomena as psychic. This allows us to maintain that only those subjects of experience whose lives unfold in the life-world, conceived of as the *wherein* and the *whereto* of experience, are capable of psychologization.

As Kirmayer once put it, "An integrated theory of somatization must show how bodily experience shapes and in turn is shaped by social processes" (1984b, 253). *Mutatis mutandis*, one can say the same about psychologization. Phenomenology of the life-world, conceived of as the *wherein* and the *whereto* of experience, provides an account of the fundamental presuppositions that underlie an integrated theorization of psychologization.

BETWEEN HOMELINESS AND HOMELESSNESS: DISCORDANCE IN THE LIFE-WORLD

By now it must be clear that such processes as somatization and psychologization are possible only insofar as the subject of pain is an embodied subjectivity, conceived of as a person in the life-world. With this thesis, we come to recognize the contribution that phenomenology can make in the framework of those fields of research that are focused on somatization and psychologization. Yet one cannot stop with this realization, since the opposite also holds true: an inquiry into the conditions that underlie somatization and psychologization can also enrich our understanding of the life-world.

To show that such is the case, let us ask: How are we to understand the ubiquitous presence of such phenomena as somatization and psychologization? We can obtain an answer by taking four analytic steps. First, it must be shown that persons are expressive beings. Second, it must be further demonstrated that the life-world functions not only as the medium of expression, but also as the general context, within which certain expressions are delegitimized. Third, one has all the reasons needed to maintain that when direct expressions are delegitimized, the person devises indirect modes of expression. Fourth, building on the foregoing realizations, one can further surmise that the processes of somatization and psychologization are modes of communication that transform the person's body into a veiled metaphor and a coded message. Let us address these claims in some detail.

As we know from Husserl's *Cartesian Meditation*s, the *Crisis of the European Sciences*, and many other published and unpublished research manuscripts (many of which have been recently compiled in *Husserliana XXXIX*), the life-world, conceived of as a cultural and sociohistorical world, is a constitutive formation that relies on the constitution of other egos as human subjectivities. The constitution of the Other is what liberates the subject of experience from solipsistic loneliness: it allows this subject to recognize that there are other beings capable of the first-person perspective on the world. Yet how exactly can this subject recognize the Other not just as a thing, but as a consciousness of things? Here we come across the realization that is of crucial importance for our purposes: I can recognize the Other as the source of another perspective on the life-world *only if the Other is given as an expressive being*—as a being whose embodied presence brings an inner world to expression, conceived of as a specific perspective on the life-world.[9] Clearly, just as the constitution of the intersubjective life-world presupposes that I recognize other subjectivities as other persons, it also, correlatively, presupposes that other subjectivities recognize me as a person. In the absence of such a double recognition, the constitution of the intersubjective life-world would not be possible. Only if other subjectivities are given to me as beings who possess inwardness, and only if I myself am given to them as such a being, can the life-world be constituted. *The recognition of Others as expressive beings belongs to the a priori of the life-world.*

Let us not forget that the person constitutes the life-world as a particular homeworld, which, conceived of as a particular field of self-evidences, differs from alien-worlds, conceived of as other fields of other self-evidences. Arguably, this means that the life-world facilitates only *some* expressions, namely, those expressions that harmonize with the established configurations of sense that differentiate a particular homeworld from alien-worlds. This further means that, besides facilitating certain expressions, the life-world, conceived of as a homeworld, also delegitimizes other expressions, namely, those expressions that sharply conflict with the established self-evidences that lie at the core of a particular life-world. Besides being the horizon within which the person can express his feelings, thoughts, and emotional dispositions, the life-world also, and simultaneously, functions as a preemptive context that delegitimizes the expression of other thoughts, other feelings, and other emotional dispositions.[10]

This realization is of crucial importance for our purposes: it brings into question the qualification of the homeworld as a surrounding world, whose constitution relies upon concordant experience. According to a claim that Husserl often repeats in his analysis of the homeworld in his research manuscripts,[11] the homeworld, conceived of as a world that is valid both for me and for my own community, is given in concordant experience.[12] Husserl's claims to the contrary notwithstanding, the ubiquitous presence of such processes as somatization and psychologization bears witness to the contrary fact that the homeworld is correlated with highly discordant experiences, many of which either cannot be brought into harmony, or at least have not been successfully harmonized with each other. The very presence of those experiences, whose expression in a particular homeworld is delegitimized, forces us to rethink the presumably harmonious nature of specific homeworlds.

What exactly is a homeworld? In Husserl's phenomenology, this notion does not have a strictly defined sense. It is clear that in the genetic account of world-constitution, Husserl draws a distinction between different constitutive levels. Husserl identifies the lowest level as the primordial world, that is, the world that is not yet social, not yet historical, not yet cultural—the world that is correlated with one's own experience, insofar as this experience is considered within the framework of the primordial reduction. Husserl identifies the homeworld as the second constitutive layer. In contrast to the primordial world, the homeworld is already an intersubjective, cultural, and historical world. The discovery of the alien-worlds belongs to the third level of world-constitution. This discovery is of crucial importance for the constitution of the objective world, since it enables one to draw a distinction between the world as such and one's own surrounding world. Finally, the objective world, conceived of as the world that embraces all the different homeworlds, is the fourth and final stage of world-constitution.

Within such a typology, it might seem that the life-world, conceived of as a homeworld, should be conceived of as a world given in concordant experience. In contrast to the constitution of alien-worlds, this world appears to be free of the conflicts that arise at the third constitutive level. It should therefore not surprise us that Husserl consistently speaks of the homeworld as the world that is given in concordant experience. However, Husserl's own more detailed account of the constitution of the homeworld brings such a view into question.

Husserl conceives of the homeworld as a synthetic unity that embraces a number of different personal worlds (see appendix XII to Husserl 1973b). He claims that everyone has his own private world, which needs to be distinguished from the communal homeworld. If such is the case, it remains unclear why Husserl would qualify the homeworld as a world correlated with concordant experience and why he would thereby exclude the possibility of conflicts that emerge between these "private worlds" and the communal homeworld.

Moreover, let us not overlook that each and every homeworld is generative and historical, which means that each homeworld continuously takes on new characteristic features. It is not clear at all how one is to reconcile homeworld's historicity with the presumed fact that it is always constituted through concordant experience. Furthermore, let us not overlook that, in Husserl's writings, the concept of the homeworld functions as a highly plastic term. The room in which a small child lives can function as the child's homeworld, as can the house, the street, the neighborhood, the city-territory, and, finally, the country-territory. In the long run, even the whole earth can one day become humanity's homeworld. Such being the case, it is by far not clear why Husserl would qualify the homeworld as a world correlated with concordant experiences and why he would thereby exclude the possibility of numerous conflicts that routinely emerge between different "homeworlds," conceived of as synthetic elements, or constitutive parts, of one's actual homeworld.

According to Husserl, a homeworld is largely made up of mythical convictions (see Husserl 1973b, 217). In light of this qualification, it remains unclear why one should assume that the mythical convictions that emerge in one's home must always and necessarily harmonize with the convictions prevalent in the street. So also, why should the "mythical convictions" characteristic of one's neighborhood necessarily harmonize with the "mythical convictions" of the city? In fact, myths themselves bring into question the presumably homogeneous nature of experience, which underlies the constitution of one's homeworld. It suffices to recall Sophocles' Antigone, whose conflict with King Creon over the burial of her brother Polinyces brings to light the irresolvable conflicts between different homeworlds that not just Antigone, but also Creon and Euridyce, as well as Haemon have to live through. One does not have the right to ignore conflicts of this nature in philosophical accounts of the constitution of the life-world. The undeniable presence of these conflicts compels us to abandon the view concerning the concordant nature of that experience, through which, presumably, our homeworlds are given to us. This claim cannot be justified phenomenologically.

If it is indeed true that we have no basis to qualify the homeworld as a world that is correlated with concordant experience, then we need to also question Husserl's view that the homeworld is a world in which a person feels "homely" ("die Welt, in der er *heimisch* ist" [Husserl 2008, 154]).[13] This is what the processes of somatization and psychologization teach us. They suggest that the person, conceived of as a fundamentally expressive being, is both at home and homeless in the life-world. They intimate that the life-world functions as a horizon, within which expression is both legitimated and proscribed. Yet no matter how inhibitive the concrete structures of the life-world might be, they cannot alter the person's fundamentally expressive nature. Being by nature an expressive being in the life-world, the person cannot help but search for ways to resolve the paradox he now confronts. We can understand somatization and psychologization as ingenious solutions to the outlined paradox. The tension that has arisen between the two concepts of the homeworld (homeworld conceived of as a field of expressibility and as a field that delegitimizes expressibility) can be overcome on the basis of *indirect* speech. Somatization and psychologization demonstrate that when direct expression is forbidden, the person transforms his own body into a hidden metaphor. What cannot be expressed in words will have to be expressed somatically.

Here we once again stumble against the vital function of embodiment. In the case of somatization, we do not just apperceive the tensions we live through in the life-world, but also transfigure them into highly ambiguous phenomena, which can be understood either as coded messages or as somatic phenomena. So also, in the case of psychologization, we are not just affected by somatic ruptures and traumas, but we also reshape them into phenomena, which lend themselves to a no less ambiguous understanding. Such ingenious transformations of one's somatic and psychic feelings into metaphors, which simultaneously express and mask what is being expressed, significantly enrich the structures of communication, so much so that the meaning of expressions under consideration obtains a layered structure. It is not just that one can now express indirectly what, under different circumstances, one could have formulated more straightforwardly. Besides becoming a coded message, the indirect expression just as strongly voices one's incapacity to speak out in a direct way. The person thereby simultaneously expresses her refusal to be silenced as well as the fact that she is being silenced; she brings to language what she could have done otherwise, yet at the same time voices her incapacity to do so otherwise.

The somatizing and psychologizing agents need not be aware of their own transformative powers. This means that the paradox and its resolution here described can occur not only at the conscious but also at the preconscious level of experience: the person is either unaware of them or is aware of them, yet refuses to acknowledge their presence. We will still have an occasion to return to this issue. For the moment, let us stress that the person's prereflective capacity to mask and modify feelings, emotions, and thoughts by turning them into disguised expressions renders these processes intelligible.

Just as these processes are largely preconsciousness, so also they are largely noncognitive: the person is not conscious of them thematically and explicitly, but is aware of them only nonthematically and implicitly. The fact that we are confronted here with prereflective modes of expression means that the person, as the somatizing and psychologizing agent, seeks not only the understanding of others, but also, simultaneously, she searches for explicit and thematic self-understanding. Quite likely we are confronted here with an important reason why some forms of pain—I have in mind different kinds of chronic pain—refuse to come to an end: when interpreted as a form of somatization or psychologization, pain proves to be a heavily disguised metaphor, which not just others but the sufferer as well find unfathomable.

At the outset of experience, pain is often lived as a hostile and meaningless feeling-sensation. We can understand its meaninglessness and its hostility in terms of a conflict that arises between the sufferer's experience and the established configurations of sense that make up the core of a particular homeworld. There are good reasons to suggest that in the cases of somatization and psychologization, the sufferer recognizes the meaninglessness of original experiences. This more or less tacit recognition might be self-imposed, as happens when the processes in question are triggered by the inability to express emotions, either due to one's own psychological disposition or to the expressive limits of a particular language. So also, the recognition of the meaninglessness of one's original experience can be imposed from the outside, when direct expression is proscribed due to sociocultural and political reasons. In both cases, the processes of somatization and psychologization can be conceived of as conscious or unconscious attempts to express the inexpressible and permeate meaninglessness with meaning.

Yet there is a price to pay for such acts of transformation and reinterpretation. Just as the somatizing and psychologizing sufferer recognizes the meaninglessness that characterizes original experiences (otherwise, she would lack the motivation needed to somatize or psychologize original experiences), she is also aware, either implicitly or explicitly, that the transformed expressions of these experiences camouflage their original meaninglessness. Due to her inherently expressive nature, the somatizing or psychologizing sufferer cannot help but turn to indirect modes of expression, yet one can also hypothesize that at the same time she knows too much and thus recognizes the phony nature of these expressions. The somatizing and psychologizing sufferer has thus devised highly sophisticated means to play hide-and-seek with herself. She deludes herself while recognizing delusions as delusions. Arguably, some forms of pain refuse to come to an end, not because the subject of experience knows too little, but because she knows too much, no matter how nonthematic and implicit this knowledge might be.

From this one can draw an important implication: the person, conceived of as the subject of somatization and psychologization, must be a deeply split being, whose self-givenness lacks clarity and distinctness. The person is given to herself, not only because she can both reflectively and prereflectively grasp herself, but also because she can both reflectively and prereflectively express herself. However, the processes of somatization and psychologization demonstrate that these forms of self-expression can be masked almost impenetrably. The person, conceived of as the subject of somatization and psychologization, hides not only from others, but also from herself. The person is a fundamentally expressive being who knows how, while expressing herself, to simultaneously keep a safe distance from herself.

MASOCHISM AND SOMATIZATION

In this study, pain has been conceived of as *an aversive bodily feeling with a distinct experiential quality, which can be given only in original firsthand experience, either as a feeling-sensation or as an emotion.* The foregoing analysis of somatization and psychologization clarifies in greater detail how we are to understand the emotional dimension of pain experience. By now it must be clear that we run the risk of misunderstanding the nature of pain experience when we draw too sharp a distinction between the so-called nonintentional feeling-sensations and intentional feelings, which include emotions. One should stress, however, that the phenomenology of somatization and psychologization is important not only for this reason. The analysis provided in this chapter also enables us to address another worry, which concerns the existence of masochism. What sense are we to make of the love of pain, be it sexual or nonsexual, in light of the proposed definition? It is not hard to see that any love of pain constitutes a serious challenge to the proposed conception. If, as the definition suggests, pain is an aversive feeling whose experiential quality is distinctly disagreeable and unpleasant, then it seems that masochistic pleasures are just not possible and that we simply do not know what we are talking about when we describe them as the love of pain. Yet arguments of such nature are worthless in phenomenology: it is senseless either to deny or to ignore experiential phenomena for the sole reason that they cannot be reconciled with the proposed conception.

It seems that one could dissolve this dilemma by arguing that any kind of masochistic pleasure is perplexing only insofar as we identify the object of pleasure with pain itself. No matter how self-evident this identification might seem to be, it might nonetheless prove untenable. We find such a view already in Cicero:

> No one rejects, dislikes, or avoids pleasure itself, because it is pleasure, but because those who do not know how to pursue pleasure rationally encounter consequences that are extremely painful. Nor again is there anyone who loves or pursues or desires to obtain pain of itself, because it is pain, but occasionally circumstances occur in which toil and pain can procure him some great pleasure. To take a trivial example, which of us ever undertakes laborious physical exercise, except to obtain some advantage from it? (Cicero 1914, bk. 1, sec. 323)

According to such a perspective, the object of masochistic pleasures is not pain itself but the pleasure that we reap from pain. Such a view suggests that, as far as sexual masochism is concerned, whipping, trampling, spanking, hair-pulling, biting, or scratching is experienced as painful, while the accompanying sexual pleasures are deeply pleasant. Here is how Colin Klein characterizes such an approach to sexual masochism: "The line goes, crudely, what's painful is the whipping, what's pleasant is the sex, and there is no mystery in either case" (2015b, 170).[14] No mystery, one should nonetheless add, apart from the following: pains are, by definition, unpleasant. If so, how can they be conceived of as a necessary means toward the attainment of superior pleasures? It is one thing to dissolve the above-mentioned dilemma by claiming that masochistic love is the love of pleasures, and not of pains. It is an altogether different thing to explain how pain, which is by definition unpleasant, could constitute a necessary condition of greater pleasures.

Let us return to Cicero: no one "loves or pursues or desires to obtain pain of itself, because it is pain" (1914, bk. 1, sec. 323). What exactly are we to understand by "pain" here? As I argued in chapter 2, pain is a stratified phenomenon, and as I further showed in chapter 3, not each and every pain is lived as what Roger Trigg (1970) calls a "whole pain experience." There are various ways in which consciousness can apprehend pain sensations. As we saw, besides being apprehended as painful, these sensations can also be regarded with indifference. In the present case, we are confronted with a different scenario: pain sensations can also be apprehended as pleasurable. Yet how can consciousness apprehend its pain sensations as pleasurable if these sensations, as shown in chapter 3, are inherently disagreeable and unpleasant?

In light of this dilemma, the phenomenological thesis that no experience is ever lived in isolation, but always in a larger horizon of experience, gains its philosophical relevance. Pain sensations are never lived in isolation from other experiences, but as moments within a large context of experience, and it is this very contextual framework that enables us to resolve this dilemma. To claim that a masochist derives pleasure from pain is not to deny the obvious fact that the masochist finds pain disagreeable and unpleasant.[15] Yet insofar as these pain sensations are lived as moments within the experiential field, they can be apprehended functionally, as necessary conditions of greater pleasure. When pain sensations are apprehended as functions that provoke greater pleasure, they can be lived as both painful and pleasurable.

To clarify how this takes place, let us turn back to Cicero: although no one loves, pursues, or desires pain, because it is pain, "occasionally circumstances occur in which toil and pain can procure him some great pleasure" (1914, bk. 1, sec. 323). There are various ways to clarify these circumstances. In Colin Klein's recent study, we come across a compelling account of one way that relies upon what Klein calls "the experience of flirting around the edge" and that he identifies as the basis of the *"penumbral* theory of masochism":

> What appears to be common to, and probably distinctive of, cases of masochistic pleasure as such is this process of pushing a painful feeling just to the limits of unendurability. Call this the *penumbral* theory of masochism. Masochistic pleasure is possible in cases where pains are in the shadowy border just shy of being too much to bear. So we can elaborate the structure of masochistic pleasures a bit further: the masochist is in pain (or some other negative experience). Pain is painful. That pain is almost, but not quite, too much to bear. Having a pain that is almost, but not quite, too much to bear is, under the right circumstances, pleasant. (2015b, 177)

In short, the pain the masochist lives through is indeed painful, while the experience of finding oneself at the limits of unbearability is pleasant: so runs the penumbral theory of masochism. This theory demonstrates how pain can be functionalized within the larger context of experience and be transformed into a necessary means through which one can attain distinct pleasures. There are, however, other ways for pain to be functionalized. To see this, it is crucial not to overlook that in the case of masochism, the function of pain need not be that of provoking greater pleasures; *it can also be that of diminishing other forms of distress.* To demonstrate this, we need to recall the foregoing discussion of somatization and psychologization.

As we saw above, these processes do not unfold entirely behind the person's back, and they are largely motivated by the person's belief that once transformed, the experiences in question will be more easily dealt with, either by the person himself or by those around him. On the basis of the foregoing discussion, I would suggest that the love of physical pain, taken in all its diverse modalities, derives from psychological suffering and distress, which the person finds unbearable and from which he therefore must find a way to escape. In this regard, to love one's pain is to cover up more disturbing forms of suffering, which need to be transformed into somatic pain if they are to be manageable. The phenomenology of somatization and psychologization brings to light that the love of physical pain is one of the ingenious ways that enable the person to conceal the psychological forms of suffering he finds unbearable. That is, the love of physical pain derives from the search to liberate oneself from psychological suffering and to reassure oneself that the source of one's misfortunes is "pain, and only pain, nothing more than that." It should therefore come as no surprise that masochism has always been the love of largely controllable pain, and never, say, the love of chronic pain (see Stoller 1991). To love pain is to love its controllability, insofar as it can be conceived of as a substitute for what is uncontrollable.[16]

Let us conclude with two sets of reflections. The first set concerns the relevance of the proposed phenomenology of pain for philosophical anthropology; the second set concerns the imperative theory of pain, which plays a prominent role in the contemporary philosophy of pain.

First, let us return to our guiding concern in the last two chapters of this study: Of what relevance is the phenomenology of pain for philosophical anthropology? Clearly, to engage in the phenomenology of pain within the framework of philosophical anthropology does not mean to focus on human pain alone. Rather, to be relevant for philosophical anthropology, the phenomenology of pain must relate to our understanding of what it means to be human.

Phenomenology invites us to conceive of the human being as a *person* in the *life-world*, understanding both terms in the rich senses that phenomenology provides them with. In light of the analysis here offered, we can further qualify the person as a fundamentally *expressive* being. Besides being an agent of experience, the person is also a subject concerned with the meaningfulness of her experiences, at least in the sense that this subject can never be satisfied with their senselessness and is always willing to rebel against their senselessness. We could qualify an act of meaning as an expressive act insofar as we understand expression in a sufficiently broad sense, which includes both verbal and nonverbal expressions. The experiences the person lives through call for their expression, verbal or nonverbal, for by bringing them to expression we bestow sense upon them, or at least protest against their senselessness.

As we saw, not all lived-experiences can be expressed within the framework of a concrete life-world. Conceived of as a concrete cultural and sociohistorical world, the life-world both facilitates and represses the person's capacity to express her lived-experiences. Insofar as the person's capacity to express her experiences is suppressed, the person obtains the motivation needed to search for *indirect* modes of expression. We can consider it a mark of the person's extraordinary ingenuity that she can transform her own lived-experiences into modes of indirect expression. *When lived-experience cannot be spoken about, it starts speaking metaphorically itself.* Even more remarkably, the person can conceal her own expressivity not only from others and the world at large, but even from herself. This occurs when the person internalizes the imposed suppression of her capacity to express those lived-experiences that call for expression. Under such circumstances, the indirect modes of expression remain hidden from the person.

There is an important implication to be drawn from the recognition that the structures of the concrete life-world both facilitate and repress the capacity to express one's lived-experiences. This realization invites one to further claim that human beings, conceived of as persons in the life-world, are the beings who are both at home and homeless in the life-world. Finding themselves in the structures of a concrete life-world, which simultaneously facilitate and repress their capacity to come to terms with their own experience, they have to live the tension that arises between the sense of homelessness and the feeling of being at home in the life-world. One thereby recognizes one's own homelessness, while nonetheless being unable to escape the concrete spatiotemporal limits of one's own existence. One thus has to live the tension between freedom and determination, reflective self-transparency and self-opacity, the will to come to terms with and to escape one's own experience.

Let us turn to the second set of concerns. To claim that pains are imperative is to contend that they are sensations with a content and that this content comes in the form of a command to protect the injured part of the body. This theory, its proponents maintain, accounts for the biological purpose of pain: Much like hunger and thirst, pain protects our bodily integrity. It does so by placing a direct command upon the body to recover. One cannot help but listen to this command, and insofar as one listens to it, one recovers.

The foregoing discussion of somatization and psychologization significantly enlarges the sense in which one can understand the imperatives of pain. Pain does indeed try to tell us something, yet the meaning of what it says is not obvious from the start. It is therefore hard to agree with Colin Klein when he argues, with an eye on pain, that "imperatives are directly and nondeliberatively action-guided" (2015b, 5). In the case of somatization, the meaning of pain is not to be found at the level of its somatic manifestation; in the case of psychologization, its form of expression might not be somatic. More generally, as David Bakan once put it,

> To attempt to understand the nature of pain, to seek to find its meaning, is already to respond to an imperative of pain itself. No experience demands and insists upon interpretation in the same way. Pain forces the question of its meaning, and especially of its cause, insofar as cause is an important part of its meaning. In those instances in which pain is intense and intractable and in which its causes are obscure, its demand for interpretation is most naked, manifested in the sufferer asking, "Why?" (1968, 57–58)

I would contend that the fundamental imperative inscribed in the experience of pain is not that of "stop," but rather that of "listen," and while the understanding of some commands does not require deliberation, other commands call for heedful decoding and interpretation. It is not true that, as Klein puts it, insofar as pains are conceived of as commands, they are noninformative. We are all familiar with commands to understand. Insofar as pain is a command to listen, it is also a command to understand, and, arguably, one of the reasons why pains so often refuse to come to an end derives from our incapacity to understand them. In a sense, the experience of chronic pain (which is awkwardly left out of consideration in the imperative theories of pain) might be likened to a resounding message, which the intended recipients either do not acknowledge as a message or fail to understand. The processes of somatization and psychologization bring to light that one of the central reasons why chronic pain refuses to cease concerns our inability to understand these pains *as coded messages* or *indirect modes of expression*, which cannot be grasped as straightforward commands.

CONCLUSION

·····································

A phenomenological account of pain must be methodical and systematic; yet, for principal reasons, it cannot be comprehensive. Pain is a remarkably complex phenomenon, so complex, in fact, that it is simply inevitable that any account would leave some important aspects of pain experience out of consideration. Although the reasons behind some omissions might be strategic, it would be a matter of self-conceit and self-deceit for any investigator to suggest that all omissions have been planned in advance. Any analysis of pain, including phenomenologically oriented investigations, can be only provisional. This is probably the reason—and, one might add, a good reason, too—why so many studies of pain are written without a concluding chapter.

Yet a conclusion of a study need not be conceived of as a set of final words. It can also serve a different purpose, namely, it can hint at further directions that research in the field can take. With this in mind, let me briefly sum up the results of this study, yet only so as to show why I take them to be of importance for future research.

We were guided by three fundamental tasks: methodological, conceptual, and anthropological. While addressing the methodological orientation of phenomenological research, we were concerned with the exact meaning in which any study of pain could be qualified as phenomenological. According to the view defended in this study, the methods of the phenomenological epoché, the phenomenological reduction, and eidetic variation constitute the three fundamental and indispensable principles of phenomenologically oriented pain research. Yet, as I further argued, these principles are necessary, although not sufficient. It would be a matter of a common confusion to conceive of the method of eidetic variation as nothing more than a set of imaginative variations that are undertaken by a certain factual investigator. So as to avoid such a misunderstanding, I have argued that imaginative variations must be supplemented with factual variations. Such a supplementation, I have maintained, provides the reasons needed to identify phenomenology as a dialogically oriented discipline. Besides that, I have further argued that

CONCLUSION   189

static phenomenology, conceived of as a methodological outlook based on the three fundamental methods mentioned above, must be supplemented with the principles of genetic phenomenology. Such, then, are the fundamental principles of phenomenological research. According to the view defended in this study, an investigation has the right to call itself phenomenological insofar as it subscribes to such a methodological orientation.

Of what significance are such methodological reflections? First and foremost, I should stress the vital importance of raising the question itself, namely, the question that concerns the exact sense in which any investigation could be identified as phenomenological. It is all too common to understand phenomenology in a loose sense, as any kind of analysis that is conducted from the first-person point of view. Yet such a broad characterization of phenomenology is deeply confusing, if only because it suggests that various autobiographies, empirically oriented analyses, introspectionist reports, and even psychologistic studies can be labeled as phenomenological. Especially when it comes to applied research, many investigations that identify themselves as phenomenological are not phenomenological in the methodological sense of the term. In light of such circumstances, the methodological reflections offered here prove highly helpful in that they enable us to circumvent many confusions in the field. In this regard, the identification of the fundamental principles that underlie phenomenological research serves two important goals: it provides the means needed to identify with precision the central standpoints in the field as well as the most important insights that are entrenched in these standpoints; it also enables other fields of research to recognize the importance of phenomenological research by distinguishing between phenomenological studies of pain and other kinds of autobiographies, pain narratives, and introspectionist or even psychologistic accounts, which only purport to be phenomenological.

Second, these reflections also provide future research with a strong methodological footing: they clarify the fundamental orientation that must guide a phenomenologically oriented research. Phenomenology is first and foremost a method, hence the vital importance of familiarizing oneself with the fundamental principles that underlie this method. In such areas as pain research, there is the danger of misconceiving phenomenology as a field of research that pays close attention to the first-person experiences, yet, presumably, cannot do anything more than remind us of the need to be attentive to lived-experience. It is of utmost importance to correct such a caricature of phenomenology, and there is no better way to do this than by clarifying the fundamental methodological orientation that underlies phenomenological research.

Third, I have argued that by supplemented imaginative variations with factual variations, one transforms pure phenomenology into a dialogical phenomenology. I consider it to be a significant limitation that such a dialogical orientation is missing from the phenomenology of pain in its current form. Especially in light of the tremendous progress that has been made in a large variety of fields that make up the contemporary science of pain, the phenomenology of pain runs the risk of becoming an isolated and anachronistic field if it single-handedly dismisses the intellectual discussions that pervade other disciplines. Phenomenology should not become a victim of its own (presumably methodological) purity.

Fourth, it is only to be expected that some will question either the necessity or even the legitimacy of those methodological principles that I have defended here. Is it true that the method of eidetic variation is crucial for phenomenology? Moreover, is it true that imaginative variations must be supplemented with factual variations and that such a supplementation transforms pure phenomenology into dialogical phenomenology? To these two questions we can add a third one: Is it not true that phenomenology is neither a doctrine nor a school of thought, but, rather, a particular style of thought? Clearly, one does not need to subscribe to the fundamental principles of Husserlian phenomenology if one wants to call one's investigation phenomenological! One can only welcome such reflections and controversies, and especially because, currently, there are no phenomenological studies of pain that would have spelled out those phenomenological principles that must underlie and guide phenomenologically oriented research. The methodological reflections I have offered here will have fulfilled a highly important function even if, instead of being accepted at face value, they provoke other researchers to present a different set of methodological principles as fundamental to phenomenologically oriented pain research. Just as the more general question that concerns the nature of phenomenology as such, so also the more specific question that concerns the nature of phenomenology of pain must retain its abiding validity and overarching significance.

The second fundamental task of this study was conceptual. The goal has been to provide the concept of pain with a definition that would be grounded in phenomenological principles. I have argued that the established definition of pain, which was endorsed by the International Association for the Study of Pain (IASP), and which suggests that "pain is an unpleasant sensory and

CONCLUSION

emotional experience associated with actual or potential tissue damage, or described in terms of such damage" (Merskey and Bogduk 1994, 209), is for various reasons unacceptable. First, methodologically, this definition relies on presuppositions that lack phenomenological justification. Second, thematically, it fails to account for the specific nature of pain experience. I have further maintained that other definitions of pain we come across in the science of pain suffer from similar shortcomings. My goal in this study has been to work out a new definition of pain that would be grounded in the fundamental methodological principles that underlie phenomenologically oriented pain research. Building on the basis of the methodological orientation as presented in chapter 1, I have argued that *pain is an aversive bodily feeling with a distinct experiential quality, which can be given only in original firsthand experience, either as a feeling-sensation or as an emotion.*

I consider this definition of pain, taken along with the justification that I have provided it with, to be one of the most important accomplishments of this study. There are a number of reasons why a novel definition of pain is much needed in pain research in general, and in the phenomenology of pain in particular. First, even though it is not unprecedented in the science of pain to lament that the IASP definition of pain entails many shortcomings, to this very day a viable alternative is missing. One thus claims that this established definition does not do justice to the lived-experience of pain, that it suffers from biomedical reductionism, and that it relies upon body-mind dualism. To this one sometimes adds that this definition leads one to conceive of pain as a "thing" that is somehow different from the embodied subjectivity that experiences it (see Quintner et al. 2008). I have aimed to offer a phenomenological definition of pain that would not be affected by these shortcomings.

Second, as far as the phenomenology of pain is concerned, even though one commonly recognizes that a phenomenological investigation cannot rely on the IASP definition, to this very day we still lack a sufficiently nuanced alternative. As far as phenomenology is concerned, Christian Grüny (2004) and Abraham Olivier (2007) in their noteworthy studies present phenomenologically oriented conceptions of pain. However, although both studies are rich not only in terms of analysis but also in terms of the implications one can draw from them, neither the view that pain is a "blocked movement of flight" (*eine blockierte Fluchtbewegung* [Grüny 2004, 25]), nor the contention that pain is a "disturbed bodily perception bound to hurt, affliction or agony" (Olivier 2007, 198) can be conceived of as viable definitions of pain. I have already alluded to the reasons for this in my introductory remarks:

nausea, vertigo, heartburn, the sensations of excessive heat and cold, of hunger and thirst, even itches and pressure can also be described in such a fashion. Such being the case, the conceptions of pain proposed by Grüny and Olivier cannot be conceived of as definitions of pain, since they do not provide us with the differentia.

Third, the definition of pain offered in this study must be of importance for empirically oriented pain research. Not only does this definition provide much-needed conceptual clarity, but it also, and especially because it is grounded in phenomenological principles, enables the empirical researcher to avoid different forms of reductionism that otherwise continue to afflict pain research.[1]

Fourth, the current study will have fulfilled an important function if it provokes other phenomenologists, or those working in other fields, to contest its validity. One can only welcome such controversies in the field, if only because they promise to significantly enrich the phenomenological understanding of pain experience.

The third fundamental goal of this study concerned the significance of phenomenology of pain for philosophical anthropology. My goal has been to demonstrate that the phenomenological concept of the person that we come across in Husserl's phenomenology not only provides us with the possibility to conceptualize the embodied subjectivity as the subject of pain, but it also, and no less importantly, enables us to analyze the depersonalizing and repersonalizing nature of pain experience. Moreover, still within the framework of a philosophical anthropology, my goal has been to demonstrate that a phenomenological approach, which considers the life-world as the ultimate horizon of pain experience, enables us to conceptualize such processes as somatization and psychologization, which so often affect the human experience of chronic pain.

Such a way of conceptualizing pain experience carries a number of important implications. First, as far as philosophical implications are concerned, I consider it a task of vital importance to return to the once prevalent, while nowadays almost entirely forgotten view, according to which, philosophical reflections on pain can provide us with fundamental insights into the nature and limits of human existence. As Max Scheler noted in the opening lines of his essay "On the Meaning of Suffering," the first version of which he completed in 1916, "A doctrine on *the meaning of pain and suffering* was, *in all lands, at all times, in the whole world* at the core of the teachings and directives which the great religious and philosophical thinkers gave to men" (1992, 121; emphasis

CONCLUSION   193

added—SG). While still accepted as self-evident by Scheler, such a conviction has vanished, as though without a trace, from the contemporary philosophy of pain. It is my view that the philosophy of pain can regain its far-reaching significance only if it finds an appropriate way to revitalize such fundamental concerns. Yet we know the common argument against such a view. Is it not steeped in metaphysical assumptions, which have lost their validity for us, and especially in light of the tremendous progress that we come across in the science of pain? Much like magic or alchemy, metaphysics of pain might fascinate us and captivate our attention and interest, yet it appears to be impossible to support the claims it makes with reliable evidence. With these common objections in mind, I would suggest that the phenomenology of pain provides a viable via media between metaphysics of pain, on the one hand, and the naturalistically oriented science of pain, on the other hand. It provides us with the means needed to address the fundamental significance of pain experience *within the boundaries of a philosophical anthropology*, which does not commit the researcher either to any kind of metaphysical postulates or to any kind of naturalistic assumptions. Rather, the philosophical anthropology of which I speak here must be grounded in those fundamental phenomenological principles, which have been addressed in detail in this study.

Second, conceptualizing pain within the boundaries of a philosophical anthropology is also of great importance because it provides the researcher with the possibility to open a much-needed dialogue between phenomenology, on the one hand, and a number of disciplines that address "pain as human experience" (to refer to one outstanding study in cultural anthropology; see Good et al. 1994), on the other hand. A number of disciplines in the human and social sciences have provided highly intriguing studies of human pain; what is more, many of these studies, and especially in the anthropology of pain, entail a broad phenomenological orientation, which anthropologists further support with references to classical phenomenological literature. It is unfortunate that to this day, these studies appear little appreciated among philosophers in general and phenomenologists in particular. By addressing pain within the framework of philosophical anthropology, phenomenology puts itself in the position to open a dialogue with cultural anthropology, cultural psychopathology, history, psychoanalysis, sociology, and other disciplines. One can conceive of the analysis offered in the last two chapters of this study as the initial set of steps in this direction.

Let me conclude with a few remarks on some issues that, for one reason or another, have not been explored in this study. The first important limitation concerns the absence of explicit reflections on the pain of nonhuman animals. One might wonder if this highly important theme does not lie at the limits of phenomenological research. After all, can phenomenology offer anything else besides a set of analyses that rely on how phenomena manifest themselves in first-person experience? Yet what could this first-person experience be if not *human* experience? In light of these questions, let me stress again that according to the view defended here, phenomenology should not be confused with any kind of autobiography, "pain narratives," introspectionism, or psychologism. I would thus maintain that there are no good reasons to claim that reflections on the pain of nonhuman animals take us beyond the limits of phenomenological research. Although I have not pursued this subject matter in this study, let me nonetheless remark in passing that the methodological framework presented here provides the fundamental basis to study not only human pain, but also animal pain, from a phenomenological point of view. Moreover, let me especially stress that the concept of pain I have presented here is not meant to qualify only human pain, but also characterizes the pain of nonhuman animals. I would thus contend that this study, even though it has not focused on the pain of animals explicitly, provides the methodological and conceptual basis to address animal pain—a theme that will have to be undertaken in other investigations.

One more limitation is worthwhile mentioning: in this study, I have had little to say about the ethical implications that follow from the phenomenology of pain. One of the reasons for this relates to the fact that here I have been concerned with pain, as it is given in original first-person experience. I have left the ethical questions concerning *the pain of others* out of consideration. The reasons behind this omission are methodological. A study that is focused on ethical issues surrounding the experience of pain would have been a significantly different kind of investigation than the one I have aimed to offer here. This study should provide a strong methodological and conceptual basis to carry out such a task for anyone who might wish to ground such an ethical investigation in phenomenological principles.

NOTES

• •

INTRODUCTION

1. As Virginia Woolf famously put it, "English, which can express the thoughts of Hamlet and the tragedy of Lear has no words for the shiver or the headache. . . . The merest schoolgirl when she falls in love has Shakespeare or Keats to speak her mind for her, but let a sufferer try to describe a pain in his head to a doctor and language at once runs dry" (1967, 194). Or in Elaine Scarry's no less famous words, "Physical pain does not simply resist language but actively destroys it, bringing about an immediate reversion to a state anterior to language, to the sounds and cries a human being makes before language is learned" (1985, 4). According to both Woolf and Scarry, the resistance to any kind of language-based articulation is not just incidental but essential to what pain is as such.

2. To emphasize this point, in the note that accompanied the IASP definition of pain, it is further stated that "pain is always subjective" (Merskey and Bogduk 1994, 209).

3. The association between pain and actual or potential tissue damage, suggested by this definition, introduces further phenomenological problems. For the moment, let us leave these difficulties aside and focus exclusively on pain as experience.

4. This does not mean that the phenomenology of pain must be indifferent to how pain is addressed in either the natural or the human sciences. Quite on the contrary, here I will argue that especially when it comes to pain research, phenomenology must be pursued *dialogically*. Still, no matter how open a phenomenological approach might be, phenomenology is not reducible either to pain biology or to pain sociology. We face here two central methodological ambitions of this study: to spell out those methodological commitments that make up the core of phenomenologically oriented pain research and to demonstrate how phenomenology can be pursued dialogically. Both issues will be addressed in detail in chapter 1.

5. To be sure, one cannot ignore Drew Leder's contributions to the phenomenology of pain that we come across in *The Absent Body* (1990) and in *The Distressed Body* (2016). While Leder's investigations are of great significance for this study, I nonetheless have to stress that these two outstanding book-length investigations are not focused exclusively on the phenomenology of pain. So also, one cannot overlook Frederik J. J. Buytendijk's *Pain: Its Modes and Functions* (1962), as well as his other shorter studies of pain. While Buytendijk's analysis will be of great significance in the following study, and especially in chapter 6, it nonetheless has to be admitted that as far as methodology is concerned, his study is not explicitly phenomenological. So also, one has to acknowledge the significance of the shorter studies by Agustín Serrano de Haro (2011, 2012, and 2017); Tetsuya Kono (2012); Dermot Moran (2010); Katherine J. Morris (2013); John Russon (2013); Fredrik Svenaeus (2000, 2015, 2018); Panos Theodorou (2014); as well as Martin Kusch and Matthew Ratcliffe (2018). However, none of them have provided book-length contributions to the phenomenology of pain. We are thus left with the conclusion that Grüny's and Olivier's above-mentioned

196   NOTES TO PAGES 5–14

studies are the only available book-length studies on the phenomenology of pain. Last, one also has to acknowledge the relevance of the classical analyses of pain undertaken by Carl Stumpf (1907 and 1916); Franz Brentano (1907 and 1968); Edmund Husserl (2000); Max Scheler (1973 and 1992); Edith Stein (1989); Maurice Merleau-Ponty (1962 and 1963); and Jean-Paul Sartre (1956). However, in these studies, pain emerges only as a marginal theme. One could say that everyone here listed has offered prolegomena to a more thorough phenomenology of pain, which still needs to be worked out in detail.

6. As Gary B. Madison once put it, phenomenology, conceived of as a philosophical tradition, is unified by a certain style of thinking, which is expressive of the phenomenological attitude, whose essentials consist of "an unremitting aversion to all forms of metaphysical reductionism and an abiding concern for the integrity of our own lived experience of things both human and natural" (2004, 446).

7. There are different ways to read this book. Those readers who are interested in methodological issues will find chapter 1 of importance. Its significance is not limited to the phenomenology of pain. Rather, what is in question here concerns the very sense in which any investigation whatsoever can be identified as phenomenological. It is deeply unfortunate that this central methodological question is for the most part ignored in phenomenologically oriented pain research. Without addressing this question explicitly, we are not in the position to say if any analysis has the right to be identified as phenomenological. No matter how central this methodological analysis might be, the analysis offered in chapter 1 also has its downside: at the end of that chapter, it will not yet be clear how what is said here enriches our understanding of pain experience. Therefore, those readers who are not concerned with methodological issues can skip the analysis offered in this chapter and start reading this book with chapter 2, which focuses on the question concerning the intentional nature of pain experience.

8. Even though the question concerning animal pain does not lie beyond the boundaries of phenomenological analysis, in the framework of this study, and especially in the last two chapters, I will focus mainly on *human* pain. I do not doubt that animals are persons of a certain kind and that their lives unfold in the life-world of a certain kind. Yet how exactly is one to delimit the specifically animal personhood and the specifically animal life-world? Moreover, how does pain affect and transform the animal personhood and the animal life-world? These important questions lie beyond the scope of this investigation.

CHAPTER 1. METHODOLOGICAL CONSIDERATIONS

1. As the following analysis will make clear, the method of factual variations is to be conceived not so much as a separate method, but as an addendum designed to adjust and supplement the method of eidetic variation. By contrast, the genetic method constitutes an independent phenomenological method.

2. "I am *not negating* this 'world' as though I were a sophist; I am *not doubting its factual being* as though I were a skeptic; rather I am exercising the 'phenomenological' epoché which also *completely shuts me off from any judgment about spatiotemporal factual being*" (Husserl 1983, 61).

NOTES TO PAGES 15–21

3. Although the concepts of the epoché and the phenomenological reduction are closely linked, it is important to distinguish between them. Dan Zahavi presents both the difference and the inseparability of these two methods in a clear and convincing way: "The epoché is the term for our abrupt suspension of a naïve metaphysical attitude, and it can consequently be likened to a philosophical gate of entry. In contrast, the *reduction* is the term for our thematization of the correlation between subjectivity and world" (2003, 46).

4. It would thus be a misunderstanding to think (as one commonly does) that phenomenology initiates a transition from the analysis of the world to the analysis of consciousness, or experience. Should one hold on to such a view, one would find it quite incomprehensible why Husserl in his later published and unpublished manuscripts would have transformed the life-world (*Lebenswelt*) into a central theme in phenomenology. Rather than inviting us to turn our attention away from the world, phenomenology summons us to focus our attention on the world of experience, which it does by initiating a move from the world of real things, as given in the natural attitude, to the world of pure, intentional phenomena. It should therefore come as no surprise that building our analysis on the basis of the phenomenological method, in chapter 7 we will turn to the analysis of pain and the life-world. This we will do in full conformity with the fundamental phenomenological principles.

5. This being said, in chapter 5, however, when we turn to the relationship between pain and embodiment, it will prove necessary to broaden the field of analysis. This broadening, to which I refer here, will prove indispensable, and it will enable us to see that mundane phenomenology relies upon transcendental phenomenology.

6. According to Husserl, there is no need for an endless modification of different variants. At a certain point of reflection, the identity of the essence comes into view: one recognizes that no matter what other variations one will subject the phenomenon to, it will continue to show the same essential features.

7. As we will see in in the fourth section of this chapter, this realization provides one of the central reasons for supplementing static phenomenology with genetic methodology.

8. In phenomenology, various forms of reductionism (psychologism, physicalism, naturalism, culturalism, etc.) should be carefully distinguished from various reductions, and especially from the phenomenological reduction. As we saw in the last section, the phenomenological reduction is a methodological procedure that relies upon the phenomenological epoché and that leads the phenomenologist back to the field of pure experience. By contrast, reductionism, taken in all its diverse forms, is conceived as an uncritical commitment to theoretical hypotheses. These hypotheses lack phenomenological justification because they are ungrounded in the field of pure experiences. Moreover, these hypotheses block access to the field of experiences. For these two central reasons, reductionism, conceived in all its modalities, is the very opposite of the reduction, conceived of as the gate of entry into phenomenology.

9. Psychologistic reductionism constitutes one of the main reasons that underlie the marginalization of pain and illness in philosophical literature. As Havi Carel remarks, "Phenomenology has played a role in the history of psychiatry that has not been paralleled in somatic medicine" (2016, 19). One should stress that in phenomenological psychiatry, we do not come across the same kind of reductionism that we face in phenomenologically oriented literature on illness and pain. Precisely, therefore,

research in phenomenological psychiatry is more advanced than research in the phenomenology of illness or pain.

10. To further pursue the analogies between the phenomenology of pain and the phenomenology of illness, one could say the following: the phenomenology of pain needs to follow in the footsteps of S. Kay Toombs, whose research was motivated by the search for the eidetic features of illness, which characterize *all* illness and not just the idiosyncratic features of her own particular disease. As Toombs has it, "The eidetic characteristics of illness transcend the peculiarities and particularities of different disease states and constitute the meaning of illness-as-lived. They represent the experience of illness in its qualitative immediacy" (1987, 229). Toombs identified five such features: loss of wholeness, loss of certainty, loss of control, loss of freedom to act, and loss of the familiar world (1987, 229). She further supplemented these five essential elements with an account of their constitutive features, such as bodily impairment and a profound sense of loss of total bodily integrity.

11. Here I will argue against the view that phenomenology can be qualified as introspectionism. However, one can also add that Eastern meditative practices do no follow the introspective method either. As Varela, Thompson, and Rosch point out, rightly, to my mind, "The mindfulness meditator would say that the introspectionists were not actually aware of mind at all; they were just thinking about their thoughts" (1993, 32). By this we are to understand that while the mindfulness meditator is concerned with the nature of experience *as experienced*, the introspectionist method decomposes experience into certain elements and trains the subjects to interpret their own experience in terms of these elements. What we have here is an appropriation of a third-person approach within the framework of reflection on experience. As Varela, Thompson, and Rosch have it, "It is precisely to cut through the attitude of introspection that mindfulness/awareness meditation exists" (1993, 32).

12. The standpoint of Price and Aydede (2005, 251), marked as it is by openness to phenomenology, confuses phenomenology with introspectionism, interpreted in three ways: either as a higher-order perception (HOP) or as a higher-order thought (HOT), or as both.

13. The inconsistencies concern such statements as "This is the purest blue anyone can perceive!" versus "No, it *isn't*, it has a faint but perceptible trace of green in it!" or, "This conscious experience of jealousy shows me how much I love my husband!" versus "No, this emotional state is not love *at all*, it is a neurotic, bourgeois fear of loss!" (see Metzinger 2003, 591).

14. In this regard, it is hard to agree with Varela, Thompson, and Rosch, who in *The Embodied Mind* maintain that "in a sort of philosophical introspection—which he called the 'intuition of essences' (*Wesenschau*)—Husserl tried to reduce experience to these essential structures and then show how our human world was generated from them" (1993, 16).

15. In Husserl's phenomenology, we come across different conceptions of open possibility, both practical and theoretical (see, in this regard, Mohanty 1984). In the present context, open possibility does not so much refer to the practical "I can" (and thus to potentialities predelineated in the horizon of a perceptual experience), but to the theoretical "I can conceive so and so."

16. One might object that dialogical phenomenology, as here presented, is nothing more than a piece of marketing. In response to this objection, I would especially stress that all my reference to dialogical phenomenology should be conceived as

NOTES TO PAGES 31–33

an invitation to pursue phenomenology by engaging in dialogue with other disciplines. This is especially called for in the phenomenology of pain, which has a lot to learn from various sciences, and especially from cognitive science, psychology, and psychoanalysis. The absence of a dialogical approach is exactly the reason why I find *certain conceptions* of eidetic variation problematic: as mentioned, relying too much on phantasy and first-person experience, one all-too-often conceives of this method as an excuse to practice phenomenology at a safe distance from all other intellectual discussions, without engaging in any dialogue with what takes place in other sciences. Indeed, to the best of my knowledge, there is not a single dialogically oriented phenomenological study of pain. I would contend that the reason for this is methodological: the available studies do not supplement eidetic variation with factual variation.

17. In phenomenological literature, Husserl was the first to conceptualize the distinction between static and genetic phenomenology. The relationship between these phenomenological methods is notoriously ambiguous and problematic. For Husserl's own explicit account of the distinction between them, see Husserl 2001, 624–34.

18. These difficulties are so far-reaching that in the critical discussions of these methods, the common strategy is to avoid methodological questions altogether and to focus exclusively on the description of the thematic (rather than methodological) differences between static and genetic phenomenology. We will return to this issue below.

19. In the *Logical Investigations*, the distinction between descriptive psychology and empirical psychology plays a fundamental role. While the task of empirical psychology is to provide genetic explanations, the goal of pure phenomenology, conceived of as descriptive psychology, is to offer pure descriptions of immanent experiences.

20. "It may well be that we have inherited dispositions for knowledge from the knowledge of past generations; but for the question concerning the meaning and value of what we know, the genetic story of this heritage of knowledge is as indifferent as is that of our gold currency to its real value" (Husserl 1983, 45).

21. As Anthony Steinbock has emphasized especially strongly, static analyses are in a sense *ontological*, and they provide *leading clues* for genetic constitutive analysis: "Once we become clear about *what* consciousness is as a structure and *how* this 'what' is constituted, maintains Husserl, the result of our static analyses can function as leading clues to *how* consciousness arises out of consciousness through genetically functioning modes of 'motivation,' that is, the relations of conditioning obtaining between the motivated and the motivating" (1995a, 45). To avoid some misunderstandings, I should further add that even though Steinbock in the study I have just quoted (as well as in more recent works) has made a strong case for a tripartite methodological division in Husserl's phenomenology (namely, the division between static, genetic, and generative phenomenology), in the context of this investigation, I will conceive of generative phenomenology not as a separate methodological framework, but as a particular addendum and a further development of genetic phenomenology. For this reason, in the framework of this chapter, I will keep to the general distinction between static and genetic phenomenology and will not address generative methodology separately.

22. In Husserl's words, "The mode of genesis is only given with the genesis of essence" (2001, 627).

23. As Bernet, Kern, and Marbach point out, even though Husserl from around 1920 onward constantly maintained the two-part division of transcendental

phenomenology into a static and genetic mode, he "did not elaborate clearly enough the methodology of genetic, constitutional analysis" (1993, 196).

24. From a historical perspective, one can note that Husserl's discovery of the genetic method and his turn to genetic phenomenology go hand in hand with his explicit interest in how the so-called Cartesian path to the reduction is to be complemented with other paths—and especially the path through psychology. This is by no means a coincidence. The new path to the reduction provides the methodological point of access to genetic phenomenology. In light of this circumstance, it becomes understandable why, in critical discussions, the difference between static and genetic phenomenology is usually addressed by focusing on the thematic fields rather than methodological commitments. Such a strategic decision is understandable, although only in part. To be sure, we need to be aware of the differences between the subject matters of static and genetic phenomenology, for only with the help of such an understanding can we meaningfully pursue an inquiry into methodological differences. Nonetheless, mere understanding of the differences between the thematic fields of static and genetic phenomenology does not suffice if we are to understand the methodological differences between them.

25. This becomes especially clear in Husserl's (1970) last and unfinished *The Crisis of European Sciences and Transcendental Phenomenology*. Besides this work, suffice it to briefly refer to the second volume of Husserl's (1959) *First Philosophy*. In this lecture course, which Husserl delivered in 1923–24, the path to the reduction through psychology is conceptualized as a genetic alternative to the Cartesian path that was privileged in the earlier studies that fall under static phenomenology.

26. Here we need to be especially cautious, as my remarks can easily lead to a misunderstanding. The second path to the reduction is not set against the universal ambitions of the first path. Rather, the second path is guided by the insight that the universal epoché and the universal reduction must be performed not at the beginning, but "at the end," that is, after one has demonstrated how each and every mundane experience can be reabsorbed within the phenomenological field. For Husserl's own account of the transition from the psychological to the universal epoché and the universal reduction, see Husserl 1959, §48.

27. Thus, in *First Philosophy II*, Husserl contends that each and every empirical act of mundane experience can be transformed into a transcendental act. He further adds a telling example: "I wish that the nice winter weather continues." When I transform this mundane wish into a transcendental experience, I do not have a transcendental wish alongside the mundane. Rather, the mundane wish is nothing other than a peculiar apperception that derives from my own experiential belief. See Husserl 1959, 82–83.

28. Or, as Sebastian Luft puts it, "Whether I take my point of departure from mundane consciousness and reduce to its transcendental 'counterpart,' or if I inquire back from the pre-given life-world to its constituting achievements, I arrive at transcendental (inter)subjectivity as the 'absolute being' that constitutes the world" (2004, 217).

29. Here, and in what follows, the term "intentional" is to be understood with relation to the phenomenological concept of intentionality.

30. One could further qualify all these acts in terms of the "as if," and this is exactly what allows us to qualify them as reproductive. Thus, if I remember, phantasize, or anticipate shaking my friend's hand, I live through this very experience in the mode of the "as if." Admittedly, Husserl often uses this expression, "as if" ("*als ob*"), to indicate what is specific to phantasy consciousness. In the present context, I

NOTES TO PAGES 37–51

employ this term in a broader sense, as Husserl also does, as a characteristic feature of all reproductive acts, be they positional (memory and anticipation) or neutralized (phantasy and image consciousness).

31. We do not just perceive phenomena but apperceive them: what we see in them or know about them always already exceeds the boundaries of their self-givenness. Or as Husserl has it: "Apperception: a consciousness that is conscious of something individual that is not self-given in it (self-given does not mean being contained in perception in an intimately inherent manner); and it is called apperception to the extent that it has this trait, even if it has something in addition that is self-given in it" (2001, 625).

32. This is true not only of the path to the reduction through psychology, but also of the ontological path. As Husserl's research manuscripts compiled in the A VII group (and subsequently published in *Husserliana XXXIX*) demonstrate, the phenomenological analysis of the life-world is to a large degree "a theory of world apperceptions."

CHAPTER 2. PAIN AND INTENTIONALITY

1. Stumpf offered his first systematic reflections on pain in his article "Über Gefühlsempfindungen" (1907). Brentano's critique of this standpoint is to be found in Brentano 1907, 119–25. Stumpf's subsequent response to Brentano can be found in Stumpf 1916.

2. Commenting on Michel Henry's analysis of pain, John Protevi remarks that "there is no intentional object constitution in the experience of pain, just pain as a purely immanent experience of life revealing itself to itself: a self-manifestation or self-appearance" (2009, 71).

3. Some terminological clarifications are in place. In *Ideas I*, Husserl interprets intentionality as composed of three moments: *hyle*, *noesis*, and *noema*. Husserl further argues that *hyle* and *noesis* make up two real (*reel*) moments of intentional acts. While the *noesis* is the form that animates the sensuous matter, *hyle* is the sensuous matter that is animated by the form. Hyletic elements are of three different kinds. They are (1) the sensuous contents that present the sensible determinations of an object; (2) various feelings, such as sensuous pleasure and pain; and (3) instinctual drives, such as bodily desire. By contrast to *hyle* and *noesis*, the *noema* is not a real (*reel*) content of an intentional act. Rather, this term denotes the object of intentionality. The noema is the object at which the meaning-intention is directed. One could qualify it as the intentional content of experience, or as the objective correlate of the conscious intention, or simply as the object as it is intended.

4. "Feelings are those outpouring atmospheres, which have their own spatiality, even though they are without place" (Schmitz 2009, 23; my translation—SG).

5. Let us note in passing that here Scarry might have touched on one of the central reasons why in the definition of pain offered by the International Association for the Study of Pain, pain is tied associatively to tissue damage. In light of Scarry's remarks, such a strategic gesture becomes understandable, even though, phenomenologically, it is unjustifiable.

6. Admittedly, Stumpf's followers reject this line of reasoning and argue that obtrusiveness constitutes a distinct characteristic of feeling-sensations. Yet, according to

those committed to the noematic conception of pain, Stumpf's followers beg the question in their reasoning: they do not explain in detail how a particular group of sensations can share the same characteristic with appearances. According to the perspective of Brentano's followers, the only way to provide an explanation is to transform a sensation into an appearance. But if so, then any explanation of this issue would land Stumpf's followers in a performative contradiction.

7. One might object that the phenomenological concept of the lived-body is much more appropriate to qualify the subject of pain. Nonetheless, one has to admit that to feel pain *in* particular parts of one's body presupposes one's capacity to objectify it.

8. See especially Husserl 1989, §36 and §37. Here Husserl provides us with a highly relevant distinction between lifeless and animated bodies, conceived of as two essentially different kinds of nature, identified by him as material and animal nature. While it is undeniable that all material things, irrespective of whether they are lifeless or animated, can be touched by other things, only with animated things, that is, only with the lived-body (*Leib*), does touching give rise to sensings (*Empfindnisse*). The sensings (*Empfindnisse*) in question can be of various kinds: touch, pressure, warmth, and coldness are some examples. According to Husserl of *Ideas II*, pain is also an *Empfindnis*. We will still have occasion to come back to pain as *Empfindis* in chapter 5, where we will address this concept in the framework of Husserl's phenomenology. For a detailed analysis of pain, conceived of as *Empfindnis*, in relation to Merleau-Ponty's phenomenology, see Grüny 2004, 51–100.

9. One should not overlook that in his more programmatic studies, Husserl has provided this schema with significant modifications. For instance, in §§15–16 of *Ideas II*, Husserl argued that the schema remains deficient insofar as one only takes into account things in isolation and ignores their embeddedness in the environment. However, according to Husserl of *Ideas II*, the recognition of this deficiency does not require that one give up the schema. Rather, this deficiency means that the schema needs to be supplemented, not abandoned. Admittedly, in his more mature writings, Husserl becomes more critical of the schema's validity. Still, concerning the schema's phenomenological legitimacy, see Kenneth Williford's (2013, 501–19) study, which provides a systematic overview of the debate surrounding this issue as well as a strong defense of the legitimacy of the apprehension—content of apprehension schema.

10. Following Husserl, here we conceive of the founding/founded relation not just "ontologically," but also logically or epistemologically. To clarify this issue, let us ask: Couldn't a pain in my leg be founded on the fact that someone kicked it? This appears to be the case "ontologically": it is certainly conceivable that being kicked in the leg would provoke the experience of pain. However, just as we do not always experience pain when our legs are kicked, so also, we can experience pain in the leg when nobody kicks it. This means that the relation between being kicked in the leg and experiencing pain in the leg is *not* a founding relation in the logical or epistemological sense of the term, for no necessity binds them to each other. To conceive of the founding/founded relation not only "ontologically," but also logically and epistemologically, is to maintain that, for instance, color is founded on extension. Indeed, nothing can be colored that is not extended. This also applies to the above-mentioned example of the politician, who can be happy about the election results if, and only if, the election results are available and he is familiar with them. By contrast, there is no necessity that binds one's experience of pain to any other occurrences. Such being the case, one has a full right to claim that even though the experience of pain is often founded

NOTES TO PAGES 55–58

"ontologically," it is not a founded experience in the logical or epistemological sense of the term.

11. As Agustín Serrano de Haro suggests, "Concerning pain or pleasure we certainly deal with a conscious experience, but it is a non-intentional one, a state of mind in which nothing at all is primarily grasped or represented, in which by itself there is no objective term towards which a conscious intention is directed. . . . In conclusion, pain is not an intentional object grasped or apprehended, nor is it either an act of grasping and feeling; it is only sensation and affective" (2011, 388).

12. In Husserl's words, "Our sensations here receive an objective 'interpretation' or 'taking-up.' They themselves are not acts, but acts are constituted through them, wherever, that is, intentional characters like a perceptual interpretation lay hold of them, and as it were animate them. In just this manner it seems that a burning, piercing, boring pain, fused as it is from the start with certain tactual sensations, must itself count as a sensation. It functions at least as other sensations do, in providing a foothold for empirical, objective interpretations" (2000, 573).

13. One could object to the interpretation I offer here and argue that it fails to account for the important difference between pain sensations, on the one hand, and those sensations that form the material content of perception, on the other. The objection runs as follows: How are we to understand the fact that Husserl, employing the "apprehension—content of apprehension" schema to analyze the structure of perceptual consciousness, does not end up with the view that perceptually given objects are stratified phenomena even though, according to the interpretation I propose here, he paves the way for the recognition of the stratified nature of pain experience? In response to this objection, I have to concede that the *Logical Investigations* do not provide us with sufficient resources to draw a clear distinction between pain sensations and those sensations that form the content of perceptual consciousness. To answer this objection, it is necessary to turn to Husserl's later works, and especially to the crucial distinction between *Empfindungen* (sensations) and *Empfindnisse* (sensings) that we come across in *Ideen II* (and elsewhere). When we turn in chapter 5 to Husserl's analysis of the body in *Ideen II*, we will address this distinction in detail. For the moment, we can briefly answer the objection as follows: in contrast to perception, which is to be conceived as the apprehension of *Empfindungen* (sensations), pain is not an *Empfindung*, but an *Empfindnis*. Sensations (*Empfindungen*) remain abstract before they are apperceived; they are *dependent* moments of perceptual experience. By contrast, sensings (*Empfindnisse*) such as pain can be felt both at the nonintentional hyletic level and at higher levels of experience that are already shaped by different kinds of apperceptive consciousness; they are *independent* moments of a full-fledged pain experience. In short, pain is a stratified phenomenon, while perceptual objects are not, because pain is an *Empfindnis*, which can still be felt before it is subsumed under apprehensive consciousness, even though it can also become a moment of such apprehensive consciousness.

14. As Husserl puts it in a footnote, "Naturally I reject Brentano's doctrine that presentative acts, in the term of acts of feeling-sensations, underlie acts of feeling" (2000, 574).

15. This argument, one could add, is a reinterpretation of the classical argument concerning the evidence of pain that Descartes had provided in his *Principles*. Descartes maintained that while the experience of pain is clear, it is not distinct. Insofar as it is clear, the experience of pain is indubitable. Yet insofar as it is not distinct,

consciousness confounds it with sensations in different parts of the body. Thus, in the case of a toothache, insofar as pain is clear, it is meaningless to doubt whether or not I am in pain. Yet, since pain lacks distinctness, it is not uncommon to misidentify pain's location. According to the interpretation I am here proposing, Husserl's stratified conception of adequate and inadequate evidence that accompanies the experience of pain is a reinterpretation of Descartes's approach, which relied on the nonstratified distinction between clear and distinct evidence.

16. I consider it to be an undeniable phenomenological fact that I can feel pain only *within my own lived-body*, nowhere else (in chapter 5, the relationship between pain and embodiment will be addressed in much greater detail). By contrast, the other intentional objects of which we speak here are not localizable within our own lived-bodies, and, therefore, they are verifiable intersubjectively. In light of this difference, one has the full right to claim that the distinction between what lies within and what lies without is of crucial importance for any phenomenologically oriented theory of pain.

17. Does this mean that painful intensity is a matter of intentionality, not of sensibility? If so, would it not be a matter of consistency to draw the conclusion that the painful character of our pains depends on reflective acts? Both questions are to be answered with a no. It is crucial to stress that even though the intensity of pain manifests itself within the horizon of sensibility (it is felt, rather than being apprehended objectively), nonetheless, the greater the intensity of the feeling-sensations, such as pains, the greater the likelihood that they will absorb our attention, thereby becoming the intentional objects of our consciousness.

18. One might wonder, how compatible is Sartre's phenomenology with that of Husserl? Do we not face here two significantly different kinds of phenomenological projects, which are guided by different goals, which rely on different methodological principles, and which unfold on different levels of experience? These polemical questions bring us back to the difficult problem that concerns the unity of the phenomenological movement. I have already touched on this issue in the introduction. In the present context, let me stress that the current study is exclusively focused on the phenomenon of pain and that one of its goals is to show what the phenomenological movement has to contribute to the science of pain. Even though the current study subscribes to the methodological principles of Husserlian phenomenology, it does not need to limit itself to any partisan view at the expense of ignoring the variety of contributions that we come across in phenomenology as a whole. While this study is committed to the fundamental methodological principles of Husserlian phenomenology, its fundamental objective is to develop a phenomenology of pain in a dialogical fashion, by bringing it into dialogue not only with other phenomenological views, but also with those disciplines that know nothing of phenomenology. In light of such an open orientation, we have the full right to keep at a distance from this conflict of interpretations, as we turn to different phenomenological accounts of pain experience that we come across in different phenomenological frameworks.

19. Regarding Sartre's notion of facticity, consider the following: "While it is necessary that I be in the form of being-there, still it is altogether contingent that I be, for I am not the foundation of my being; on the other hand, while it is necessary that I be engaged in this or that point of view, it is contingent that it should be precisely in this view to the exclusion of all others. This twofold contingency which embraces a necessity we have called the *facticity* of the for-itself" (Sartre 1956, 408).

NOTES TO PAGES 63–76

20. This is what Drew Leder has called "the centripetal mode" of the experience of pain: "Centripetal movement is one 'directed inward toward a center or axis.' . . . Our sensory experience, normally directed ecstatically upon the world, is now forced inward in a centripetal fashion. We no longer see, hear, feel the world *through* our bodies: instead the body itself becomes what we feel, the center or axis of thematic attention. As often as we turn outward we are pulled back by the insistent call of pain, back to the crampy stomach, the headache, the throbbing foot" (1984–85, 255).

21. The relationship between pain and suffering is twofold. On the one hand, as is the case with a cancer victim, physical pain is the cause of suffering. On the other hand, as is the case with virtually all stressful experiences, nonphysical suffering is the source of pain. In the present context, I will address only the first type of suffering, namely, suffering that is triggered by physical pain.

22. Using Heideggerian terminology, one could say that we face here the transformation of the body's readiness-to-hand (*Zuhandenheit*) into its presence-at-hand (*Vorhandenheit*). As Drew Leder has elegantly put it, "We look at the painful body as though from a distance, prod it, point at it, take it to the doctor for examination. The alienation and objectification consummated in the modern medical encounter merely extends a phenomenological shift already begun by the illness. The painful body surfaces as a *thing*. . . . It has betrayed us. . . . We are bound together now as reluctant partners, and after serious pain we may never regain our former trust" (1984–85, 262).

23. Here we speak *exclusively* of physiological localization of pain. As we will see in chapter 5, a phenomenological theory of pain must draw a distinction between two different forms of pain localization: besides being localized in one's physical body (*Körper*), pain can also be localized in one's lived-body (*Leib*). In the present context, we leave the second form of pain localization out of consideration.

CHAPTER 3. THE PHENOMENOLOGY OF PAIN DISSOCIATION SYNDROMES

1. The analysis undertaken in chapter 2 allows us to identify two scenarios of when pain can be experienced as a mere sensation. This can happen (1) either when pain remains *nonobtrusive*, for then the motivation is missing to transform the contents of experience into forms of intentional experience; or (2) at the *onset of pain experience*, since some experiential contents must first be lived through if consciousness is to notice them, single them out, focus on them, and apperceive them as painful.

2. Consider in this regard Sartre's brief analysis of the suffering of a psychaesthenic, as proposed in *The Imaginary* (2004). According to Sartre, there is a real and irreducible difference between the real distress of a cancer victim and the "pain" of a psychaesthenic who is convinced that he is suffering from cancer pain. "Without doubt we could find, in the case of imagined pain, an absolutely wild person, having lost all control, thrown into a panic, nervous and despairing. Nothing of this—neither the starts, nor the cries when the limb they imagine to be ailing is touched—is acted in the absolute sense of the word. . . . It is indeed true that such victims cannot prevent themselves from screaming. . . . But nothing—neither starts nor moans—can make it real suffering" (Sartre 2004, 143). Indeed, while the patient suffering from

cancer pain does all that is in his power to reduce the effects of his pain and suffering, the psychaesthenic, by contrast, invests all his energy into the production of pain and suffering. According to Sartre, such a magical production is not realizable, which is something that the psychaesthenic knows quite well, and thus, the deep nature of his cries largely relies upon the unrealizable nature of his project.

3. As Drew Leder has it, "Pain has a unique qualitative feel that sets it off from other sensory experiences: namely, it *hurts*. Pain is the very concretization of the unpleasant, the aversive. It places upon the sufferer what I will term an *affective call*. One's attention is summoned by the gnawing, distasteful quality of pain in a way that it would not be by a more neutral stimulus" (1990, 73).

4. More than fifty years ago, Bruce Aune argued against the intrinsic incorrigibility of such utterances as "I am in pain." Aune contended that we must give up our ingrained empiricism and the inappropriate way it invites us to think of pain: "We must not suppose, after all, that we begin our lives with a wholly natural, pre-conceptual understanding of what pain is, and then, after linguistic training, we come to understand that *this* and *that* are to be called 'pain,' that the time to say 'I am in pain' is when I have *this*. To suppose such a thing is obviously to trail clouds of empiricist error, to signal one's allegiance to the Myth of the Given" (1965, 56).

5. Or as Grüny has it, "Der Schmerz tut (jemandem) weh. Dieses Wehtun, das in traditionellen Begriffen als emotionale Komponente oder Reaktion verstanden wurde, ist es, was den Schmerz zum Schmerz macht, und diese Feststellung verliert ihre Trivialität, wenn man sie zu explizieren versucht" (2004, 20).

6. "When the patient is not directly asked to report on his condition, he does not 'attend' to it or 'think' about it to the same extent as before the operation and, when not thus reacting to it, does not appear to be 'in pain'" (Barber 1959, 439).

7. The account I here offer is further corroborated by neurological explanations, which suggest that these patients have the sensation of pain, yet they do not have the appropriate emotive and behavioral reaction toward their pain.

8. Consider in this regard Williford's observation, which we come across in his analysis of Husserl's concept of hyletic data: "Certain types of hyletic structures may indeed be fit by their natures for certain types of representative and behavioral functions and not others—it is hard, for example, to imagine a complete inversion of pleasure and pain keeping all behaviors constant" (2013, 510). In the case under discussion, we face a pathological apprehension precisely because the content of experience is not (to use Williford's expression) fit for the apprehension.

9. Could one not say the reverse? After all, these patients report that they feel what they identify as pain only when they are asked about it. Could one, therefore, not contend that these patients do not feel pain at the nonintentional level of experience but, on the contrary, only at the intentional level, conceived of as a reflective, cognitive, and objectifying level of experience? I think these questions need to be answered negatively. The stratified conception of pain I am presenting here suggests that pain simply cannot be lived merely at the intentional level; if it is not lived through as a sensation, it is not lived through at all; and if it is not lived through, one does feel it. I believe this holds for all feelings and emotions: in contrast to perceptual and conceptual objects, if one does not feel emotionally given objects, one cannot constitute them at the intentional level either. In such cases, they remain empty of all feeling-related intentionality.

NOTES TO PAGES 84–97

10. One should note in passing that Grahek does not treat pain hypersymbolia as an instance of painfulness without pain. Rather, for him, the condition called "pain affect without pain sensation" (Grahek 2007, 108) provides such an instance. We will soon turn to the analysis of this alleged syndrome.

11. One might wonder: Could it not be so that threat hypersymbolia is a case of prereflective, nonintentional experience of threat? As we just saw, the patients suffering from this syndrome find their lot humiliating because their bodies react in a way contrary to how they want them to react. Should one not claim that here we are confronted with a case where the body reacts nonintentionally to pain, while the patient himself, at the intentional level, does not experience any pain? I do not think that such an interpretation is convincing. Most importantly, threat hypersymbolia is not an instance of prereflective, nonintentional experience of pain simply because the patients suffering from this condition are well aware that they are in pain. This basic fact provides sufficient reason to contend that the patients experience pain intentionally. However, they cannot experience it merely intentionally if only because, as I have been arguing, pain as such is a feeling, a lived-experience. One thus has to admit that, despite all the tensions between the subject of pain (however one is to conceive of such a subject) and the body, threat hypersymbolia is an instance that illustrates how pain can be experienced both pre-intentionally and intentionally, although in the absence of pain-inducing stimuli.

12. As Grahek has it, pain asymbolics "are quite capable of discriminating, differentiating, and localizing the damaging or potentially damaging stimuli whenever they are applied to any part of their bodies, and they do feel pain therefrom. However, the pain that these patients feel does not represent for them any damage or potential damage to their bodies" (2007, 80).

13. This view is further confirmed by Rubins and Friedman, whose study of four cases of AP led them to claim that "all our patients showed mixed aphasia" (1948, 563). Their study further shows that in the case of these patients, "spelling of simple monosyllabic words was usually correct, although several trials were frequently necessary. Longer ones could not be spelled at all" (1948, 563). These remarks point toward a rather common relation between AP and some kind of aphasia, including word deafness.

CHAPTER 4. PAIN AND TEMPORALITY

1. Admittedly, in Husserl's phenomenology, the concept of the "as if" (*als ob*) is employed sometimes in a broader and sometimes in a narrower sense. In the broader sense, the term refers to all forms of reproductive consciousness. In the narrower sense, it designates the specific way in which objects are given to phantasy consciousness and image consciousness. According to Husserl, both phantasy consciousness and image consciousness intend their objects in the mode of *neutralized presentifications (neutralisierte Vergegenwärtigungen)*. In the present context, I employ the concept of the "as if" in the broader sense of the term, conceiving of it as a characteristic feature that distinguishes reproductive consciousness, taken in its diverse modalities, from original consciousness.

2. For instance, the short Text Nr. 35, which focuses on the reduction to the streaming present, *ends* with a question: "What is, then, the stream of presence?" (Husserl 2006, 139; my translation—SG). The very fact that Husserl raises this question at the very end, rather than at the beginning of the manuscript, suggests that the exact meaning of the living present remains problematic not only for Husserl's interpreters, but also for Husserl himself.

3. With regard to the first sense, it suffices to observe that, clearly, pain is not lived at the level of time-constituting consciousness; the temporality of pain is necessarily given as constituted duration. So also, with regard to the second sense, it suffices to remark that pain is experienced not only impressionally, but also retentionally and protentionally: pain is lived in its temporal duration (a pain that would be lived only impressionally wouldn't really matter to us, since as soon as one would experience it, one would instantly overcome it). Finally, with regard to the fifth sense, we can note that, as we already know from our earlier considerations, the field of presence in which pain is lived refuses to be measured in terms of the categories of objective time. In fact, as we will still see, pain belongs to the group of traumatic experiences that disturb and disrupt the constitution of objective time.

4. This issue will be addressed in detail in chapter 5.

5. According to Roger Trigg, Kaplan's interpretation of the case, which I have presented above, "seems to suggest that the writing is in fact an 'avowal' on the part of an unconscious portion of the personality, but this is to say that the pain is 'unconscious' (or perhaps 'subconscious') and therefore unfelt, which involves us in a straight contradiction" (1970, 67). Yet the fact that pain is unconscious does not mean that pain is unfelt. The distinction drawn between implicit and explicit modes of consciousness implies that one can live through many feelings and emotions nonthematically. We will still have an occasion to return to this issue.

6. One might wonder: Why is this distinction between what one lives through implicitly and what one is conscious of explicitly so strongly linked to temporality? Aren't we faced here with two significantly different issues? I do not think so, and for a very basic reason. We are speaking here of feelings and consciousness of feelings. Yet feelings as such can be lived only *in the present*. Clearly, a feeling that belongs either to the past or to the future is not an actual feeling; it becomes actual when it is lived, and it can be lived only in the present.

7. "A pain in my knee is a sensation that I mind having; so 'unnoticed pain' is an absurd expression" (Ryle 2009, 203). I should note in passing that Ryle's conception of pain is more complex than this brief passage might suggest, as can be witnessed especially in the question that we come across in the title of his short paper published in *Analysis* in 1954. The title of his paper reads as follows: "If a Distraction Makes Me Forget My Headache Does It Make My Head Stop Aching, or Does It Only Stop Me Feeling It Aching?" (Ryle 1954, 51). The analysis here offered suggests the following answer to this question: in the hypothetical case under consideration, one continues to be implicitly aware of one's pain (that is, one continues to *feel* pain), even though one is not explicitly conscious that one is in pain.

8. Here we have an eidetic insight into one of the essential characteristics of pain experience. A pain without any intensity would be an "unfelt pain"; as such, it would no longer be a feeling, and, therefore, we would no longer have any basis to identify it as pain.

NOTES TO PAGES 110–116

9. We come across a similar argument in David Palmer's (1975) "Unfelt Pains." However, this similar form of reasoning leads Palmer to argue for the falsity of two theses. First, according to Palmer, the thesis that "whenever we have a sensation it must be felt or noticed is false" (1975, 294). Second, another closely related thesis, namely, that "whenever we have a sensation of the sort we call pain, it must be felt or noticed can no longer be accepted" (1975, 294). For the reasons presented in this section, I do not agree with Palmer on either point. There is an important distinction to be drawn between feeling, on the one hand, and explicit consciousness (what Palmer calls "noticing"), on the other. *Not all feelings are explicitly self-conscious*: noticing that one is in pain is not the same as feeling pain.

10. Let us not overlook that this distinction between focal, unattended, and co-attended experiences is indicative of the selective nature of conscious life. *We always experience more than we can focus on explicitly.* Or, as Husserl insightfully remarks, "The seizing-upon is a singling out and seizing; anything perceived has an experiential background" (1983, 70). We can take this to mean that we can be thematically conscious of anything only when we single out and apprehend specific contents of experience, while there are many other contents that could have taken the place of the one to which consciousness has chosen to direct its interest. Yet, as we already saw, it is not enough to draw a distinction between focal and unattended experiences. Rather, the experiential background to which Husserl refers in the above-quoted passage is further differentiated into those experiences that remain unattended to (that is, unconscious experiences), as well as other experiences, which are co-attended to (that is, co-conscious experiences). Thus, insofar as we think of pain as a sensation, we can further say that pain can be experienced as a focal sensation (given in the foreground); as an unattended sensation (given in the background); and, finally, as a co-attended sensation (also given in the background).

11. Or, as Brough puts it, "I know that the past is my past, but it now seems cut adrift, no longer the phase of my life coherently preceding my present and forming the ground of my harmonious passage into the future" (2001, 39).

12. As Leder has it, "Temporal constriction is characteristic of chronic pain as well. While the body in well-being can explore the far reaches of time through memory and imagination, such possibilities constrict when we are in pain. With chronic suffering a painless past is all but forgotten. While knowing intellectually that we were once not in pain we have lost the bodily memory of how this felt" (1990, 76).

13. Both the depersonalizing and the repersonalizing nature of chronic pain will be addressed in detail in chapter 6.

14. The influence of early experience on the subsequent experience of pain has also been demonstrated experimentally (see Melzack and Scott 1957, 155–61; and Melzack and Wall 2008, 20–21).

15. Moreover, anticipating the analysis of embodiment in the next chapter, we could say the following: while explicit memory is the memory of consciousness, implicit memory is the memory of the body.

16. More recently, we come across the analysis of this study in Zangwill 1983; Fuchs 2008; and Feinstein, Duff, and Tranel 2010.

17. The same neurons respond both to visual and to noxious stimulation. Because of brain damage, the patients suffering from this syndrome cannot help but associate visual and noxious stimulations. Due to the power of associations, visually detected threats produce an actual experience of pain in the patients.

18. The psychological reasons concern the common worry shared by a number of pain patients. Presumably, the failure to identify external causes that underlie the patient's pain experience would provoke the suspicion that the pain the patient complains of is just "in the patient's mind": it is only imaginary, the patient herself is to blame for it, and thus, she is not in need of a physician, but a psychiatrist. It thereby becomes understandable why the patients would have a strong psychological motivation to believe that the pain they suffer from is triggered externally.

CHAPTER 5. THE BODY IN PAIN

1. *When I say that I am in pain, what does the "I" refer to?* This is the question that I here wish to identify as the question concerning the subject of pain.

2. As S. Kay Toombs observes in *The Meaning of Illness*, "In providing a phenomenological description, the phenomenologist is committed to the effort to begin with what is given in immediate experience, to turn to the essential features of what presents itself as it presents itself to consciousness, and thereby to clarify the constitutive activity of consciousness and the sense-structure of experiencing" (1993, xi).

3. The distinction drawn here between pain and suffering should not be taken to mean that while pain is exclusively physical, suffering is just as exclusively psychological. When we turn in chapter 7 to the analysis of such processes as somatization and psychologization, it will become clear that such is by no means the case. In the present context, we are not yet in the position to address these issues, which will be at the center of our attention in the last two chapters of this study.

4. It is worth noting that the recognition that pain is an experiential phenomenon is strongly pronounced in some of the founding legends of Western civilization, which we come across in the book of Genesis. As David Bakan insightfully remarks, "Pain, having no other locus but the conscious ego, is almost literally the price man pays for the possession of a conscious ego, as the biblical story of Adam and Eve in the Garden of Eden so strongly suggests: Eve, having eaten of the Tree of Knowledge, must bear her children in pain. . . . Certainly the most effective devices available for the elimination of pain are exactly those which eliminate consciousness entirely" (1968, 71–72).

5. Here, as well as in the book as a whole, the concept of spirit is to be understood in the sense that this concept has received in phenomenology. We are to understand this concept as the English translation of the German *Geist*, which refers to the intersubjective culture, as contrasted with the realm of nature. Conceived of phenomenologically, spirit encompasses all cultural achievements, understood as expressions of (inter)subjective activity. This concept thus refers to art, religion, politics, everything that is addressed in the human sciences (*Geisteswissenschaften*). The spiritual world (*geistige Welt*), of which Husserl speaks in *Ideas II* and elsewhere, refers to a world in which persons interact with each other *as persons*, and not just as natural objects.

6. In this regard, it is quite telling that in his analysis of the lived-body as the field of sensings, Husserl (1989, §36) does not merely claim that the lived-body is the bearer of sensations; rather, he claims that the lived-body is the bearer of *localized* sensations.

NOTES TO PAGES 134–142

7. "Joy and sorrow are not in the heart as blood is in the heart. Sensations of touch are not in the skin as pieces of organic tissue are" (Husserl 2006, 5; my translation—SG).

8. Tadashi Ogawa (1983) provides a compelling response to such an accusation in his analysis of Husserl's phenomenology of the lived-body. According to Ogawa, the very fact that this constitution relies on tactual rather than visible sensations indicates that Husserl's phenomenology overcomes the dualism in question: with the help of the concept of *Empfindnisse*, it discovers behind all duality a more primordial unity. In the present context, I do not want to focus on the primordial unity that underlies the split between the disembodied consciousness and the physiological body. Rather, here I wish to ask: What phenomenological sense does it make to qualify the body as a constitutive accomplishment? I take this qualification to mean that, as seen from the standpoint of Husserlian phenomenology, the body is myself (insofar as I apperceive myself as embodied), as well as something other than myself (insofar as the body is constituted). My goal here is to show that such a paradoxical split is of great significance for the phenomenological understanding of pain experience.

9. "The situation is somewhat different as regards extra-Bodily things which through their relation to man have likewise assumed Ego-meanings, e.g., words, goods, aesthetic values, Objects to be used, etc. They have indeed a 'meaning,' but they have no soul" (Husserl 1989, 102).

10. As Dermot Moran insightfully observes, "Husserl, Scheler and Edith Stein all claim that feelings such as pain and pleasure take place 'at a distance from the ego'" (2010, 1).

11. For this reason, it would be phenomenologically incorrect to qualify the body in pain as the absolute here, although given in a somewhat modified form, say, as the absolute, confining, and restrictive *here* that has lost access to all that is *there*. What is absolutely here remains out of sight. By contrast, the body in pain is plainly "in sight": in extreme cases, it becomes the one and only object of experience, which absorbs all attention.

12. A detailed inquiry into the relation between pain and the life-world will be provided in chapter 7.

CHAPTER 6. THE PHENOMENOLOGY OF EMBODIED PERSONHOOD

1. Admittedly, a number of phenomenologically oriented thinkers would be willing to claim that the lived-body is not something that I have, but something that I am. For instance, in a recently published study, Fredrik Svenaeus writes: "The body is not only ours, it is *us*" (2018, 5). I do not share this view. It seems to me that it expresses a phenomenologically unjustified bias of a healthy body, which either does not know or refuses to accept the body's refusal to be me, which was addressed in chapter 5. I do not find it surprising that, as far as Svenaeus's study is concerned, soon after identifying the self with the body, he introduces a split between them, as witnessed in his brief analysis of what happens when "the person, whose body it is, appears to be permanently gone" (2018, 5). Indeed, Svenaeus introduces the concept of the suffering

person in chapter 2 of his analysis, and it is here that we come across implicit reasons why the identification of the body with the self lacks phenomenological justification. Here we encounter the analysis of what happens when the lived-body "displays an alien character in showing up as an obstacle and a limitation" (Svenaeus 2018, 25). Here also we encounter the claim that "the suffering of pain is actually a way of not being at home in one's body" (2018, 25). How can the body have such an alien character and how can I be not at home in my body if I myself am my body? The analysis offered here relies upon a more basic split between the body and the self, which in the present chapter I will aim to conceptualize by not conflating the concepts of the lived-body and the person.

2. Consider also Viktor von Weizsäcker's reflections: "Ist er, der Schmerz, ein Ich-Zustand oder ein Es-Zustand? Gehört er mir oder der Umwelt? Bezeichnet er mich oder ein Nicht-Ich? Sicher gehört er nicht einem Außending an wie die Farbe, die Form, die Elastizität jenem Gummiballe. Aber er gehört auch nicht so nur zu mir wie meine geheimen Gedanken" (2011, 266–67).

3. In his highly influential study, in which he argued that medicine is too preoccupied with the *causes* of pain and too indifferent to the *meaning* it has for the *person* who suffers it, Eric Cassell (1978) drew a distinction between the concepts of the person and of the self. According to Cassell, selfhood is "self-concerned" and is somehow cut off from what in phenomenology is called intersubjectivity and the lifeworld. By contrast, the concept of the person does not suffer from such a shortcoming. Much like Svenaeus (2018, 23), I also have philosophical concerns about such a distinction. It forces us to overlook the highly intriguing phenomenological analyses of the self that we come across in the literature. For this reason, in the present study I will use the terms "person" and "self" interchangeably, although, admittedly, there are other ways besides the one offered by Cassell to distinguish between them. However, as far as my current purposes are concerned, these other phenomenological distinctions are irrelevant.

4. By imprisoning the person in the field of presence and cutting him off from the painless past and the painless future, chronic pains force the self to reconstitute his or her own selfhood by reestablishing new types of fundamental relations that make up the core of personhood.

5. Building on the basis of Husserl's analysis in §85 of *Ideen I*, Serrano de Haro has recently argued that the ego, understood as the subjective pole of the stream of consciousness, must be conceived of as the subject of pain: "No pain can be thought without an ego, no aversive sensation without a subject who suffers it" (2018, 8); and as Serrano de Haro further added, "We could surely say this the other way around as well: there is no subjectivity without pain; an ego pole who never came to experience pain is unthinkable" (2018, 8). This is an important realization, if only because it forces us to abandon the common tendency to think of Husserl's concept of the pure ego in the Kantian fashion, as an absolute ego that does not relate in any shape or form to the concrete ego, conceived of as an active and passive subject of action and affection. Besides forcing us to rethink some central themes in phenomenology, this realization also compels us to admit that pain is not asubjective: "As a matter of principle, [pain] is subjective and centripetal: it needs an ego-pole" (Serrano de Haro 2018, 10). My goal, in the present context, is not to deny the validity of these well-founded phenomenological claims, but to complement them with insights that rely on other phenomenological sources. The recognition that the subject of pain is

NOTES TO PAGES 145–149

the *person* does not contradict the view that it is also the ego, since the ego, being the centering point of the stream of experiences, is described as the very core of personhood. Nonetheless, more can be said about the person conceived of as the subject of pain than we could say about the pure ego fulfilling this very function. In the present context, of central importance is the realization that by recognizing the person as the subject of pain, we have all the means needed to address the depersonalizing and the repersonalizing characteristics of pain experience.

6. Or, as Maria Villela-Petit has it, the nature of the natural attitude "is no longer what we have to deal with when we cultivate our garden or that of the blue sky we contemplate with delight, not even that of a movingly beautiful body. . . . Rather, it is what we have in mind when, through a change of attitude, we envisage things in a theoretical way" (2007, 208).

7. Pure nature, conceived of naturalistically, is a modification of the life-world, conceived of personalistically. This realization does not exclude the possibility that the naturalistic modification of the personalistic attitude enables us to find out a large variety of truths about the world, which would otherwise lie beyond our reach. One could say about the naturalistic modification what Husserl famously said about Galileo: this modification is both revealing and concealing; revealing, in that it discloses unseen dimensions of reality; concealing, in that it lacks the inner awareness that it is a modification of the personalistic attitude.

8. It is important not to confuse motivation with mechanistic causality. While causality rules over *nature*, motivation finds its place within the horizon of *understanding*. Motivation refers to "what moves me, what makes me act and accomplish such and such operations (as for example theoretical acts)" (Villela-Petit 2007, 210). If, when I leave my apartment, I see dark clouds in the sky, I feel motivated to bring an umbrella with me, just as when I realize that I am running late for an important meeting, I feel motivated to catch a taxi. Motivation is a peculiar kind of nonmechanistic causality that relies upon the person's capacity to discriminate between different possibilities, granting some more and others less weight. These differentiations rely upon subjective expectations and exclude objective necessity. The person always remains free to choose certain plans over others as well as to engage in these rather than other activities. Thus, no matter how dark and heavy the clouds might be, I can always choose not to bring an umbrella with me; no matter how important the meeting, I might choose not to take a taxi.

9. See in this regard Matthew Ratcliffe's account of the phenomenology of sickness, which emphasizes the contrast between estrangement and belonging and which revolves around the insight that "existential feelings are *partly* constitutive of selfhood" (2008, 120) and that "the phenomenology of self, whatever else it might involve, is not dissociable from existential feelings" (121). In this regard, of fundamental importance is the realization that chronic pain brings about a profound transformation in existential feelings by transforming the space of possibilities that these feelings make manifest. This transformation is to be conceived in terms of diminution, and, therefore, it must be conceived of as a depersonalizing experience.

10. Such is the case not only with chronic but also with transient and acute pain. While in the usual flow of experience, the person identifies herself with the lived-body, "the tooth in which there is pain becomes 'the tooth that hurts me,' an 'it' which is no longer 'me'; and its extraction is not an injury to the ego but a saving of the ego from assault" (Bakan 1968, 77).

214   NOTES TO PAGES 149–151

11. Or as Brian—Byron J. Good's interviewee—puts it, "And then it goes back into my conflict about my body. Is it my body? Is it my thinking process that activates physical stresses? Or . . . is it the other way around?" (Good 1994a, 35). Consider also the observations of Gordon Stuart, a thirty-three-year-old writer who is dying from cancer: "The feeling there is something not me in me, an 'it,' eating its way through the body. I am the creator of my own destruction. These cancer cells are me and yet not me. I am invaded by a killer. . . . Cancer makes us think of a lingering torture, a being eaten away from inside. And that is what it's been like for me" (Kleinman 1988, 148).

12. As Buytendijk so insightfully puts it, "We are not tormented by some foreign agent . . . it is our own body. My own hand, my head, hurts me. The organs of the body, the heart, kidneys, stomach function in a manner which is hidden and unconscious as far as I am concerned: now they refuse to serve, they are in revolt against me: they torment and rob me of my power over myself. This senseless abandonment of the human being to pain has its direct result in a cleavage of the self and the body" (1962, 30).

13. These references to Kleinman's, Jackson's, and Good's studies are meant to illustrate the philosophical fruitfulness of anthropological studies of pain. It is highly regrettable that to this day, the phenomenologically oriented anthropologists and the phenomenologically minded philosophers have shown little interest in each other's works. In this regard, Katherine J. Morris's (2013) recent study is a noteworthy exception. This work reconstructs the main reasons that have led medical anthropology to consider phenomenologically relevant themes. This study also spells out the main phenomenologically resonant themes that have emerged from anthropological studies of pain.

14. These four kinds of disturbance are not unique to the experience of pain; they also aptly characterize other forms of affliction, such as illness. Yet chronic pain does not affect the body the way illness does. This is something we already know from chapter 5: *while illness affects the whole body* (and thus we would never say that our head or our lower back is ill), *chronic pain is always located within the body* (and thus it is always our head or our lower back that is in pain). Due to its localizability, chronic pain renders the relation between the self and the body profoundly paradoxical. On the one hand, the body in pain could be characterized as both subject and object. On the other hand, the body in pain could be further said to be both subservient and insubordinate to the self.

15. We come across an intriguing analysis of the responsive dimension of pain experience in Juan-David Nasio's psychoanalytic study *The Book of Pain and Love*, which suggests that "above all, pain is an *affect*, an ultimate affect. . . . It is like a final struggle that attests to life and to our power to regain ourselves. One does not die from pain. As long as there is pain, we also have the available forces to fight against it and continue living" (2004, 15). This very same responsive dimension also plays a role in Drew Leder's analysis of pain. According to Leder, "Pain exerts a *telic demand* upon us. While calling us to the now, its distasteful quality also establishes a futural goal: to be free of pain" (1990, 77). This very same dimension is also of significance in Sartre's analysis: "Pain-consciousness is a project towards a further consciousness which would be empty of all pain; that is, to a consciousness whose contexture, whose being-there would be not painful" (1956, 438). Last, let me also remark that we come across the same responsive dimension in David Bakan's study: "Pain is the demand on the conscious ego to work

NOTES TO PAGES 151–159

to bring the decentralized part back into the unity of the organism. Pain is the imperative to the ego to assume the responsibility of telic centralization, the ego itself having emerged as a result of telic decentralization" (1968, 72).

16. As seen from the phenomenological standpoint, it would be a mistake to understand such responses as merely physiological reflexes. Exclusively physiological explanations fail to take into account the role of the body's implicit memory, which was addressed in chapter 4 (see also Fuchs 2008, 65–81).

17. Max Scheler's "Meaning of Suffering," which was originally completed in 1916, provides us with a richer typology of what Scheler (1992, 110) identifies as different types of spiritual interpretations of pain and suffering. Scheler speaks of the teachings of the Buddha, which endorse indifference and extinction as goals of salvation. He further speaks of the dulling of pain to the point of apathy (the asceticism of Epictetus and the Stoics), or the heroic struggle against pain (the active heroism of Heracles, which Scheler identifies as the ancient attitude par excellence), or of pain's suppression to the point of the realization that it is an illusion (Stoicism). So also, Scheler speaks of the view endorsed in the Old Testament, which interprets suffering as a penalty and as earthly realization of divine justice. For Scheler (1992, 87), all these different forms of what Weizsäcker calls "Schmerzarbeit" need to be distinguished from the Christian teaching, which identifies *sacrifice* as the true meaning of all pain and suffering.

18. "The work of pain (*Schmerzarbeit*) is not essentially a conversion of energy, but rather essentially a decision (*Entscheidung*). . . . The work of pain is actually a matter of decision, which cannot be expressed energetically. . . . The outcome of the work of pain is de-cision (*Ent-scheidung*): restoration of the unity of the self after the ejection of the It (*Es*)" (Weizsäcker 2011, 273; my translation—SG).

19. This theme will be addressed in detail in chapter 7.

20. One could characterize these distinctions as the most established distinctions in the phenomenology of medicine in general. We find them in the works of Edmund Pellegrino, Paul Tournier, Viktor Kestenbaum, Arthur Kleinman, Byron Good, Alfred Tauber, S. K. Toombs, James and Kevin Aho, among others.

21. No one else has maintained as strongly as Elaine Scarry that pain, unlike other feelings, resists verbal objectification: "Thus Sophocles's agonized Philoctetes utters a cascade of *changing* cries and shrieks that in the original Greek are accommodated by an array of formal words (some of them twelve syllables long), but that at least one translator found could only be rendered in English by the uniform syllable 'Ah' followed by variations in punctuation (Ah! Ah!!!!)" (1985, 5).

22. As the philosopher-physician Alfred Tauber argues in his award-winning study, *Confessions of the Medicine Man*, "So much of our discontent can be traced back to the too little time the physician spends with a client, and how poorly a true dialogue develops. . . . Beyond obtaining information that may be important in tending to the patient's particular medical needs, a patient's own description of the illness presents the physician with the problem of suffering, with the profound disruption, uncertainty, and pain that disease imposes. To ignore this aspect of illness is to deny the patients' fundamental humanity and relegate them to the status of object. Only a relational construct, deliberately and carefully effected, can counteract this attitude" (2002, 109–10). Or as Luchuo E. Bain remarks in a recent study, "As a primary care physician, it has become clearer to me that a good number of patients visit doctors just to be listened to. . . . Active listening . . . may be fading

from the priorities of contemporary medicine. . . . Alas, I am, like all persons at some point in their lives, also a patient, and I often feel frustrated by my treating physicians' attendance to a computer, rather than listening, examining or talking to me" (2018, 2).

23. This prejudice has been brought into question both in narrative medicine and in psychoanalysis. As Salman Akhtar (2012, 81–103) argues in his recent study, *Psychoanalytic Listening*, listening to one's own associations, emotions, impulses, and actions provides the analyst with a deep source of information not only about himself, but also about the analysand and is especially helpful during the turbulent moments of clinical work. Yet the exact reasons why listening-to-oneself proves so helpful in such circumstances remain unexplored in either narrative medicine or psychoanalysis. In this regard, a dialogue between these fields and phenomenology is much needed.

24. The foregoing analysis invites us to conceive of the person as a being whose self-constitution relies upon four fundamental relations: self-relation, relation to one's body, relation to others, and relation to the environment. Yet, just as importantly, the person is a being who can lose the distinctly personal characteristics that are established on the basis of such four relations. However, this loss in its own turn motivates the person to reconstitute his or her own selfhood. It will be our task in the next chapter to deal with the implications that are central to philosophical anthropology more straightforwardly.

CHAPTER 7. PAIN AND THE LIFE-WORLD

1. Dere et al. (2013, 10) note in their recent study that such a conception of both phenomena is dominant in contemporary research.

2. For a survey of the "geography of somatization," which details the diverse studies of somatization that were undertaken in Asia, Africa, North and South America, and Europe, see Kirmayer 1984a, 162–74.

3. To what degree can such processes as psychologization and somatization be incorporated into phenomenology? One might suspect that they are expressive of quasi-Cartesian dualism, which the phenomenological concept of the lived-body was meant to replace. One might suspect that they rely on a phenomenologically illegitimate conception of *soma* and *psyche*, a conception that suggests *soma* and *psyche* are some kind of independent entities, which, despite their ontological independence from each other, somehow interact with each other. One might therefore hold the view that the analysis of somatization and psychologization relies on that kind of metaphysics, which from the start phenomenology was eager to displace. For this reason, one might hold the view that these processes cannot be incorporated into phenomenology. I do not find these misgivings persuasive. The empirical analyses of these processes bring to light something significantly different, namely, that *soma* and *psyche* are inextricable from each other, so much so that those processes we usually conceive of as specifically somatic are never purely somatic, but in a good sense also psychic, and *vice versa*. Such processes as somatization and psychologization could not be as prevalent as they are—in fact, *they could not occur at all*—if *soma* and *psyche* were independent from each other.

NOTES TO PAGES 172–176

4. As Husserl has it, "The contrast between the subjectivity of the life-world and the 'objective,' the 'true' world, lies in the fact that the latter is a theoretical-logical substruction, the substruction of something that is in principle not perceivable, in principle not experienceable in its own proper being, whereas the subjective, in the life-world, is distinguished in all respects precisely by its being actually experienceable" (1970, 127).

5. For a detailed and insightful analysis of Husserl's concepts of concordance (*Einstimmigkeit*) and discordance (*Unstimmigkeit*), see Steinbock 1995a, 129–38; and Steinbock 1995b.

6. I have addressed these three senses of the life-world in detail in part 3 of *The Origins of the Horizon in Husserl's Phenomenology* (see Geniusas 2012, 177–224).

7. As Drew Leder insightfully remarks in a somewhat different context, "Reflective awareness rests on that which necessarily eludes it. The phenomenologist of the body is already, and necessarily, a hermeneut. To explore the region of the body most hidden from awareness is merely to extend this hermeneutical approach" (1990, 37).

8. One might wonder, and with good reasons, Of what therapeutic relevance is such a phenomenology of somatization? Does it help the pain patients to know that their somatic suffering derives from various tensions they have experienced, or continue to experience, in the life-world? It is a well-known fact that when the patients hear from their physicians that the pains they suffer from are instances of somatization, they interpret such an explanation as a sign that they have been abandoned by their physicians. It is common for pain patients to think that their physicians' inability to identify the organic causes of their pains equals their refusal to recognize the legitimacy of their somatic suffering (see, e.g., Bullington 2013; and Slatman 2018). In light of such circumstances, the phenomenological thesis that many of our pains are instances of somatization that derive from various tensions we experience in the life-world does not appear to help the pain patients. Quite on the contrary, one might worry that if the phenomenological thesis that is presented and defended here is accepted by the health-care providers, then it would only worsen the condition of the patients and exacerbate their suffering. In response, I would like to stress two interrelated points. First, it is crucial to draw a distinction between understanding the nature of somatic suffering and helping the patients confront their suffering. Unfortunately, the two do not always go hand in hand. The goal of a phenomenological study is first and foremost to understand the phenomenon, and I openly admit that further steps need to be taken so that this understanding could fulfill a therapeutic function. Second, it is not enough to observe that this or any other account of pain experience entails adverse therapeutic implications. One must further clarify the reasons that underlie such undesirable consequences. Clearly, these reasons have little to do with the phenomenological account per se. Rather, they concern the widespread and unfounded conviction that only the form of somatic suffering that has organic causes can be identified as real suffering. This conviction not only limits our theoretical capacity to understand somatic suffering; it also hinders the practical chances of the patients to come to terms with the true nature of their own experiences.

9. In the present context, expression is to be understood in a highly broad sense, which is not limited to linguistic expression. The embodied being of other human and nonhuman animals must be expressive of an inner life if we are to recognize them as lived-bodies. We must distinguish this general sense of expression from a more restricted sense, which concerns linguistic expressions. Concerning the significance

of *linguistic* expression for the transcendental world-constitution, see also Husserl 1973b, 224. Here Husserl argues that the fundamental difference between human beings and nonhuman animals concerns language and expression. For this very reason, argues Husserl, our world is fundamentally different from the surrounding world of animals. Linguistic expressions convey a possible experience, which itself becomes part and parcel of our cultural and sociohistorical surrounding world.

10. The general issue of social delegitimization, as well as the more specific ways in which the person transforms the body into a vehicle of expression by taking on specific pathologies, has been addressed in feminist literature, with a special focus on the woman's body. See in this regard especially Iris Young's "Throwing Like a Girl" (1980); Janice McLane's "The Voice on the Skin" (1996); and Susan Bordo's *Unbearable Weight* (2004). These studies focus on restricted spatiality of embodiment, self-mutilation as a form of expression, and, finally, weight loss, anorexia, and bulimia as modes of social response. As far as the phenomenology of pain is concerned, the role of social delegitimization still remains to be investigated in all the necessary detail.

11. Many of these manuscripts have been compiled in *Husserliana XV* and *Husserliana XXXIX*. See Husserl 1973b, especially Texts Nr. 14 and Nr. 27, along with the appendixes that accompany them. See also Husserl 2008, especially appendix XI to Text Nr. 16; also Text Nr. 17 and Text Nr. 35.

12. See, for instance, Husserl 1973b, 216. Or, as Husserl puts it in a different manuscript, "What 'the' world is for us, and that it is, arises out of our experience (*Erfahrung*), out of the all-binding, concordant streaming experience" (1973b, 218; my translation—SG). One should not overlook that Husserl does not only speak of the concordance that unfolds within the framework of our personal lives, but that he also explicitly recognizes the concordance of the communal life of experience ("Einstimmigkeit des gemeinshaftliches Erfahrungslebens") (see Husserl 1973b, 222).

13. Or, as Husserl puts it in a different manuscript, "I, as the subject of experience, have the next surrounding world, the 'near world,' which we could also call the *homeworld*, conceived of as the world, in which I feel at home due to my own experience" (1973b, 221; my translation—SG). In this manuscript, Husserl further qualifies the homeworld as a well-known and familiar surrounding world, whose familiarity derives from the acquisitions of my own experience.

14. Klein refers to such an account as a "debunking explanation." He does not believe such an explanation is capable of accounting for masochistic pleasures. In Klein's view, debunking accounts must be replaced with contextual accounts, of which there are two kinds. While some rely on the intuition that the object of masochistic pleasure is some composite state of the world, others contend that the object is a composite sensation. Klein himself defends the second possibility. See Klein 2015b, 167–82.

15. As George Pitcher once put it, the masochist "does not find the pain inflicted by the whipstrokes of his sexual partner pleasant. What an absurd idea! If he did find them pleasant, he would look for a more aggressive mate. No, the pain is fearfully unpleasant, and that is precisely why it excites him, precisely why he wants it. Without the suffering, the whole exercise is pointless" (1970, 485).

16. One might argue that there is yet another way to conceive of masochistic pain as pleasurable. One could be deeply convinced that one is deserving of punishment and one could interpret physical pain as a form of punishment. Under such circumstances, one might be even in search of masochistic pains and one could experience them as deeply pleasurable. I would argue, however, that here we face one particular

NOTES TO PAGE 192

instance of the general structure described above: one experiences pain as pleasurable insofar as it relieves one of greater forms of suffering. In this particular case, the general feeling that one is deserving of punishment is exactly what causes one greatest distress and the masochistic pain relieves one of that distress.

CONCLUSION

1. I consider it self-evident that just as an empirical researcher has much to learn from phenomenology, so also a phenomenologist has much to learn from concrete empirical research. It is fully conceivable that empirical investigations of concrete types of pain experience would compel a phenomenologist to revise the definition of pain here proposed. This is, however, an open and not a motivated possibility. To repeat the central insight that was worked out in chapter 1, a phenomenologist must couple imaginative variations with factual variations, many of which find their inspirations in concrete empirical investigations.

BIBLIOGRAPHY

Aho, Kevin, ed. 2018. *Existential Medicine: Essays on Health and Illness*. New York: Rowman & Littlefield.

Akhtar, Salman. 2012. *Psychoanalytic Listening: Methods, Limits, and Innovations*. New York: Routledge.

American Psychiatric Association. 2000. *Diagnostic and Statistical Manual of Mental Disorders*. 4th ed. Washington, DC: American Psychiatric Association.

Armstrong, David M. 2002. *Bodily Sensations*. New York: Routledge & Kegan Paul.

Augustine. 2006. *The Confessions*. Edited by Michael P. Foley. Translated by F. J. Sheed. Indianapolis, IN: Hackett.

Aune, Bruce. 1965. "On the Complexity of Avowals." In *Philosophy in America*, edited by Max Black, 35–57. Ithaca, NY: Cornell University Press.

Aydede, Murat, ed. 2005. *Pain: New Essays on Its Nature and the Methodology of Its Study*. Cambridge, MA: MIT Press.

Baier, Kurt. 1962. "Pains." *Australasian Journal of Philosophy* 40 (1): 1–23.

———. 1964. "The Place of a Pain." *Philosophical Quarterly* 14 (55): 138–50.

Bain, Luchuo E. 2018. "Revisiting the Need for Virtue in Medical Practice: A Reflection Upon the Teaching of Edmund Pellegrino. *Philosophy, Ethics, and Humanities in Medicine* 13 (4): 1–5.

Bakan, David. 1968. *Disease, Pain, and Sacrifice: Toward a Psychology of Suffering*. Boston, MA: Beacon Press.

Baker, Lynne R. 2000. *Persons and Bodies: A Constitution View*. Cambridge: Cambridge University Press.

Barber, Theodore X. 1959. "Toward a Theory of Pain: Relief of Chronic Pain by Prefrontal Leucotomy, Opiates, Placebos, and Hypnosis." *Psychological Bulletin* 56 (6): 430–60.

Benveniste, Daniel. 2015. "Free Association and the Search for Psychological Meaning in Everyday Life." https://benvenistephd.com/wp-content/uploads/2019/01/free.pdf.

Bernet, Rudolf, Iso Kern, and Eduard Marbach. 1993. *An Introduction to Husserlian Phenomenology*. Evanston, IL: Northwestern University Press.

Berthier, Marchcelo, Sergio Starkstein, and Ramon Leiguarda. 1988. "Asymbolia for Pain: A Sensory-Limbic Disconnection Syndrome." *Annals of Neurology* 24 (1): 41–49.

Bordo, Susan. 2004. *Unbearable Weight: Feminism, Western Culture, and the Body*. Berkeley: University of California Press.

Brand, Paul W., and Philip Yancey. 1997. *The Gift of Pain*. Grand Rapids, MI: Zondervan.

Brentano, Franz. 1907. *Untersuchungen zur Sinnespsychologie*. Leipzig: Duncker & Humblot.

———. 1968. *Vom sinnlichen und noetischen Bewusstsein*. Edited by Oskar Kraus. Leipzig: Meiner Verlag.

Brough, John B. 2001. "Temporality and Illness: A Phenomenological Perspective." In *Handbook of Phenomenology and Medicine*, edited by S. Kay Toombs, 29–46. Dordrecht: Kluwer.

Bullington, Jennifer. 2013. *The Expression of the Psychosomatic Body from a Phenomenological Perspective*. Berlin: Springer.

Buytendijk, Frederik J. J. 1962. *Pain: Its Modes and Functions*. Translated by Eda O'Shiel. Chicago: University of Chicago Press.

Carel, Havi. 2016. *Phenomenology of Illness*. Oxford: Oxford University Press.

Carman, Taylor. 1999. "The Body in Husserl and Merleau-Ponty." *Philosophical Topics* 27 (2): 205–26.

Cassell, Eric J. 1978. *The Healer's Art: A New Approach to the Doctor-Patient Relationship*. London: Penguin.

———. 2001. "The Phenomenon of Suffering and Its Relationship to Pain." In Toombs, *Handbook of Phenomenology and Medicine*, 371–90.

Chapman, C. Richard, Yoshio Nakamura, and Leticia Y. Flores. 2000. "How We Hurt: A Constructivist Framework for Understanding Individual Differences in Pain." In *Individual Differences in Conscious Experience*, edited by Robert G. Kunzendorf and Benjamin Wallace, 17–44. Amsterdam: John Benjamins.

Charon, Rita. 2006. *Narrative Medicine: Honoring the Stories of Illness*. Oxford: Oxford University Press.

Chen, Ya-Chun, Michaela Auer-Grumbach, Shinya Matsukawa, Manuela Zitzelsberger, Andreas C. Themistocleous, Tim M. Strom, Chrysanthi Samara, et al. 2015. "Transcriptional Regulator PRDM12 Is Essential for Human Pain Perception." *Nature Genetics* 47: 803–8.

Churchland, Paul M., and Patricia Smith Churchland. 1981. "Functionalism, Qualia, and Intentionality." *Philosophical Topics* 12 (1): 121–45.

Cicero. 1914. *On Ends*. Translated by H. Rackham. Cambridge, MA: Harvard University Press.

Claparède, Édouard. 1911. "Recognition et moïté." *Archives de Psychologie* 11: 79–90.

Dearborn, George. 1932. "A Case of Congenital Pure Analgesia." *Journal of Nervous and Mental Disease* 75: 612–15.

Degenaar, Johannes J. 1979. "Some Philosophical Considerations on Pain." *Pain* 7 (3): 281–304.

Dennett, Daniel C. 1991. *Consciousness Explained*. Boston, MA: Little, Brown.

Dere, Jessica, Jiahong Sun, Yue Zhao, Tonje J. Persson, Xiongzhao Zhu, Shuqaio Yao, R. Michael Bagby, and Andrew G. Ryder. 2013. "Beyond 'Somatization' and 'Psychologization': Symptom-Level Variation in Depressed Han Chinese and Euro-Canadian Outpatients." *Frontiers in Psychology* 4 (377): 1–13.

Dickinson, Emily. 1960. *The Complete Poems of Emily Dickinson*. Edited by Thomas H. Johnson. Toronto: Little, Brown.

Fisette, Denis. 2010. "Descriptive Psychology and Natural Sciences: Husserl's Early Criticism of Brentano." In *Philosophy, Phenomenology, Sciences: Essays in Commemoration of Edmund Husserl*, edited by Carlo Ierna, Hanne Jacobs, and Filip Mattens, 221–53. Dordrecht: Springer.

BIBLIOGRAPHY

Feinstein, Justin S., Melissa C. Duff, and Daniel Tranel. 2010. "Sustained Experience of Emotion after Loss of Memory in Patients with Amnesia." *Proceedings of the National Academy of Sciences* 107 (17): 7674–79.

Foucault, Michel. 2012. *The Birth of the Clinic: An Archaeology of Medical Perception*. Translated by A. M. Sheridan. London: Routledge.

Freeman, Walter, and James W. Watts. 1950. *Psychosurgery in the Treatment of Mental Disorders and Intractable Pain*. Oxford: Blackwell.

Fuchs, Thomas. 2008. "Das Gedächtnis der Schmerzen." In *Leib und Lebenswelt: Neue philosophisch-psychiatrische essays*, 37–81. Kusterdingen: Die Graue Edition.

———. 2013. "Temporality and Psychopathology." *Phenomenology and the Cognitive Sciences* 12 (1): 75–104.

Gallagher, Shaun. 1998. *The Inordinance of Time*. Evanston, IL: Northwestern University Press.

———. 2012. *Phenomenology*. Hampshire: Palgrave Macmillan.

Geniusas, Saulius. 2012. *The Origins of the Horizon in Husserl's Phenomenology*. Dordrecht: Springer.

———. 2013. "On Naturalism in Pain Research: A Phenomenological Critique." *Metodo* 1 (1): 1–10. http://www.metodo-rivista.eu/index.php/metodo/article/view/14/4.

———. 2014a. "The Origins of the Phenomenology of Pain: Brentano, Stumpf and Husserl." *Continental Philosophy Review* 47 (1): 1–17.

———. 2014b. "The Subject of Pain: Husserl's Discovery of the Lived-Body." *Research in Phenomenology* 44 (3): 384–404.

———. 2015. "Max Scheler and the Stratification of the Emotional Life." *The New Yearbook for Phenomenology and Phenomenological Philosophy*. Vol. 14, edited by Ludger Hagedorn and James Dodd, 355–77. London: Routledge.

———. 2016. "Max Scheler's Phenomenology of Pain." *Frontiers of Philosophy in China* 11 (3): 358–76.

———. 2017a. "Pain and Intentionality." In *Perception, Affectivity, and Volition in Husserl's Phenomenology*, edited by Roberto Walton, Shigeru Taguchi, and Roberto Rubio, 113–36. Dordrecht: Springer.

———. 2017b. "Phenomenology of Chronic Pain: De-Personalization and Re-Personalization." In *Meanings of Pain*, edited by Simon van Rysewyk, 147–64. Dordrecht: Springer.

Gergel, Tania L. 2012. "Medicine and the Individual: Is Phenomenology the Answer?" *Journal of Evaluation in Clinical Practice* 18 (5): 1102–9.

Good, Byron J. 1994a. "A Body in Pain: The Making of a World of Chronic Pain." In Good et al., *Pain as Human Experience*, 29–48.

———. 1994b. *Medicine, Rationality, and Experience: An Anthropological Perspective*. Cambridge: Cambridge University Press.

Good, Mary-Jo DelVecchio, Paul E. Brodwin, Byron J. Good, and Arthur Kleinman, eds. 1994. *Pain as Human Experience: An Anthropological Perspective*. Berkeley: University of California Press.

Grahek, Nikola. 2007. *Feeling Pain and Being in Pain*. Cambridge, MA: MIT Press.

Grüny, Christian. 2004. *Zerstörte Erfahrung: Eine Phänomenologie des Schmerzes*. Würzburg: Königshausen & Neumann.

Gurwitsch, Aron. 1964. *The Field of Consciousness*. Pittsburgh, PA: Duquesne University Press.

Hall, K. R. L., and E. Stride. 1954. "The Varying Response to Pain in Psychiatric Disorders: A Study in Abnormal Psychology." *British Journal of Medical Psychology* 27 (1–2): 48–60.

Hardcastle, Valerie G. 1999. *The Myth of Pain*. Cambridge, MA: MIT Press.

Hardy, James D., Harold G. Wolff, and Helen Goodell. 1952. *Pain Sensations and Reactions*. New York: Hafner.

Held, Klaus. 2003. "Husserl's Phenomenological Method." In Welton, *New Husserl*, 3–31.

Hemphill, Robert E., and Erwin Stengel. 1940. "A Study on Pure Word-Deafness." *Journal of Neurology, Neurosurgery & Psychiatry* 3 (3): 251–62.

Henry, Michel. 1973. *The Essence of Manifestation*. Translated by Girard Etzkorn. The Hague: Martinus Nijhoff.

Hill, Christopher S. 2005. "Ow! The Paradox of Pain." In Aydede, *Pain*, 75–98.

Hill, Harris E., Conan H. Kornetsky, Harold G. Flanary, and Abraham Wikler. 1952. "Effects of Anxiety and Morphine on Discrimination of Intensities of Painful Stimuli." *Journal of Clinical Investigation* 31 (5): 473–80.

Hoogenraad, Tjaard U., L. M. Ramos, and J. van Gijn. 1994. "Visually Induced Central Pain and Arm Withdrawal after Right Parietal Lobe Infarction." *Journal of Neurology, Neurosurgery & Psychiatry* 57 (7): 850–52.

Husserl, Edmund. 1959. *Erste Philosophie (1923/4). Zweiter Teil: Theorie der phänomenologischen Reduktion*. Edited by Rudolf Boehm. The Hague: Martinus Nijhoff.

———. 1960. *Cartesian Meditations: An Introduction to Phenomenology*. Edited by Stephan Strasser. Tranlated by Dorian Cairns. The Hague: Martinus Nijhoff.

———. 1964. *The Phenomenology of Internal Time-Consciousness*. Edited by Martin Heidegger. Translated by James S. Churchill. Bloomington: Indiana University Press.

———. 1970. *The Crisis of European Sciences and Transcendental Phenomenology: An Introduction to Phenomenological Philosophy*. Translated by David Carr. Evanston, IL: Northwestern University Press.

———. 1973a. *Zur Phänomenologie der Intersubjektivität: Texte aus dem Nachlass. Erster Teil: 1905–20*. Edited by Iso Kern. The Hague: Martinus Nijhoff.

———. 1973b. *Zur Phänomenologie der Intersubjektivität: Texte aus dem Nachlass. Driter Teil: 1929–35*. Edited by Iso Kern. The Hague: Martinus Nijhoff.

———. 1977. *Phenomenological Psychology*. Translated by John Scanlon. The Hague: Martinus Nijhoff.

———. 1983. *Ideas Pertaining to a Pure Phenomenology and to a Phenomenological Philosophy*. First Book: *General Introduction to a Pure Phenomenology*. Translated by Fred Kersten. The Hague: Martinus Nijhoff. First published 1913.

———. 1988. *Aufsätze und Vorträge, 1922–1937*. Edited by Thomas Nenon and Hans R. Sepp. The Hague: Kluwer.

———. 1989. *Ideas Pertaining to a Pure Phenomenology and to a Phenomenological Philosophy*. Second Book: *Studies in the Phenomenology of Constitution*. Translated by Richard Rojcewicz and André Schuwer. Dordrecht: Springer.

———. 2000. *Logical Investigations*. Vol. II. Translated by John N. Findlay. Toronto: Humanity Books. First published 1900–1901.

BIBLIOGRAPHY

———. 2001. *Analyses Concerning Passive and Active Synthesis: Lectures on Transcendental Logic.* Translated by Anthony J. Steinbock. Dordrecht: Kluwer.

———. 2006. *Späte Texte über Zeitkonstitution (1924–1934): Die C-Manuskripte.* Edited by Dieter Lohmar. Dordrecht: Springer.

Jackson, Jean E. 1994. "'After a While No One Believes You': Real and Unreal Pain." In Good et al., *Pain as Human Experience,* 138–68.

James, William. 1980. *The Principles of Psychology.* 2 vols. New York: Dover.

Janzen, Greg. 2013. "An Adverbialist-Objectualist Account of Pain." *Phenomenology and the Cognitive Sciences* 12 (4): 859–76.

Jewsbury, Eric C. 1951. "Insensitivity to Pain." *Brain* 74 (3): 336–53.

Jünger, Ernst. 2008. *On Pain.* Translated by David C. Durst. New York: Telos Press.

Kaplan, Eugene A. 1960. "Hypnosis and Pain." *Archives of General Psychiatry* 2 (5): 567–68.

Kirmayer, Laurence J. 1984a. "Culture, Affect and Somatization: Part I." *Transcultural Psychiatric Research Review* 21 (3): 159–78.

———. 1984b. "Culture, Affect and Somatization: Part II." *Transcultural Psychiatric Research Review* 21 (4): 237–62.

Klein, Colin. 2015a. "What Pain Asymbolia Really Shows." *Mind* 124 (494): 493–516.

———. 2015b. *What the Body Commands: The Imperative Theory of Pain.* Cambridge, MA: MIT Press.

Kleinman, Arthur. 1988. *The Illness Narratives: Suffering, Healing, and the Human Condition.* New York: Basic Books.

———. 1994. "Pain and Resistance: The Delegitimation and Relegitimation of Local Worlds." In Good et al., *Pain as Human Experience,* 169–97.

Kleinman, Arthur, and Joan Kleinman. 2007. "Somatization: The Interconnections in Chinese Society among Culture, Depressive Experiences, and the Meaning of Pain." In Lock and Farquhar, *Beyond the Body Proper,* 468–74.

Kockelmans, Joseph J. 1994. *Edmund Husserl's Phenomenology.* West Lafayette, IN: Purdue University Press.

Kono, Tetsuya. 2012. "Phenomenology of Pain." Unpublished manuscript.

Kusch, Martin, and Matthew Ratcliffe. 2018. "The World of Chronic Pain: A Dialogue." In Aho, *Existential Medicine,* 61–80.

Leder, Drew. 1984–85. "Toward a Phenomenology of Pain." *Review of Existential Psychology & Psychiatry* 19 (2–3): 255–66.

———. 1990. *The Absent Body.* Chicago: University of Chicago Press.

———. 2016. *The Distressed Body: Rethinking Illness, Imprisonment, and Healing.* Chicago: University of Chicago Press.

Lewis, Thomas. 1942. *Pain.* New York: Macmillan.

Lock, Margaret, and Judith Farquhar, eds. 2007. *Beyond the Body Proper: Reading the Anthropology of Material Life.* Durham, NC: Duke University Press.

Locke, John. 2005. *An Essay Concerning Human Understanding.* Raleigh, NC: Hayes Barton Press.

Lohmar, Dieter, and Jagna Brudzi ska, eds. 2011. *Founding Psychoanalysis Phenomenologically: Phenomenological Theory of Subjectivity and the Psychoanalytic Experience.* Dordrecht: Springer.

Lotze, Hermann. 2011. *Outlines of Psychology: Dictated Portions of the Lectures of Hermann Lotze.* Toronto: University of Toronto Libraries.

Luft, Sebastian. 2004. "Husserl's Theory of the Phenomenological Reduction: Between Life-World and Cartesianism." *Research in Phenomenology* 34 (1): 198–234.

Madison, Gary B. 2004. "The Interpretive Turn in Phenomenology: A Philosophical History." *Symposium* 8 (2): 397–467.

Malcolm, Norman. 1958. "Knowledge of Other Minds." *Journal of Philosophy* 55 (23): 969–78.

McLane, Janice. 1996. "The Voice on the Skin: Self-Mutilation and Merleau-Ponty's Theory of Language." *Hypatia* 11 (4): 107–18.

McMurray, Gordon A. 1950. "Experimental Study of a Case of Insensitivity to Pain." *Archives of Neurology & Psychiatry* 64 (5): 650–67.

Melzack, Ronald, and T. H. Scott. 1957. "The Effects of Early Experience on the Response to Pain." *Journal of Comparative and Physiological Psychology* 50 (2): 155–61.

Melzack, Ronald, and Patrick D. Wall. 2008. *The Challenge of Pain*. Updated 2nd ed. London: Penguin.

Merleau-Ponty, Maurice. 1962. *Phenomenology of Perception*. Translated by Colin Smith. London: Routledge & Kegan Paul.

———. 1963. *The Structure of Behavior*. Translated by Alden L. Fisher. Boston, MA: Beacon Press.

Merskey, Harold. 1991. "The Definition of Pain." *European Psychiatry* 6 (4): 153–59.

Merskey, Harold, and Nikolai Bogduk. 1994. *Classification of Chronic Pain: Descriptions of Chronic Pain Syndromes and Definitions of Pain Terms*. 2nd ed. Seattle, WA: IASP Press.

Metzinger, Thomas. 2003. *Being No One: The Self-Model Theory of Subjectivity*. Cambridge, MA: MIT Press.

Minett, Michael S., Vanessa Pereira, Shafaq Sikandar, Ayako Matsuyama, Stéphane Lolignier, Alexandros H. Kanellopoulos, Flavia Mancini, et al. 2015. "Endogenous Opioids Contribute to Insensitivity to Pain in Humans and Mice Lacking Sodium Channel $Na_v1.7$." In *Nature Communications* 6 (8967).

Mitchell, Silas Weir. 1872. *Injuries of Nerves and Their Consequences*. Philadelphia, PA: J. B. Lippincott.

Mohanty, Jitendramath N. 1984. "Husserl on 'Possibility.'" *Husserl Studies* 1 (1): 13–29.

Moran, Dermot. 2000. *Introduction to Phenomenology*. London: Routledge.

———. 2009. "The Phenomenology of Personhood: Charles Taylor and Edmund Husserl." *Colloquium* 3 (1): 80–104.

———. 2010. "Pain That Takes Place at a Distance from the Ego: The Experience of Inner Spatiality in Husserl and Stein." Unpublished manuscript.

———. 2014. "Defending the Transcendental Attitude: Husserl's Concept of the Person and the Challenges of Naturalism." *Phenomenology and Mind* 7: 30–43.

Morris, David B. 2010. "Intractable Pain and the Perception of Time: Every Patient Is an Anecdote." In *Evidence-Based Chronic Pain Management*, edited by Cathy Stannard, Eija Kalso, and Jane Ballantyne, 52–64. Oxford: BMJ Books.

Morris, Katherine J. 2013. "Chronic Pain in Phenomenological/Anthropological Perspective." In *The Phenomenology of Embodied Subjectivity*, edited by Rasmus T. Jensen and Dermot Moran, 167–84. Dordrecht: Springer.

BIBLIOGRAPHY

NANDA (North American Nursing Diagnosis Association). 1996. *Nursing Diagnoses: Definitions and Classification, 1997–1998*. Philadelphia, PA: NANDA Press.

Nasio, Juan-David. 2004. *The Book of Love and Pain: Thinking at the Limit with Freud and Lacan*. Translated by David Pettigrew and François Raffoul. Albany: State University of New York Press.

Nelkin, Norton. 1986. "Pains and Pain Sensations." *Journal of Philosophy* 83: 129–47.

———. 1994. "Reconsidering Pain." *Philosophical Psychology* 7 (3): 325–43.

Nietzsche, Friedrich W. 2000. *On the Genealogy of Morals*. In *Basic Writings of Nietzsche*, translated and edited by Walter Kaufmann, 437–600. New York: Random House.

Ogawa, Tadashi. 1983. "'Seeing' and 'Touching,' or, Overcoming the Soul-Body Dualism." *Analecta Husserliana* 16: 77.

Olivier, Abraham. 2007. *Being in Pain*. Frankfurt am Main: Peter Lang.

Palmer, David. 1975. "Unfelt Pains." *American Philosophical Quarterly* 12 (4): 289–98.

Pellegrino, Edmund D., and David C. Thomasma. 1981. *A Philosophical Basis of Medical Practice: Toward a Philosophy and Ethic of the Healing Professions*. New York: Oxford University Press.

Pete, Steven. 2012. "Congenital Analgesia: The Agony of Feeling No Pain." *BBC News Magazine*, 17 July 2012. http://www.bbc.com/news/magazine-18713585.

Peter, Sebastian von. 2010. "The Temporality of 'Chronic' Mental Illness." *Culture, Medicine, and Psychiatry* 34 (1): 13–28.

Peucker, Henning. 2008. "From Logic to the Person: An Introduction to Edmund Husserl's Ethics." *Review of Metaphysics* 62 (2): 307–25.

Pitcher, George. 1970. "The Awfulness of Pain." *Journal of Philosophy* 67 (14): 481–92.

Ploner, Markus, Hans-Joachim Freund, and Alfons Schnitzler. 1999. "Pain Affect without Pain Sensation in a Patient with a Postcentral Lesion." *Pain* 81 (1–2): 211–14.

Ploner, Markus, Joachim Gross, Lars Timmerman, and Alfons Schnitzler. 2002. "Cortical Representation of First and Second Pain Sensation in Humans." *Proceedings of the National Academy of Sciences* 99 (19): 12444–48.

Pötzl, Otto, and Erwin Stengel. 1937. "Über das Syndrom Leitungsaphasie-Schmerzasymbolie." *Jahrbuch der Psychiatrie* 53: 174–207.

Price, Donald D., and Murat Aydede. 2005. "The Experimental Use of Introspection in the Scientific Study of Pain and Its Integration with Third-Person Methodologies: The Experiential-Phenomenological Approach." In Aydede, *Pain*, 242–73.

Protevi, John. 2009. "Philosophies of Consciousness and the Body." In *The Continuum Companion to Continental Philosophy*, edited by John Mullarkey and Beth Lord, 69–92. London: Continuum.

Quintner, John L., Milton L. Cohen, David Buchanan, James D. Katz, and Owen D. Williamson. 2008. "Pain Medicine and Its Models: Helping or Hindering?" *Pain Medicine* 9 (7): 824–34.

Ratcliffe, Matthew. 2008. *Feelings of Being: Phenomenology, Psychiatry and the Sense of Reality*. Oxford: Oxford University Press.

———. 2013. "Phenomenology, Naturalism and the Sense of Reality." In *Phenomenology and Naturalism: Examining the Relationship between Human Experience and Nature*, edited by Havi Carel and Darian Meacham, 67–88. Cambridge: Cambridge University Press.

Ricoeur, Paul. 1987. *A l'école de la phénoménologie*. Paris: Vrin.

Rubins, Jack L., and Emanuel D. Friedman. 1948. "Asymbolia for Pain." rchives of Neurology & Psychiatry 60 (6): 554–73.

Russon, John. 2013. "Haunted by History: Merleau-Ponty, Hegel and the Phenomenology of Pain." *Journal of Contemporary Thought* 37 (Summer): 81–94.

Ryle, Gilbert. 1954. "Report on Analysis 'Problem' No. 4: 'If a Distraction Makes Me Forget My Headache Does It Make My Head Stop Aching, or Does It Only Stop Me Feeling It Aching?'" *Analysis* 14 (3): 51–52.

———. 2009. *The Concept of Mind*. London: Routledge.

Sartre, Jean-Paul. 1956. *Being and Nothingness: An Essay on Phenomenological Ontology*. Translated by Hazel E. Barnes. New York: Washington Square Press.

———. 1970. "Intentionality: A Fundamental Idea of Husserl's Phenomenology." *Journal of the British Society for Phenomenology* 1 (2): 4–5.

———. 2004. *The Imaginary: A Phenomenological Psychology of the Imagination*. Translated by Jonathan Webber. London: Routledge.

Scarry, Elaine. 1985. *The Body in Pain: The Making and Unmaking of the World*. New York: Oxford University Press.

Schacter, Daniel L. 1987. "Implicit Memory: History and Current Status." *Journal of Experimental Psychology* 13 (3): 501–18.

Scheler, Max. 1973. *Formalism in Ethics and Non-Formal Ethics of Values: A New Attempt toward the Foundation of an Ethical Personalism*. Translated by Manfred S. Frings and Roger L. Funk. Evanston, IL: Northwestern University Press.

———. 1974. *Max Scheler (1874–1928): Centennial Essays*. Edited by Manfred S. Frings. The Hague: Martinus Nijhoff.

———. 1992. "The Meaning of Suffering." In *On Feeling, Knowing, and Valuing: Selected Writings*, edited by Harold J. Bershady, 82–115. Chicago: University of Chicago Press.

Scheper-Hughes, Nancy. 2007. "Nervoso." In Lock and Farquhar, *Beyond the Body Proper*, 459–67.

Schilder, Paul, and Erwin Stengel. 1928. "Schmerzasymbolie." *Zeitschrift für die gesamte Neurologie und Psychiatrie* 113 (1): 143–58.

———. 1931. "Asymbolia for Pain." *Archives of Neurology & Psychiatry* 25 (3): 598–600.

Schmitz, Hermann. 2009. *Der Leib, der Raum und die Gefühle*. Bielefeld: Aisthesis Verlag.

Serrano de Haro, Agustín. 2011. "Is Pain an Intentional Experience?" In *Phenomenology 2010*. Vol. 3, *Selected Essays from the Euro-Mediterranean Area*, edited by Ion Copoeru, Pavlos Kontos, and Augustin Serrano de Haro, 386–95. Budapest: Zeta Books.

———. 2012. "New and Old Approaches to the Phenomenology of Pain." *Studia Phenomenologica* 12: 227–37.

———. 2017. "Pain Experience and Structures of Attention: A Phenomenological Approach." In van Rysewyk, *Meanings of Pain*, 165–80.

———. 2018. "Husserl on Physical Pain." Unpublished manuscript.

BIBLIOGRAPHY

Slatman, J. 2018. "Reclaiming Embodiment in Medically Unexplained Physical Symptoms." In Aho, *Existential Medicine*, 101–14.

Smith, Quentin. 1977. "A Phenomenological Examination of Husserl's Theory of Hyletic Data." *Philosophy Today* 21 (4): 356–67.

Stein, Edith. 1989. *On the Problem of Empathy*. Translated by Waltraut Stein. Washington, DC: ICS Publications.

Steinbock, Anthony J. 1995a. *Home and Beyond: Generative Phenomenology after Husserl*. Evanston, IL: Northwestern University Press.

———. 1995b. "Phenomenological Concepts of Normality and Abnormality." *Man and World* 28 (3): 241–60.

Stoller, Robert J. 1991. *Pain and Passion: A Psychoanalyst Explores the World of S & M*. New York: Plenum Press.

Stumpf, Carl. 1907. "Über Gefühlsempfindungen." *Zeitschrift für Psychologie und Physiologie der Sinnesorgane* 44: 1–49.

———. 1916. "Apologie der Gefühlsempfindungen," *Zeitschrift für Psychologie und Physiologie der Sinnesorgane* 75: 104–40.

———. 1924. "Carl Stumpf." In *Die Philosophie der Gegenwart in Selbstdarstellungen*. Vol. 5, edited by Raymond Schmidt, 205–65. Leipzig: Meiner.

Sullivan, Mark, and Wayne Katon. 1993. "Somatization: The Path between Distress and Somatic Symptoms." *APS Journal* 2 (3): 141–49.

Svenaeus, Fredrik. 2000. "Das Unheimliche: Towards a Phenomenology of Illness." *Medicine, Health Care and Philosophy* 3 (1): 3–16.

———. 2015. "The Phenomenology of Chronic Pain: Embodiment and Alienation." *Continental Philosophy Review* 48 (2): 107–22.

———. 2018. *Phenomenological Bioethics: Medical Technologies, Human Suffering, and the Meaning of Being Alive*. London: Routledge.

Szasz, Thomas S. 1975. *Pain and Pleasure: A Study of Bodily Feelings*. New York: Basic Books.

Tauber, Alfred I. 2002. *Confessions of a Medicine Man: An Essay in Popular Philosophy*. Cambridge, MA: MIT Press.

Taylor, D. M. 1965. "The Location of Pain." *Philosophical Quarterly* 15 (58): 53–62.

Thacker, Mick. 2015. "Is Pain in the Brain?" *Pain and Rehabilitation* 39: 3.

Theodorou, Panos. 2014. "Pain, Pleasure, and the Intentionality of Emotions as Experiences of Values: A New Phenomenological Perspective." *Phenomenology and the Cognitive Sciences* 13 (4): 625–41.

Thomas, Sandra P., and Mary Johnson. 2000. "A Phenomenological Study of Chronic Pain." *Western Journal of Nursing Research* 22 (6): 683–705.

Titchener, Edward B. 1973. *Lectures on the Elementary Psychology of Feeling and Attention*. New York: Arno Press.

Toombs, S. Kay. 1987. "The Meaning of Illness: A Phenomenological Approach to the Patient-Physician Relationship." *Journal of Medicine & Philosophy* 12 (3): 219–40.

———. 1990. "The Temporality of Illness: Four Levels of Experience." *Theoretical Medicine* 11 (3): 227–41.

———. 1993. *The Meaning of Illness: A Phenomenological Account of the Different Perspectives of Physician and Patient*. Dordrecht: Kluwer.

Trigg, Roger. 1970. *Pain and Emotion*. Oxford: Clarendon Press.

Tye, Michael. 2005. "Another Look at Representationalism about Pain." In Aydede, *Pain*, 99–120.

Updike, John. 1983. "Pain." *New Republic* 189 (26 December): 34.

van Rysewyk, Simon, ed. 2017. *Meanings of Pain*. Dordrecht: Springer.

Varela, Francisco. J. 1996. "Neurophenomenology: A Methodological Remedy for the Hard Problem." *Journal of Consciousness Studies* 3 (4): 330–49.

Varela, Francisco J., Evan Thompson, and Eleanor Rosch. 1993. *The Embodied Mind: Cognitive Science and Human Experience*. Cambridge, MA: MIT Press.

Vesey, Godfrey N. A. 1961. "The Location of Bodily Sensations." *Mind*, n.s., 70 (277): 25–35.

———. 1965. "Baier on Vesey on the Place of a Pain." *Philosophical Quarterly* 15 (58): 63–64.

Villela-Petit, Maria. 2007. "Naturalistic and Personalistic Attitude." In *Analecta Husserliana*. Vol. XCIII, *Phenomenology of Life: From the Animal Soul to the Human Mind*, edited by Anna-Teresa Tymieniecka, 205–18. Dordrecht: Springer.

Welton, Donn, ed. 2003a. *The New Husserl: A Critical Reader*. Bloomington: Indiana University Press.

———. 2003b. "The Systematicity of Husserl's Transcendental Philosophy: From Static to Genetic Method." In Welton, *New Husserl*, 255–88.

Weizsäcker, Viktor von. 2011. "Die Schmerzen." In *Die Schmerzen*, edited by Marcus Schiltenwolf and Wolfgang Herzog, 263–79. Würzburg: Königshausen & Neumann.

Williford, Kenneth. 2013. "Husserl's Hyletic Data and Phenomenal Consciousness." *Phenomenology and the Cognitive Sciences* 12 (3): 501–19.

Woolf, Virginia. 1967. "On Being Ill." In *Collected Essays*. Vol. 4, 193–203. London: Hogarth.

Young, Iris M. 1980. "Throwing Like a Girl: A Phenomenology of Feminine Body Comportment Motility and Spatiality." *Human Studies* 3 (1): 137–56.

Zahavi, Dan. 1998. "Self-Awareness and Affection." In *Alterity and Facticity: New Perspectives on Husserl*, edited by Natalie Depraz and Dan Zahavi, 205–28. Dordrecht: Kluwer.

———. 2003. *Husserl's Phenomenology*. Stanford, CA: Stanford University Press.

———. 2013. "Naturalized Phenomenology: A Desideratum or a Category Mistake?" In *Phenomenology and Naturalism: Examining the Relationship between Human Experience and Nature*, edited by Havi Carel and Darian Meacham, 23–43. Cambridge: Cambridge University Press.

Zangwill, Oliver L. 1983. "Disorders of Memory." In *Handbook of Psychiatry*. Vol. 1, *General Psychopathology*, edited by Michael Shepherd and Oliver L. Zangwill, 97–113. Cambridge: Cambridge University Press.

INDEX

Absent Body, The (Leder), 157, 195n5
activity and passivity, 37, 60–61, 65, 104
acute pain, 98–99, 143
adumbrations *(Abschattungen)*, 132
affective reflection, 64
Akhtar, Salman, 216n23
alienation from the body, 118, 149, 152, 212n1
alien-worlds, 173, 177–78
amnesia, 113
Analyses Concerning Passive and Active Synthesis (Husserl), 199n22
animals, 194, 196n8, 218n9
anthropology, pain in, 150, 169–70, 193, 214n13. *See also* philosophical anthropology, pain in
anticipation of pain, 83–85, 98, 113, 115–17; implicit and explicit, 116–17, 118–19
Antigone, 179
anxiety, 115
AP. *See* asymbolia for pain (AP)
apperceptions, 36–37, 40, 74, 201n31
apprehension, 52–54, 63–64, 68–69, 73, 206n8; associative, 123–24; and content of apprehension, 52–54, 60–61, 66, 73, 81–82, 91, 96, 202n9, 203n13; double, 132–33; vs. experience, 69; functional, 183–84; in masochism, 183–84
apraxia, 87
Armstrong, David, 80
"as if," 48–49, 97, 200n30, 207n1
associationist account of pain, 123–24, 125
asymbolia for pain (AP), 69, 71, 85–93, 207n12; and congenital insensitivity to pain, compared, 92; definition of, 86; and indifference to the body, 88–90; patients, as interested in pain, 90; testing, 86, 90, 91–92; and word deafness, 91, 207n13

attention, 109–10, 111, 128, 206n6; *noema* and, 50–51, 109; and pain intensity, 109–10, 204n17, 208n8
attitudes. *See* natural attitude; personalistic attitude
Augustine, 1
Aune, Bruce, 77, 206n4
awareness, thematic vs. nonthematic, 60, 121
Aydede, Murat, 22, 198n12

bad faith, 118
Baier, Kurt, 80, 126, 127
Bain, Luchuo E., 215n22
Bakan, David, 187, 210n4, 213n10, 214n15
Barber, Theodore, 81, 206n6
battle with pain, 152
becoming, sphere of. *See* genetic method
behavioral reactions to pain, 71, 76, 78; in asymbolia for pain patients, 85–86, 87; mimicking, by congenital insensitivity to pain patients, 74–75
Being and Nothingness (Sartre), 48, 62–66, 108
Being in Pain (Olivier), 5, 6, 51
Benveniste, Daniel, 158
Bernet, Rudolph, 199n23
Berthier, Marchcelo, 87, 91–92
Bible, pain in, 210n4, 215n17
biology, pain, 1–3, 79–80, 195n4; experience ignored in, 3; tissue damage in, 41–42, 195n3, 201n5
body: alienation from, 118, 149, 152, 212n1; caring about, 88–90; and embodied personhood, 143–48; as a founded phenomenon, 133; lifeless vs. animated, 202n8; as lived and not known, 63; memory of, 113; as metaphor, 176, 179–80; as object, 63–64, 214n14; as object-body *(Körper)*, 127,

body: alienation from, *(continued)*
140, 142, 165; of the Other, 62, 136,
157; otherness of, 65–66, 137–39; pain
as a feeling of, 9, 44, 49–51, 120–41;
pain's localizability within, 56, 66,
94, 95, 120, 122–30, 133–34, 211n7;
perceiving, as subject, 51; phenomenology of, 120–41; psychological attitude
rooted in, 119; relating to, 62; remembering pain, 153; response of, to pain,
151, 214n15; as secondary to experience, 45; sensitive vs. sensible, 126–27,
133–34; and social processes, 175; as
split, 137–39, 152; as two-fold unity,
133–34. *See also* lived-body *(Leib)*
Body in Pain, The (Scarry), 43, 44–45, 46,
76, 151–52, 157, 158
Book of Pain and Love, The (Nasio),
214n15
brain as the subject of pain, 144
Brand, Paul, 70–71, 81
Brentano, Franz, 42–43, 44, 45, 47, 49, 54,
58, 66, 140
Brentano-Stumpf debate, 42–50, 52,
54–55, 57–58, 201n1, 201n6; congenital
insensitivity to pain patients and, 73;
pain treatment and, 80
Brough, John B., 99, 209n11
Buddha, 215n17
Buytendijk, Frederik J. J., 43, 144, 195n5,
214n12

Carel, Havi, 21, 197n9
Carman, Taylor, 135
Cartesian Meditations (Husserl), 176
Cartesian path, 33–34, 200nn24–25. *See
also* static method
Cassell, Eric, 144, 149, 151, 156, 212n3
causal account of pain, 123, 124, 125
causalgia. *See* complex regional pain syndrome (CRPS)
centripetal mode, 205n20
certainty of pain, 47–48, 49, 58, 59, 76–77
Chapman, C. Richard, 116
Chinese Cultural Revolution, 169–70
chronic pain, 10, 98–99; as betrayal by the
body, 149; dependency forced by, 150;
as depersonalizing, 148–50; effects of,
115–16; as endless, 112; expressing,
158; as metaphor, 180, 187; person as

subject of, 143–48, 212n2, 212n4; psychogenic vs. organic causes of, 154–55;
relations disrupted by, 149–50, 152–53,
160, 214n14, 216n24; as repersonalizing, 143, 150–54, 160, 192; temporality
of, 98–99, 111–12, 118–19, 143, 153–55,
209n12, 212n4. *See also* complex
regional pain syndrome (CRPS)
Churchland, Patricia, 78
Churchland, Paul, 78
Cicero, 182, 183, 184
cingulotomy, 69, 80–82, 84, 92, 93, 96
CIP. *See* congenital insensitivity to pain
(CIP)
Claparède, Édouard, 113
C-Manuscripts (Husserl), 98, 100–105,
208n2, 211n7
cognitive reflection, 64
cognitive response to pain, 151, 152–53,
154
communication. *See* language; listening
complex experiences, 24, 29, 39, 57–58,
68, 87–88
complex regional pain syndrome (CRPS),
115–16, 209n17
congenital insensitivity to pain (CIP),
69–80; and asymbolia for pain, compared, 92; causes of, 72–73; definition
of, 69–70; and the "discovery" of pain,
74–80, 121; and episodic analgesia,
70–71; intentionality and, 71, 96;
naloxone treating, 72–73; reports of
patients with, 71–72; "throbbing"
sensation and, 72, 75
congruence *(Deckung)*, 133–34
consciousness: apperceptive, 36–37; attention and, 109–10; contents of, 52–53;
embodied, 127–28, 137–39, 141; hypnosis and, 105–7, 208n5; implicit and
explicit, 105–10, 118–19, 208n6, 209n9;
liberation of, 3–4; and the living present, 100–102; pain disrupting, 46, 47,
60, 111; vs. pain experience, 45, 109;
of past and future, 102–3; personal,
111; of presence, 98, 108; reflective,
45, 63–65, 82, 110; reinterpretation
by, 53; repression of, 107; retention by,
103; streaming, 100–102, 104; as time-
constituting, 102; transcendental, 163;
unity of, 101–4, 109, 111, 138

INDEX

Constancy Hypothesis, 53
continuity, 100–102, 104, 118
Crisis of European Sciences, The (Husserl), 139, 176, 200n25, 217n4
critiques of phenomenology, 11
CRPS. *See* complex regional pain syndrome (CRPS)
cultural worlds, pain rooted in, 7
curing vs. healing, 155–56

darkening and awakening, 103
Dearborn, George, 69
Degenaar, Johannes J., 1
delusion, 181
denial, 167
depersonalization, 38, 112, 114, 117, 139, 142–43, 192; stemming from alienation, 118, 149, 152; syndrome, 148
depression, 107, 110, 166
Dere, Jessica, 216n1
Descartes, René, 30, 203n15
description. *See* static method
descriptive psychology, 32, 199n19
dialogical phenomenology, 5, 9, 12, 27–31, 38–40, 68–96, 165, 190–93, 195n4, 198n16, 219n1
Dickinson, Emily, 153–54
disease: vs. illness, 1, 155–56; pain as manifestation of, 65–66, 67; patient's reaction to, 156
dissociation, 29, 68–96
distraction from pain, 208n7
Distressed Body, The (Leder), 195n5
doctors. *See* patient-physician encounter

eidetic variation, 7, 8, 11–12, 18–31, 39; criticism of, 19, 20–25, 30, 199n16; definition of, 18; and epoché, 18, 21; factual variation supplementing, 8, 11–12, 27–30, 39, 188, 190, 196n1, 199n16, 219n1; and field of experience, 16–17; types of possibility and, 26–27, 28
eidos, 18–19
elimination of pain, 152, 210n4
Embodied Mind, The (Varela, Thompson, Rosch), 198n14
embodied subjectivity, 136, 154, 172, 175, 191–92
emotion, 9, 44, 206n5, 206n7; and anticipation, 116, 151; in asymbolia for pain

patients, lack of, 86, 87; and bodily feelings, 167; and emotive responses to pain, 151, 152–53, 154; intentionality and, 50; pain as, 50, 164–65, 167, 175, 182, 191, 206n9; person as subject of, 146; as sensation, 54; without sensation, 69, 81. *See also* Brentano-Stumpf debate
emphasis of symptoms, 167
empirical psychology, 199n19
empiricism, 4, 206n4; findings of, as possibilities, 28–29; phenomenology conflicting with, 26–27
episodic analgesia, 70–71
epoché, 4, 6, 8, 11, 20, 34, 39; definition of, 14; eidetic variation and, 18, 21; Husserl and, 34, 196n2, 200n26; and inner dialogue, 162; and reduction, 16, 100, 197n3, 200n26; time and, 99–100
essences, 18–20, 197n6, 198n14; vs. facts, 32; vs. individual experiences, 18, 19, 23; language's effects on seeing, 30–31; morphological, 18
ethics, 194
experience, 42, 68, 76–77; vs. apprehension, 69; biology's inability to clarify, 1–2, 12; communal, 218n12; concordant, 177–78, 179; determinates of, 79; discordant, 178–79; expressing, 157–62; founded, 55, 202n10; life-world and, 172–75; meaning and, 6, 32; vs. object, 15–16, 58; vs. perception, 46, 50; priority of, 45; pure, 4, 7, 16–20, 24, 34, 88–89, 197n8, 198n15; sensory dimension fundamental to, 73–74; sequence of, 104, 111; simple vs. complex, 56–58, 68, 87; stream of, 16, 20, 21–22, 32, 138–39, 212n5, 218n12; structures of, 4, 8, 38, 45, 50, 59, 126; temporal nature of, 7. *See also* psychologization; somatization
experiential objects, relating to, 51, 55
explanation. *See* genetic method
expression, 217n9; direct and indirect, 176, 186, 218n10; life-world and, 176–77, 185–86; meaning and, 185; of pain, 157–62; in somatization and psychologization, 167, 176, 179–81, 186

facticity, pain as mark of, 63, 204n19
factual variations, 8, 11–12, 27–30, 39, 188, 190, 196n1, 199n16, 219n1

'feeling-acts, 54–55. *See also* intentionality

feeling-sensations, 42, 44–49, 54–55, 68, 80; vs. emotions, 164, 166–67, 182; first-person experience of, 59, 66; Husserl on, 203n14; intentionality founded on, 57–58, 66; obtrusiveness and, 201n6

feminist literature, 218n10

field of experience, 3–4, 16–17, 20, 34, 197n8; eidetic variation and, 16–17, 34; as field of genesis, 34–35; pain as a rupture in, 38, 51

first-person perspective, 4, 146, 189; vs. first-person condition, 24; methodology of, 4, 12–13, 22–24, 42, 59; of non-human animals, 194; of the Other, 176

First Philosophy II (Husserl), 200n25, 200n27

Fisette, Denis, 55

Flores, Leticia Y., 116

focal pain, 111, 117, 209n10

Formalism in Ethics and Non-Formal Ethics of Values (Scheler), 43, 144

foundedness, 55, 57–58, 60, 66, 96, 136–37, 202n10

Freeman, Walter, 81, 82

Freund, Hans-Joachim, 94

Friedman, Emanuel, 86, 87, 90, 91, 207n13

Fuchs, Thomas, 104, 153

functionalism, 78

function of pain, 69, 184–85, 186–87

future, 102–4; painful presence disconnected from, 111, 114, 117; pain management and, 152–53; past and, meeting-point of, 104, 105

Gallagher, Shaun, 23, 27, 39

Geist. See spirit

generative phenomenology, 199n21

genetic method, 8, 11, 12, 31–39, 162, 163, 189, 199n18, 199n22; as diachronic, 32, 34; goal of, 37; principles of, 33; psychology and, 33, 34–35, 200nn24–25; reduction and, 33–34, 200n24; significance of, for phenomenology of pain, 38, 40; static method supplemented by, 12, 31–34, 40, 162–63, 189, 197n7, 199n17, 199n23

Gergel, Tania, 24–25

Gijn, J. van, 83–84, 85, 116

Good, Byron, 149, 214n11, 214n13

Goodell, Helen, 81, 82

Grahek, Nikola, 71, 78–79, 80, 82; on asymbolia for pain, 87–88, 89, 90, 92, 93, 207n12; on brain damage, 116; on painfulness without pain, 94; on threat hypersymbolia, 83, 84, 207n10

Grüny, Christian, 5, 6, 191–92, 195n5, 206n5

Gurwitsch, Aron, 53

Hall, K. R. L., 107

Hardy, James D., 81, 82

healing vs. curing, 155–56

Heidegger, Martin, 6

Hemphill, Robert, 86, 91

Henry, Michel, 43, 201n2

Heracleitean flux, 16, 20

Hill, Christopher S., 125

Hill, Harris E., 115

homeworld, 173–74, 177–81; and alienworlds, 177–78; communal, 178; conflict in, 178–79; definition of, 173, 177, 218n13; expression and, 173, 175, 176, 179–81; homelessness in, 165; mythical convictions making up, 178–79

Hoogenraad, Tjaard U., 83–84, 85, 116

horizon, life-world as, 173

hunger, 170

Husserl, Edmund, 14; on apperceptions, 36–37; on Brentano, 203n14; dualism ascribed to, 135, 211n8; on eidetic variation, 18; and the epoché, 34, 196n2, 200n26; on genetic methods, 31–32, 199n17; on the homeworld, 218n13; on language, 49; and the life-world, 33, 163, 172–73, 176–79, 197n4, 201n32, 217n4; on mathematics, 18–19; on nature, 202n8; on open vs. motivated possibility, 26–27; on pain, 54–59; psychologism critiqued by, 21; on reduction, 15, 17, 35; on spirit, 210n5; on subjectivity, 15, 16; on temporality, 35

Husserl, Edmund, works of: *Analyses Concerning Passive and Active Synthesis*, 199n22; *Cartesian Meditations*, 176; C-Manuscripts, 98, 100–105, 208n2, 211n7; *The Crisis of European*

INDEX

Sciences, 139, 176, 200n25, 217n4; *First Philosophy II,* 200n25, 200n27; *Ideas I,* 32, 46–47, 61, 109, 196n2, 199n20, 201n3, 209n10; *Ideas II,* 51, 120, 128–29, 131–33, 137, 144–47, 163, 202nn8–9, 211n9; *Logical Investigations,* 21, 32, 52–59, 199n19, 203nn12–14; *Phenomenological Psychology,* 19; *Zur Phänomenologie der Intersubjektivität,* 218n9, 218nn12–13

Husserliana XXXIX, 176, 201n32, 218n11

Husserlian phenomenology, 5–6; characteristics of, 6–7, 8, 13–14; as descriptive science, 14; Platonism and, 18–19, 34; Sartre and, 204n18. *See also* phenomenology

hyle, 46–47, 53, 61–62, 66, 96; elements of, 201n3; and hyletic data, 206n8; and streaming consciousness, 101–2

hyperprotectiveness, 83–85

hypnosis, 105–7, 110, 208n5

I, the, 101, 128, 140–41, 212n5, 214n15. *See also* self-distantiation

Ideas I (Husserl), 32, 46–47, 61, 109, 196n2, 199n20, 201n3, 209n10

Ideas II (Husserl), 51, 120, 128–29, 131–33, 137, 144–47, 163, 202nn8–9, 211n9

illness: vs. chronic pain, 214n14; vs. disease, 1, 155–56; eidetic features of, 198n10; phenomenology of, 21, 24–25, 198n10; sufferers' viewpoint of, 24–25

Imaginary, The (Sartre), 205n2

imaginative variation. *See* eidetic variation

immanence: as field of pure experience, 16; pain and, 38, 135

imperative, pain as, 186–87, 215n15, 215n18

impressions, 101–5, 208n3

indifference to pain, 71, 86–87, 88–91, 93, 107

indubitability of pain, 47–48, 49, 58, 59, 76–77; and localizability, 120, 121–26, 135, 139

intentional feelings, 137, 164; vs. nonintentional feelings, 54–55, 57–58, 182; pain as, 45, 49–52; pain coloring, 48; pain interrupting, 44–45, 46, 47

intentionality, 42–67, 200n29, 201n2,

203nn11–12; ascription and, 55; asymbolia for pain patients and, 93, 96; clarifying the structure of, 52–54; congenital insensitivity to pain patients and, 71, 96; experience obtaining, 52–53; and foundedness, 55, 57–58, 66, 96; *hyle, noesis, noema,* and, 46–47, 61–62, 201n3; and nonintentional vs. pre-intentional, 57, 59, 207n11; obtrusiveness and, 60–61; pain disruption and, 81–82, 93, 96, 206n7; threat hypersymbolia patients and, 84, 93, 96, 207n11

International Association for the Study of Pain (IASP), 2, 41, 141, 190–91, 195n2

interpretation: of sensations, 55–56, 203n12; in somatization and psychologization, 167, 168–70, 186–87

interrupting pain, 80–82

intersubjective reflection, 64, 65–66, 161; time as achievement of, 104; and verifiability, 19–20, 25

intersubjectivity, transcendental, 17, 20, 35–36, 37, 200n28

introspectionism, 4; critique of, 23; inconsistencies in, 198n13; phenomenology and, 11, 21, 22–24, 198n11, 198n14

invariants, 18

"Is Pain an Intentional Experience?" (Serrano de Haro), 61–62

Jackson, Jean, 150, 214n13

James, William, 54, 124

Jewsbury, Eric C., 71

Johnson, Mary, 111

Jünger, Ernst, 129

Kaplan, Eugene A., 105–7, 208n5

Katon, Wayne, 166

Kern, Iso, 199n23

Kirmayer, Laurence J., 166, 167, 175

Klein, Colin, 95; on asymbolia for pain, 87, 88–89, 90; on imperatives, 186, 187; on masochism, 183, 184, 218n14

Kleinman, Arthur, 150, 169–70, 214n11, 214n13

Kleinman, Joan, 169–70

knowledge: inherited, 199n20; of pain, 65–66, 106–10, 205n22

language, 157, 159, 195n1, 206n4, 215n21, 217n9; animals and, 218n9; metaphorical, for pain, 48–49, 78–79, 134, 174–75, 186; for sensations, 48–49, 77–79
laughter, 86, 87, 88, 89, 92
Leder, Drew, 150, 205n20, 205n22, 206n3, 209n12, 214n15, 217n7
Leder, Drew, works of: *The Absent Body,* 157, 195n5; *The Distressed Body,* 195n5
Leiguarda, Ramon, 87, 91–92
leprosy, 70–71
Leriche, René, 79
Lewis, Thomas, 1
life-world, 7, 35–36, 154, 164–87, 197n4; and alien-worlds, 173, 177–78; definition of, 35, 172–73; discordance in, 175–81; experience and, 172–75, 218n12; expression and, 176–77, 185–86; at home and homeless in, 186; as horizon, 173; and "objective" world, 217n4; pain originating in, 38, 40, 172, 173–74; relation to, 165, 173; structures of, 37; transcendental intersubjectivity and, 35–36, 37, 176
listening, 157–62, 215n22; definition of, 159; goals of, 160; inner dialogue and, 161–62; to oneself, 160–61, 216n23; as pain's imperative, 187; wider therapeutic significance of, 160
lived-body *(Leib),* 121, 135–37, 165, 202n7, 204n16; as bearer of localized sensations, 129–30, 138, 142, 204n16, 205n23, 210n6; belonging to the person, 142–63; as constitutive accomplishment, 135, 136–37, 211n8; as expression of the spirit, 129, 130, 138, 139, 142; having vs. being, 211n1; as organ of will, 128, 130, 138, 139, 142; as pain's subject, 127–30, 171–72; as psychological and physical, 127, 140; as self-conscious, 130; self-distantiation and, 107, 135–36, 137–39; sensings constituting, 132–33; as split, 137–39, 152; as zero-point of orientation, 128, 129, 138, 139, 142, 211n11
living present, 100–102, 208n2
lobotomy, 69, 80–82, 84, 92, 93, 96
localizability: and ebbs and flows of experience, 134; and the I, 135, 140–41; and

indubitability, 120, 121–26, 135, 139; of pain, 56, 66, 94, 95, 120, 122–30, 133–34, 211n7; physiological, 205n23; of sensings vs. objects, 132, 134
Locke, John, 77
Logical Investigations (Husserl), 21, 32, 52–59, 199n19, 203nn12–14
Lotze, Hermann, 123
Luft, Sebastian, 200n28

Madison, Gary B., 196n6
Malcolm, Norman, 75, 76
Marbach, Eduard, 199n23
masochism, 71, 182–85, 218nn14–16; as control of pain, 184–85; penumbral theory of, 184
McGill Pain Questionnaire, 48, 78
McMurray, Gordon A., 70, 71, 72, 74
meaning: abyss of, 135; and asymbolia for pain patients, 91; excess of, 36–37; and experience, 6, 32; and expression, 185; listening to, 159; and meaningless pain, 180–81; original, 35; of pain, 43, 155, 186–87; person producing, 146, 155; somatization as expression of, 169–70, 180–81; and soul, 211n9; source of, 17, 37
Meaning of Illness, The (Toombs), 158, 160, 198n10, 210n2
"Meaning of Suffering, The" (Scheler), 43, 192–93, 215n17
mechanisms of pain, 1
medicine: chronicity in, 118; listening in practice of, 159–62, 215n22, 216n23; narrative, 159, 160, 216n23; patient's voice in, 160–61; the person in, 144; phenomenology of, 24–25, 143, 154–56, 159–62, 215n20
meditation, 22, 198n11
Melzack, Ronald, 115
memory, 112–15; implicit and explicit, 113, 114–15, 116–17, 118–19, 209n15, 215n16; of pain, body's, 153; pain forming, 113–14, 209nn14–15; of painlessness, as irreal, 112, 113, 114, 209n12; presence and, 113–15
mentality condition, 23
Merleau-Ponty, Maurice, 6, 31, 51, 135
metaphor, pain and, 48–49, 78–79, 134, 174–75, 186

INDEX

methodology, 7–40, 188–91, 196n7; central questions of, 9; first-person, 4, 12–13, 22–24, 42, 59; of intentional implications, 36; principles of, 7, 8, 12–20; static vs. genetic, 8, 11, 12, 31–39, 162, 189, 199nn17–23; structure and, 7–10

Mitchell, Silas Weir, 115

Moran, Dermot, 144, 145, 211n10

morphine, 69, 80–82, 84, 92, 93, 96

Morris, David B., 112

Morris, Katherine J., 214n13

motivation and motivationalism, 62, 63–64, 74, 80, 88–89, 147, 158–59, 186, 199n21, 205n1; apperceptive consciousness and, 37; causality and, 213n8; and masochism, 181, 184; in somatization and psychologization, 169, 171

mundane, 34–35, 36, 61, 197n5, 200nn26–27

"mythical convictions," 178–79

Nakamura, Yoshio, 116

naloxone, 72–73

Nasio, Juan-David, 214n15

natural attitude, 15, 34–35, 125, 130, 145, 197n4, 213n6; and personalistic attitude, 145–46, 147, 160, 172, 213n7; of physician, 158–59; preconceptions of, suspended, 4, 6, 32

naturalism, 3, 8, 197n8

Nelkin, Norton, 78

neurasthenia, 169–70

neutralized presentifications, 207n1

Nietzsche, Friedrich, 30, 113–14

noema, 47, 50–51, 59–60, 61–62, 109, 201n3, 202n6

noesis, 59–60, 61–62, 201n3

"not I," 101

object-body *(Körper),* 127, 140, 142, 165

objectification, 205n22; motivation for, 63–64; of pain, 46–47, 49, 56–57; pain resisting, 45, 59, 215n21; stoic, 152

objectivistic prejudice, 161

objects: vs. experience, 15–16, 58; and language for pain, 78–79; pain marking, 63

obtrusiveness of pain, 46–47, 49–50, 60, 201n6

Ogawa, Tadashi, 211n8

Olivier, Abraham, 5, 6, 43, 51, 191–92, 195n5

On the Genealogy of Morals (Nietzsche), 113–14

ontology: attitude and, 35, 145, 160; and foundedness, 55, 202n10; and ontological gap, 158–59, 160; and ontological path, 35, 201n32

organic pain, 143, 144, 154–55

"original ego," 101

original experience, 9, 42, 97–119

Other, the, 62, 64, 65–66, 136, 150, 176

pain: as ambiguous, 56–57, 59; of animals, 194, 196n8; anticipation of, 83–85, 98, 115–19; as atmosphere, 48, 51, 60, 61; as aversive feeling, 9, 42, 68, 69–96, 206n3; battle with, 152; certainty of, 47–48, 49, 58, 59, 76–77; criteria for sensitivity to, 71; defining, difficulties in, 1–2, 195nn1–2; definitions of, 2, 8–9, 41–42, 43, 141, 182, 190–92, 219n1; as depersonalizing, 38, 112, 114, 117, 139, 142–43, 192; dialogical method required by, 39–40; dissociation, 29, 68–96; elimination of, 152, 210n4; experiential quality of, 42, 68, 76–77; expression of, 157–62; as founded, 57–58, 60, 136–37, 202n10; function of, 69, 184–85, 186–87; as hyperprotective, 83–85; as imperative, 186–87, 215n15, 215n18; indifference to, 71, 86–87, 88–91, 93, 107; inferring, 74–76; inner split characterizing, 107, 152; intensity of, 46, 63–64, 109–10, 204n17; intentional vs. nonintentional, 42–67, 81–82, 203nn11–12; interrupting, 80–82; knowledge of, 65–66, 106–10, 205n22; as localizable, 56, 66, 94, 95, 120, 122–30, 133–34, 211n7; and masochism, 182–85, 218nn14–16; meaning of, 43, 155, 186–87; as mode of consciousness, 49–50; new conception of, 7, 8–9; as *noema,* 50–51; objectifying, 46–47, 49, 56–57; obtrusiveness of, 46–47, 49–50, 60, 201n6; organic, 143, 144, 154–55; as an original experience, 9, 42, 97–119, 210n18; psyche's role in, 119, 124, 154–55, 166–81, 216n3; as repersonalizing, 38, 114, 117,

pain: as ambiguous, *(continued)*
139, 142–43; spiritual aspects of, 129,
215n17; the subject of, 120, 127–30,
143, 212n2, 212n5; and suffering, the
relationship between, 43, 64–65, 67,
122, 166–70, 205n21, 210n3, 217n8; tissue
damage associated with, 41, 195n3,
201n5; types of, 98–99, 142–43, 213n10;
unfelt, 98, 107, 108–9, 208n5, 208n8,
209n9; unnoticed, 60, 108–9, 110, 121,
208n7, 209n9; as unshareable, 59, 150,
157. *See also* chronic pain; stratified
experience, pain as
Pain (Lewis), 1
pain affect without pain sensation, 69,
93–95, 96
Pain: Its Modes and Functions (Buytendijk),
195n5
pain management, 152–54
pain patients, treatment of, 69, 80–82,
154–56. *See also* patient-physician
encounter
pain research, 2–3; naturalism in, 3, 8;
phenomenology in dialogue with, 5, 9,
12, 165, 169–70, 171–72, 188; phenomenology
not relying on, 14–15; social
constructionism in, 3, 8
Palmer, David, 108, 209n9
panic attacks, 151
paradox of pain, 120–21, 149
passivity and activity, 37, 60–61, 65, 104
past, 102–4; future and, meeting-point
of, 104, 105; and memories of pain,
153–54; painful presence disconnected
from, 111, 112–15, 117, 209nn11–12,
212n4
patient-physician encounter, 156; *Leib-Körper*
distinction in, 158–59; listening
in, 159–62, 215n22; meaning in, 159;
somatization and, 217n8; temporality
and, 118–19
Pellegrino, Edmund, 148
perception: vs. experience, 46, 50; internal
vs. external, 47, 58, 60, 122, 126–27,
133–34; pain as form of, 43, 45; phenomenology
of, 51; temporality and, 36
perceptual account of pain, 124–25
person, 162–63, 165; an animal as, 196n8;
definition of, 146; as dependent on
others, 146, 147; response of, to dis-

ease, 156; response of, to pain, 152–54;
and the self, 212n3; spirit and, 210n5;
temporality and, 212n4; unique history
of, 147. *See also* depersonalization;
personhood, embodied; philosophical
anthropology, pain in
personalistic attitude, 7, 9, 141, 144–47,
160–62; definition of, 145; naturalistic
attitude derived from, 172, 213n7; pain
in, 9, 141, 145–47, 162; of patient,
158–59; spirit and, 147
personality, pain affecting, 144
personhood, embodied, 143–48; and medicine,
phenomenology of, 154–56; and
pain response, 151–54
Pete, Steven, 71, 72, 75
Peter, Sebastian von, 99
phenomena, 3–4, 14–20, 22–24, 29–30,
32–33; interpreting, 175, 179–80; natural,
15; as possibilities, 18; sensations
as physical, 84–85, 123–24; stratified,
59, 62, 84, 203n13; as unnatural, 16
phenomenological attitude, 196n6
Phenomenological Psychology (Husserl), 19
phenomenology, 126–27, 210n2; animals
in, 194, 196n8, 218n9; complex experiences
in, 24, 29, 39, 57–58, 68, 87–88;
confusion about, 22–23, 24, 25; cross-cultural,
31; definition of, 13, 196n6;
descriptive method of, 6–7, 8; dialogical,
5, 9, 12, 27–31, 38–40, 68–96, 165,
190–93, 195n4, 198n16, 219n1; diversity
within, 190; ethical implications of,
194; illness vs. pain in, 198n10; as
insular, 26–27, 30; of medicine, 24–25,
143, 154–56, 159–62, 215n20; not comprehensive,
188; significance of, 192–93;
transcendental, 17–18, 34–36, 37, 65,
163, 197n5, 199n23, 200nn27–28
philological differences, 30
philosophical anthropology, pain in, 7,
9–10, 142–63, 192–93; the life-world
and, 164–87
physicians. *See* patient-physician encounter
physiological response to pain, 71
Pitcher, George, 218n15
Ploner, Markus, 94
possibilities: eidetic variation and, 26–27,
28; empirical findings as, 28–29; open
vs. motivated, 26–27, 198n15

INDEX

Pötzl, Otto, 92
pragmatism, 4
preconceptual insight, 19, 32–33, 36, 37–38. *See also* genetic method
pregivenness, 15
pre-intentional, pain as, 57, 59–60
preobjective, pain as, 63, 67
prereflective, pain as, 62–63, 67, 207n11
presence, 98, 100–119; anticipation and, 113, 117; concretely experienced, 102–3; consciousness of, 98, 108; implicit and explicit, 105–10; as infinite sameness, 111; memory and, 113–15; pain lived in the field of, 97–98, 105, 110–12, 117–18, 208n3
presence-at-hand *(Vorhandenheit),* 205n22
Price, Donald D., 22, 198n12
primordial reflection, 64–65, 67
protention, 38, 102, 104–5, 111, 208n3
Protevi, John, 201n2
psychaesthenia, 205n2
psyche, role of, in pain, 119, 124, 154–55, 166–81, 216n3
psychoanalysis, 159, 160, 214n15, 216n23
psychogenic pain, 143, 144, 154–55. *See also* somatization
psychological reductionism, 197n9
psychologism, phenomenology as, 11, 21–22, 26
psychologization, 10, 38, 165, 166–68, 192, 216n1, 216n3; definition of, 166, 167–68; and the life-world, 175–82; masochism and, 184–85; meaning and, 187; phenomenology of, 171–72; relation and, 173; as a split, 181

Ramos, L. M., 83–84, 85, 116
Ratcliffe, Matthew, 148, 213n9
real and irreal, 52–54, 201n3
recognition as belated, 108
recollection: of painlessness, as irreal, 112, 113, 114, 209n12; perception and, 36; as reawakening, 103; sequence of, 104. *See also* retention
reduction, phenomenological, 4, 6, 8, 11, 15–18, 20, 39; and the epoché, 16, 100, 197n3, 200n26; genetic path to, 33–34, 200n24; and immanence, 16; and inner dialogue, 162; and the living presence, 101; vs. reductionism, 197n8

reduction, transcendental, 17–18, 34–35, 37
referential content, pain lacking, 44–45
reflection. *See* intersubjective reflection
reflective consciousness, 45, 63–65, 82, 110
relation, 216n24; chronic pain disrupting, 149–50, 152–53, 160; to the life-world, 165, 173
repersonalization, 38, 114, 117, 139, 142–43, 150–54, 160, 192
representationalist account of pain, 124, 125
reproductive experience, 97, 200n30, 207n1
responses to pain, 68–69, 75, 150–54; memory affecting, 154; as repersonalizing, 151–54. *See also* psychologization; somatization
retention, 38, 102–4, 111, 208n3
Ricoeur, Paul, 13
Rosch, Eleanor, 198n11, 198n14
Rubins, Jack, 86, 87, 90, 91, 207n13
Ryle, Gilbert, 108, 110, 123, 208n7

sacrifice, 215n17
Sartre, Paul, 51, 53, 118, 126–27, 204nn18–19, 214n15
Sartre, Paul, works of: *Being and Nothingness,* 48, 62–66, 108; *The Imaginary,* 205n2
Scarry, Elaine: on communicating pain, 48, 157, 158, 195n1, 215n21; on damage, 49, 201n5; on depersonalization, 151–52; on pain's indubitability, 47, 76; on pain's nonintentionality, 43, 44–45, 46
Scheler, Max, 43, 144, 150, 157, 192–93, 215n17
Scheler, Max, works of: *Formalism in Ethics and Non-Formal Ethics of Values,* 43, 144; "The Meaning of Suffering," 43, 192–93, 215n17
Scheper-Hughes, Nancy, 170
Schilder, Paul, 85–86, 89–90, 92
Schmitz, Hermann, 48, 51, 201n4
Schnitzler, Alfons, 94
self-distantiation, 107, 135–36, 137–39, 181, 211n10, 213n10, 214nn11–12
selfhood, 212n3, 213n9
semiological account of pain, 122–23, 124, 125

sensations *(Empfindungen)*, 203n13, 205n1; and appearance, 201n6; ascribed to objects of experience, 131; as central to pain experience, 73–74, 78; distinctions between, 77–79; double, 132, 133; focal, 209n10; interpreting, 55–56, 203n12; Jamesian view of, 54; lacking localizability, 95; language for, 48–49, 77–79; as nonspatial, 122–23; in psychology vs. psychophysics, 84–85, 90–93; sensings distinct from, 130–31, 203n13; tactual, 55–56, 131–32, 133, 136–37, 203n12, 211n8. *See also* feeling-sensations

sensings *(Empfindnisse)*, 51, 126, 140, 202n8, 211n8; the body as field of, 121, 128, 129–30, 133, 138–40; definition of, 131; lived-body constituted by, 132–33; as localized, 131–32; vs. objects, 125, 126; pain as, 130–33, 136–37, 202n8; pain differing from other, 137; as reflexive, 132; sensations distinguished from, 130–31, 203n13; unity of, 101–2, 133–34

Serrano de Haro, Agustín, 46, 50, 55, 61–62, 109, 110, 152, 203n11, 212n5

sickness, phenomenology of, 213n9

sleep, pain in, 46, 60

sleeplessness, pain resulting from, 62–63

Smith, Quentin, 53

social constructionism, 3

social delegitimization, 218n10

sociohistorical setting of persons, 146

sociology, pain, 3, 195n4

solipsism, phenomenology as, 11, 21, 24–25

somatization, 10, 38, 165, 166–68, 192, 216n1, 216n3; definition of, 166, 167–68; hermeneutics of, 217n7; interpretations of, 168–70; and the life-world, 174–81; masochism and, 184–85; meaning and, 186–87; patient-physician encounter and, 217n8; pervasiveness of, 166; phenomenology of, 170–71, 217nn7–8; relation and, 173; as a split, 181

soul, 136, 211n9

spirit, 129, 138, 139, 210n5; lived-body as expression of, 129, 130, 138, 139, 142; personalistic attitude and, 147

Starkstein, Sergio, 87, 91–92

static method, 33–34, 40, 162, 163, 199n18; definition of, 33; genetic method supplementing, 12, 31–34, 40, 162–63, 189, 197n7, 199n17, 199n23; as ontological, 199n21

Stein, Edith, 147

Steinbock, Anthony, 199n21

Stengel, Erwin, 85–86, 89–90, 91, 92

stimuli: asymbolia for pain patients sensing, 89, 91–92, 93, 207n12; CRPS patients sensing, 116, 209n17; lack of, 85; lack of defense against, 86

stoic objectification of pain, 152

stratified experience, pain as, 44, 57, 58–67, 68, 96, 203n15; asymbolia for pain patients and, 93; masochism and, 183; threat hypersymbolia patients and, 84; and the "whole pain experience," 73–74, 183

Stride, E., 107

structures of experience, 4, 8, 38, 45, 50, 59, 126

Stuart, Gordon, 214n11

Stumpf, Carl, 42–43, 44, 46, 47, 54, 55, 57, 66, 157, 164

subject-body *(Leib)*. *See* lived-body *(Leib)*

subjectivity, 15–16, 162, 163, 217n4; embodied, 136, 154, 172, 175, 191–92; pain necessary for, 212n5; paradox of, 139; recognizing others', 176; transcendental, 17, 35–36, 37

subject/object dichotomy, 7, 15–16, 46, 126–27, 137–38, 217n4; grammar and, 47; philological difference and, 30–31

subject of pain, 120, 127–30, 143, 212n2, 212n5

suffering, 67, 78, 166–70, 211n1; masochism and, 184–85, 218n15; meaning of, 192–93, 215n17; as melody, 64; as non-localizable, 122; and pain, relation between, 43, 64–65, 67, 122, 166–70, 205n21, 210n3, 217n8; Sartre on, 64–65

Sullivan, Mike, 166

Svenaeus, Fredrik, 211n1

synaesthesia, 27

tactile sensations, 55–56, 131–32, 133, 136–37, 203n12, 211n8

Tauber, Alfred, 215n22

Taylor, D. M., 123

temporality, 7, 35–36, 38, 97–119; of
chronic pain, 98–99, 111–12, 118–19,
143, 153–55, 209n12, 212n4; of experience, 7; focal pains and, 111, 117;
implicit vs. explicit, 98, 105–11; and
originality, 97; of pain, 95, 97–119,
153–54, 208n3; the personal and,
112; and temporal fields, 102, 103–4,
111–12, 114; therapeutic relevance of,
118; and time, distinction between,
98–100. *See also* presence
temporal proximity condition, 24
Thacker, Mick, 144
Thomas, Sandra P., 111
Thomasma, David, 148
Thompson, Evan, 198n11, 198n14
thought experiments, 29
threat hypersymbolia, 69, 83–85, 116,
207nn10–11, 209n17
time, objective, 98–100, 118; epoché
suspending, 99–100; as intersubjective
achievement, 104; and pain types, 99
time-constitution, 100–105
tissue damage, 41, 195n3, 201n5
Titchener, Edward, 84–85, 90
Toombs, S. Kay, 118, 158, 160, 198n10,
210n2
torture, 152
transcendental constitution, 133
transcendental experience, 17–18, 34–36,
37, 65, 163, 197n5, 199n23, 200nn27–28
transcendental intersubjectivity, 17, 20,
35–36, 37, 200n28
transformation in somatization and psychologization, 167
transient pain, 98, 99, 142–43, 164
Trigg, Roger, 68, 71, 74–75, 106, 183, 208n5
Tye, Michael, 78, 124

"Über Gefühlsempfindungen" (Stumpf),
201n1

unfelt pain, 98, 107, 108–9, 208n5, 208n8,
209n9
unnoticed pain, 60, 108–9, 110, 121,
208n7, 209n9
unpleasant sensations, distinguishing
between, 2, 77
Untersuchungen zur Sinnespsychologie
(Brentano), 201n1
Updike, John, 157

values, 146
Varela, Francisco J., 23, 198n11, 198n14
verbal report of pain, 71, 106–7, 215n21
verifiability, intersubjective, 19–20, 25
Vesey, Godfrey N. A., 126–27, 133, 134
Villela-Petit, Maria, 147, 213n6, 213n8

Wall, Patrick D., 115
Watts, James W., 81, 82
Weizsäcker, Viktor von, 150–51, 152, 157,
212n2, 215n18
Welton, Donn, 162
"whole pain experience," 68–69, 79–80;
masochism and, 183; spiritual aspects
of, 129; as stratified experience,
73–74
Williford, Kenneth, 202n9, 206n8
Wolff, Harold G., 81, 82
Woolf, Virginia, 195n1
word deafness, 91, 207n13
work of pain, 152, 160, 214n16, 215n18
world, 163; as actuality, 34; constitution,
177–78. *See also* homeworld; life-
world

Zahavi, Dan, 23, 29, 197n3
Zerstörte Erfahrung (Grüny), 5, 6
Zuhandenheit (readiness to hand), 128,
205n22
Zur Phänomenologie der Intersubjektivität
(Husserl), 218n9, 218nn12–13